ENGLISH
FOR EVERYONE

ENGLISH VOCABULARY BUILDER

FREE AUDIO
website and app
www.dkefe.com

Author

Thomas Booth worked for 10 years as an English-language teacher in Poland and Russia. He now lives in England, where he works as an editor and English-language materials writer, notably of course books and vocabulary textbooks.

ENGLISH FOR EVERYONE

ENGLISH VOCABULARY BUILDER

DK

DK Penguin Random House

US Editors Kayla Dugger, Jenny Siklos
Senior Editor Laura Sandford
Project Editor Thomas Booth
Senior Art Editors Amy Child, Anna Hall
Art Editors Raymond Bryant, Michelle Staples, Jemma Westing
Illustrators Edward Byrne, Michael Parkin, Gus Scott
Project Manager Christine Stroyan
Jacket Designer Surabhi Wadhwa
Jacket Editor Claire Gell
Jacket Design Development Manager Sophia MTT
Producer, Pre-production Gillian Reid
Producers Alex Bell, Anna Vallarino
Publisher Andrew Macintyre
Art Director Karen Self
Publishing Director Jonathan Metcalf

DK India
Project Art Editor Sanjay Chauhan
Art Editor Meenal Goel
Assistant Art Editor Devika Khosla
Project Editor Nisha Shaw
Illustrator Arun Pottirayil
Jacket Designer Juhi Sheth
Managing Jackets Editor Saloni Singh
Pre-production Manager Balwant Singh
Senior DTP Designer Vishal Bhatia
Managing Art Editor Sudakshina Basu
Managing Editor Rohan Sinha

First American Edition, 2018
Published in the United States by DK Publishing,
a division of Penguin Random House LLC
1745 Broadway, 20th Floor, New York, NY 10019

25 10 9 8 7 6 5 4 3
003–334973–Feb/2023

A catalog record for this book is available from the Library of Congress.
Box set ISBN 978-0-7440-8186-2
ISBN 978-1-4654-6483-5

DK books are available at special discounts when purchased in bulk for sales promotions, premiums, fund-raising, or educational use. For details, contact:
DK Publishing Special Markets,
1745 Broadway, 20th Floor, New York, NY 10019
SpecialSales@dk.com

Printed and bound in China

www.dk.com

MIX
Paper | Supporting responsible forestry
FSC™ C018179
FSC www.fsc.org

This book was made with Forest Stewardship Council™ certified paper—one small step in DK's commitment to a sustainable future.
Learn more at www.dk.com/uk/information/sustainability

Contents

How to use this book 8

GETTING STARTED

01 Countries and nationalities 10

02 Numbers 14

03 Time expressions 18

04 Daily routines 22

05 Describing things: facts 26

06 Describing things: opinions 30

07 Sharing information 34

08 Common English idioms 38

HOME

09 Around the house 42

10 Kitchen implements and toiletries 46

11 Chores and cleaning 50

12 Tools and gardening 54

13 Moving and renting 58

PEOPLE

14 The body 62

15 Clothes 66

16 Accessories and beauty products 70

17 Appearance 74

18 Personality traits 78

19 Feelings and moods 82

20 Family tree 86

21 Family and relationships 90

22 Baby equipment and toys 94

23 Education 98

24 Studying 102

25 Speaking a foreign language 106

26 Communication and beliefs 110

27 Crime and the law 114

FOOD AND DRINK

28 Meat, fish, dairy, and snacks 118

29 Fruit and nuts 122

30 Vegetables 126

31 Bread, desserts, and condiments 130

32 Drinking and eating 134

33 Eating in and eating out 138

WORK

34 Jobs 142

35 Working conditions 146

36 Industries and departments 150

37 Office equipment 154

38 Money and finance 158

39 Working 162

40 Meeting and presenting 166

41 Work and business idioms 170

42 Applying for a job 174

43 Workplace skills and abilities 178

TRAVEL

44 Transportation and travel 182

45 Driving a car 186

46 Maps and directions 190

47 Travel and accommodation 194

48 Travel and tourism 198

49 Camping and cycling 202

50 Beach 206

THE ENVIRONMENT

51 Weather and climate 210

52 Geographical features 214

53 Environmental concerns 218

ANIMALS

54 Pets and farm animals 222

55 Wild animals 226

56 Birds and bugs 230

57 Fish, whales, and sea creatures 234

ACTIVITIES

58 Free time activities 238

59 Abilities and actions 242

60 Sports 246

61 Soccer 250

62 Sports equipment and venues 254

ARTS AND THE MEDIA

63 Books and reading 258

64 Music 262

65 Movies and plays 266

66 TV 270

67 Media and celebrity 274

HEALTH

68 Sickness 278

69 Medicine and treatment 282

70 Healthy eating 286

71 Fitness and well-being 290

AROUND TOWN

72 Around town 294

73 Shopping 298

74 At the supermarket 302

75 Urban life 306

SCIENCE AND TECHNOLOGY

76 Technology and gadgets 310

77 Technology and the future 314

78 Science 318

Answers 322

Word list 340

Acknowledgments 360

How to use this book

Each unit of *English for Everyone: English Vocabulary Builder* consists of a teaching spread and a practice spread. Teaching spreads give you an illustrated vocabulary list on a particular topic. Practice spreads include a variety of exercises to reinforce what you have learned. Supporting audio for each teaching spread is available on the website and app. The best way to learn spoken vocabulary is to listen to the audio and repeat each word and phrase on the spread. If you have difficulty understanding a word or phrase, look it up in your dictionary or the word list at the back of this book.

PRACTICE SPREAD

TEACHING SPREAD

Teaching spreads

Unit number The book is divided into units. The unit number helps you keep track of your progress.

Modules Most teaching spreads are broken down into modules covering different aspects of a topic.

Module number Every module is identified with a unique number, so you can easily locate the related audio.

Write-on lines You are encouraged to write your own translations of English words to create your own reference pages.

Sample sentences Some modules show useful English phrases in the context of a sample sentence.

Definitions Idiomatic English phrases are accompanied by definitions.

Supporting graphics Visual cues help you understand and remember new vocabulary.

Audio support All teaching modules are supported by audio recordings to help you recognize and pronounce spoken vocabulary.

Practice exercises

Each teaching spread is followed by exercises that help to fix new words and phrases in your memory. Working through the exercises will help you to remember what you have learned and to use and recognize new English vocabulary. Answers are provided for every exercise.

Listening exercise This symbol indicates that you should listen to an audio track in order to answer the questions in the exercise.

Exercise number Each exercise is identified with a unique number, so you can easily locate answers.

Exercise instruction Each exercise is introduced with a brief instruction, telling you what you need to do.

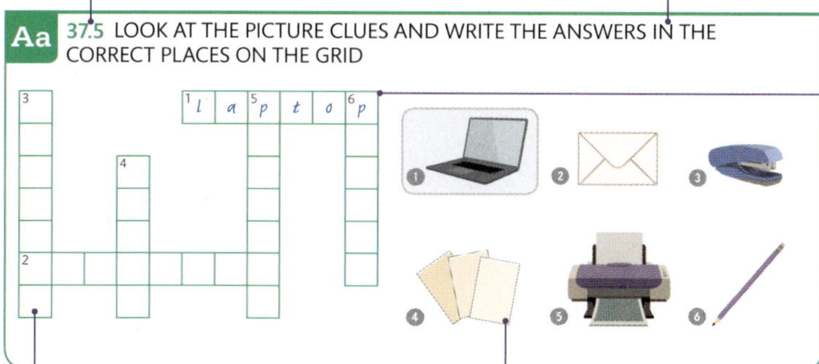

Sample answer The first question of each exercise is answered for you, to help make the task easy to understand.

Space for writing You are encouraged to write your answers in the book for future reference.

Supporting graphics Visual cues are given to help you understand the exercises.

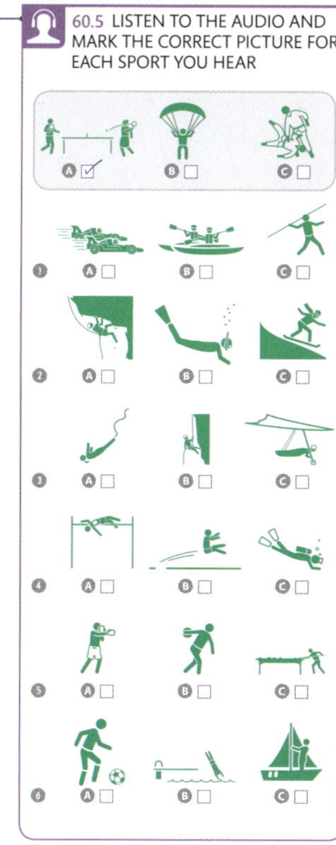

Audio

English for Everyone: English Vocabulary Builder features extensive supporting audio resources. Every word and phrase in the teaching spreads is recorded, and you are encouraged to listen to the audio and repeat the words and phrases out loud, until you are confident you understand and can pronounce what has been said.

SUPPORTING AUDIO
This symbol indicates that audio recordings of the words and phrases in a module are available for you to listen to.

LISTENING EXERCISES
This symbol indicates that you should listen to an audio track in order to answer the questions in the exercise.

FREE AUDIO
website and app
www.dkefe.com

Answers

This book is designed to make it easy to monitor your progress. Answers are provided for every exercise, so you can see how well you have understood and remembered the vocabulary you have learned.

Answers Find the answers to every exercise printed at the back of the book.

Exercise numbers Match these numbers to the unique identifier at the top-left corner of each exercise.

01

1.3
1. India
2. Germany
3. Mongolia
4. Egypt
5. Canada
6. Thailand
7. Slovakia
8. Russia
9. Japan

1.4
1. Indonesia
2. France
3. China
4. Pakistan
5. South Korea
6. Brazil
7. Singapore
8. Argentina

01 Countries and nationalities

1.1 COUNTRIES

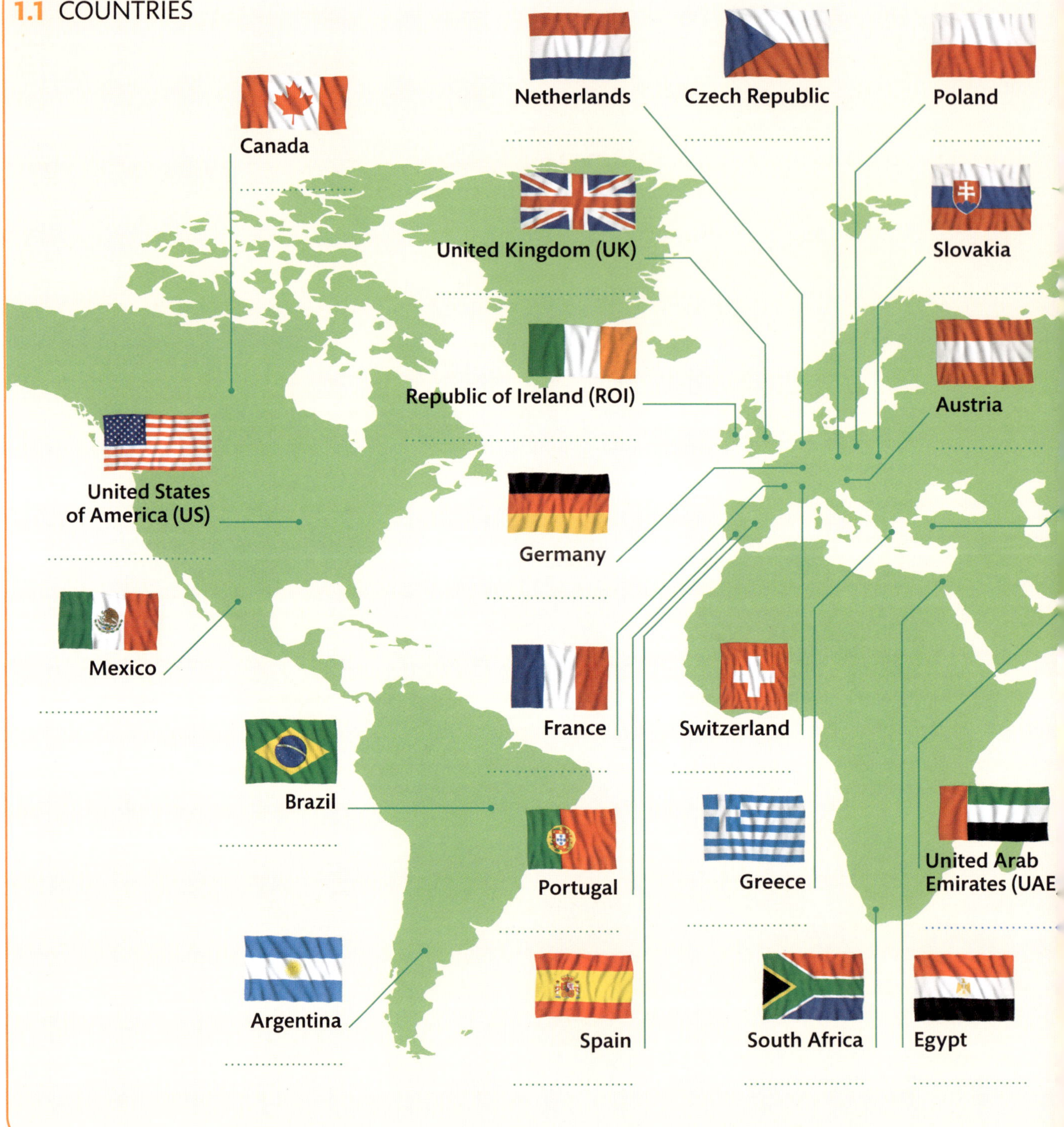

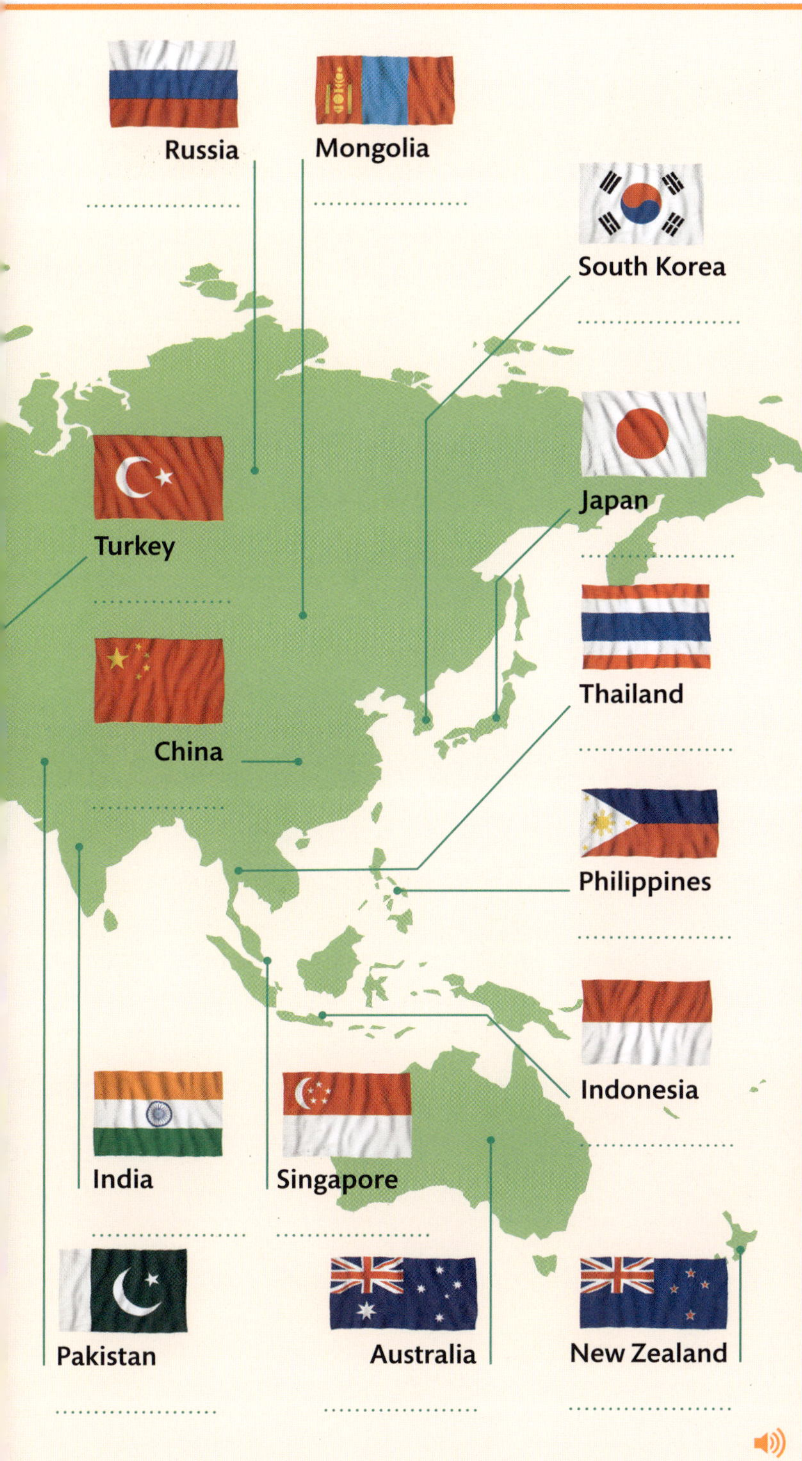

1.2 NATIONALITIES

USA	→	American
Canada	→	Canadian
Mexico	→	Mexican
Brazil	→	Brazilian
Argentina	→	Argentinian
UK	→	British
France	→	French
Russia	→	Russian
Spain	→	Spanish
Portugal	→	Portuguese
Poland	→	Polish
Greece	→	Greek
Turkey	→	Turkish
Egypt	→	Egyptian
China	→	Chinese
Japan	→	Japanese
India	→	Indian
Pakistan	→	Pakistani
Mongolia	→	Mongolian
Australia	→	Australian
Germany	→	German
Switzerland	→	Swiss
Austria	→	Austrian

Aa 1.3 MARK THE CORRECT COUNTRY FOR EACH FLAG

- South Korea ☑
- China ☐
- France ☐

1
- France ☐
- India ☐
- Greece ☐

2
- Brazil ☐
- Canada ☐
- Germany ☐

3
- Mongolia ☐
- Argentina ☐
- New Zealand ☐

4
- Pakistan ☐
- Indonesia ☐
- Egypt ☐

5
- Canada ☐
- Philippines ☐
- Mexico ☐

6
- Thailand ☐
- Turkey ☐
- Portugal ☐

7
- Indonesia ☐
- India ☐
- Slovakia ☐

8
- China ☐
- Australia ☐
- Russia ☐

9
- Poland ☐
- Japan ☐
- Turkey ☐

Aa 1.4 FIND EIGHT MORE COUNTRIES IN THE GRID THAT MATCH THE FLAGS

S G A H A I F M C S S
T A R P Q H R E V O I
M E G E M P A X D U N
P R E N T A N I I T G
M E N I C K C C B H A
E E T I A I E O D K P
C H I N A S Y T A O O
X J N A M T Q L A R R
B I A B R A Z I L E E
C I N D O N E S I A C

1

2

3

4

5

6

7

8

1.5 LISTEN TO THE AUDIO AND CIRCLE THE WORDS YOU HEAR

	Argentina	Australian	Australia
1	India	Indian	Indonesian
2	Spanish	Polish	Turkish
3	Greece	Egypt	Greek
4	Thailand	Poland	Netherlands
5	Chinese	Japanese	Portuguese
6	Germany	German	Japan
7	Mongolian	Australia	Mongolia
8	China	Chinese	Canada

1.6 WRITE THE WORDS FROM THE PANEL IN THE CORRECT GROUPS

COUNTRIES	NATIONALITIES
Russia	Russian

United Kingdom / UK Japanese Poland
~~Russia~~ Polish Pakistan Japan
Pakistani British ~~Russian~~

1.7 WRITE THE CORRECT COUNTRY UNDER EACH FLAG

South Africa

1 ______

2 ______

3 ______

4 ______

5 ______

6 ______

7 ______

8 ______

9 ______

02 Numbers

2.1 NUMBERS

1 one	2 two	3 three	4 four	5 five	6 six
7 seven	8 eight	9 nine	10 ten	11 eleven	12 twelve
13 thirteen	14 fourteen	15 fifteen	16 sixteen	17 seventeen	18 eighteen
19 nineteen	20 twenty	21 twenty-one	22 twenty-two	30 thirty	40 forty
50 fifty	60 sixty	70 seventy	80 eighty	90 ninety	100 a / one hundred

2.2 ORDINAL NUMBERS

1st first	2nd second	3rd third	4th fourth	5th fifth	6th sixth	7th seventh
8th eighth	9th ninth	10th tenth	11th eleventh	12th twelfth	20th twentieth	21st twenty-first

2.3 LARGE NUMBERS

100 — a / one hundred

250 — two hundred and fifty

1,200 — one thousand two hundred

200 — two hundred

1,000 — a / one thousand

1,000,000 — a / one million

3,846 — three thousand, eight hundred and forty-six

82,043 — eighty-two thousand and forty-three

234,407 — two hundred and thirty-four thousand, four hundred and seven

3,089,342 — three million, eighty-nine thousand, three hundred and forty-two

2.4 FRACTIONS, DECIMALS, AND PERCENTAGES

$1/8$ an eighth

$1/4$ a quarter

$1/3$ a third

$1/2$ a half

$3/5$ three fifths

0.5 nought point five

1.7 one point seven

3.97 three point nine seven

1% one percent

99% ninety-nine percent

Aa 2.5 MATCH THE NUMBERS TO THE CORRECT WORDS

10 → ten	twenty
1. 12	ten
2. 20	twelve
3. 30	thirteen
4. 110	thirty
5. 13	seventeen
6. 1,100	eight
7. 17	one hundred and ten
8. 8	one thousand, one hundred

Aa 2.6 REWRITE THE WORDS, CORRECTING THE SPELLINGS

14 foreteen *fourteen*

1. 100 a hundrid ______
2. 8th eighttth ______
3. 1,000 a thousend ______
4. 40 fourty ______
5. 13 threeteen ______
6. 20th twentyeth ______
7. 19 ninteen ______
8. 90 ninty ______
9. 12th twelvth ______
10. 50 fivty ______

2.7 LISTEN TO THE AUDIO AND MARK THE CORRECT NUMBER FOR EACH WORD YOU HEAR

	A	B	C
Example	40 ☑	14 ☐	4 ☐
1	91 ☐	19 ☐	90 ☐
2	12 ☐	20 ☐	21 ☐
3	1,200 ☐	120 ☐	102 ☐
4	413 ☐	430 ☐	403 ☐
5	300 ☐	13 ☐	30 ☐
6	127 ☐	173 ☐	172 ☐

2.8 WRITE THE CORRECT WORDS NEXT TO EACH NUMBER

2.5 *two point five*

1. 1,200 ____________
2. 342 ____________
3. 750 ____________
4. 6.3 ____________
5. 542 ____________
6. 45% ____________
7. 3.95 ____________

2.9 WRITE THE CORRECT WORDS UNDER EACH FRACTION

$\frac{3}{5}$ *three fifths*

1. $\frac{1}{3}$ ____________
2. $\frac{1}{2}$ ____________
3. $\frac{1}{4}$ ____________
4. $\frac{2}{3}$ ____________

03 Time expressions

3.1 THE CALENDAR

day

week

two weeks / fortnight (UK)

month

weekend

year

decade (1990–1999)

century (2000–2099)

millennium (1000–1999)

Monday (MON)

Tuesday (TUE)

Wednesday (WED)

Thursday (THU)

Friday (FRI)

Saturday (SAT)

Sunday (SUN)

January (Jan)

February (Feb)

March (Mar)

April (Apr)

May (May)

June (Jun)

July (Jul)

August (Aug)

September (Sept)

October (Oct)

November (Nov)

December (Dec)

3.2 SEASONS AND FREQUENCY

day

night

morning

afternoon

evening

spring

summer

fall (US)
autumn (UK)

winter

minute

hour

once a week

twice a week

three times a week

every day

every other day

hourly

daily

weekly

monthly

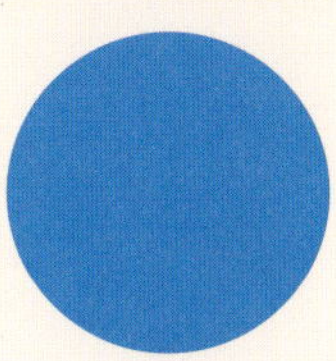
always

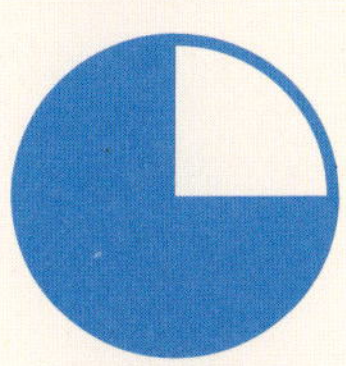
usually

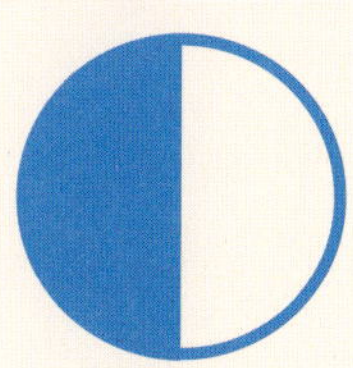
often

sometimes

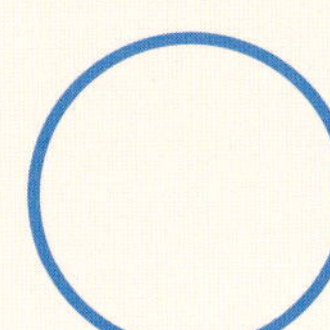
never

Aa 3.3 COMPLETE THE WORD FOR EACH PICTURE, FILLING IN THE MISSING LETTERS

J a n u a r y

1 

T _ e _ d _ y

2 

d _ c _ d _

3 

N _ v _ m _ _ r

4 
w _ _ k

5 

A _ _ u _ t

6 
y _ _ r

Aa 3.4 CIRCLE THE WORD THAT DOES NOT BELONG IN EACH LIST

	Monday	(August)	Wednesday
1	October	day	week
2	evening	hour	afternoon
3	December	Friday	March
4	millennium	fall	spring
5	winter	night	morning
6	sometimes	century	always
7	summer	spring	minute
8	month	hourly	weekend
9	day	week	often

Aa 3.5 LOOK AT THE PICTURE CLUES AND WRITE THE ANSWERS IN THE CORRECT PLACES ON THE GRID

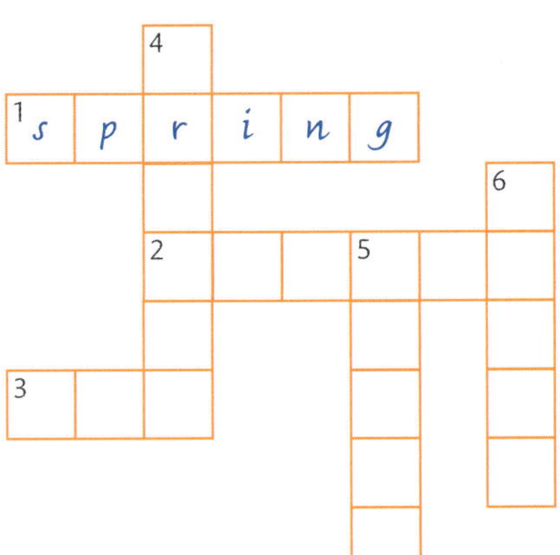

1 

2 

3 

4 

5 

6 

3.6 LISTEN TO THE AUDIO AND MARK THE CORRECT PICTURE FOR EACH WORD YOU HEAR

	A	B	C
(example)	Jul ☐	Jun ☑	Apr ☐
1	 ☐	 ☐	 ☐
2	THU ☐	TUE ☐	SUN ☐
3	2000 – 2099 ☐	1000 – 1999 ☐	 ☐
4	Sept ☐	Dec ☐	Oct ☐
5	 ☐	 ☐	 ☐
6	 ☐	 ☐	 ☐
7	WED ☐	MON ☐	FRI ☐

3.7 MARK THE BEGINNING AND ENDING OF EACH WORD OR EXPRESSION IN THE CHAIN OF LETTERS, THEN WRITE THE WORDS YOU FIND

millennium|weeklyseptemberafternoonhourlysometimeseverydayusuallytwiceaweek

millennium

1 ____________

2 ____________

3 ____________

4 ____________

5 ____________

6 ____________

7 ____________

8 ____________

04 Daily routines

4.1 DAILY ROUTINES

alarm goes off

to wake up

to get up

to take / have a shower

to take / have a bath

to put on make-up

to shave

to wash your hair

to dry your hair

to iron a shirt

to get dressed

to brush your teeth

to wash your face

to brush your hair

to make the bed

to have / eat breakfast

to do the housework

to leave the house

to go to work

to go to school

to catch the train

to catch the bus

to drive

to arrive late

to start work

to have a break

to have / eat lunch

to finish work

to leave work

to work overtime

to go home

to buy groceries

to cook dinner

to have / eat dinner

to clear the table

to listen to the radio

to watch TV

to check your emails

to have / drink tea or coffee

to do / wash the dishes

to walk the dog

to read a newspaper

to go out with friends

to go to a café

to call a friend / your family

to do homework

to put the children to bed

to take out the trash (US) / rubbish (UK)

to feed the dog / cat

to go to bed

Aa 4.2 MARK THE CORRECT PICTURE FOR EACH EXPRESSION

to get up

A ☑ B ☐ C ☐

❶ to put on make-up

A ☐ B ☐ C ☐

❷ to get dressed

A ☐ B ☐ C ☐

❸ to work overtime

A ☐ B ☐ C ☐

❹ to buy groceries

A ☐ B ☐ C ☐

❺ to clear the table

A ☐ B ☐ C ☐

Aa 4.3 MATCH THE PICTURES TO THE CORRECT EXPRESSIONS

❶ 

❷ 

❸ 

❹ 

❺ 

to go to school

to wash the dishes

to arrive late

to wash your face

to do the housework

to put the children to bed

Aa **4.4** WRITE THE CORRECT EXPRESSION UNDER EACH PICTURE

to watch TV

1 ______

2 ______

3 ______

4 ______

5 ______

6 ______

7 ______

8 ______

9 ______

10 ______

11 ______

12 ______

13 ______

14 ______

4.5 LISTEN TO THE AUDIO, THEN NUMBER THE PICTURES IN THE ORDER YOU HEAR THEM

A ☐

B ☐

C ☐

D ☐

E ☐

F ☐

G 1

H ☐

I ☐

J ☐

K ☐

L ☐

05 Describing things: facts

5.1 COLORS (US) / COLOURS (UK)

red

yellow

green

dark green

pale green

blue

purple

pink

white

gray (US)
grey (UK)

black

brown

orange

cream

navy blue

5.2 MATERIALS

plastic

wood

paper

wool

leather

metal

glass

fabric

denim

silk

5.3 ADJECTIVES

big

small / little

wide

narrow

deep

high

low

heavy

light

shallow

clean

dirty

hot

cold

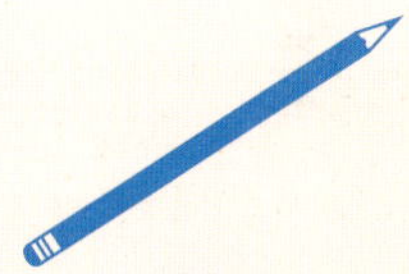
long

loud

quiet

thin

thick

short

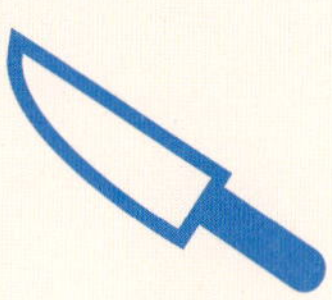
sharp

tight

loose

near

far

Aa 5.4 REWRITE THE WORDS, CORRECTING THE SPELLINGS

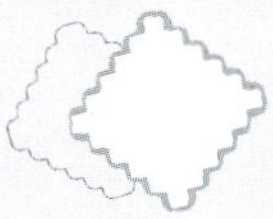
wite
white

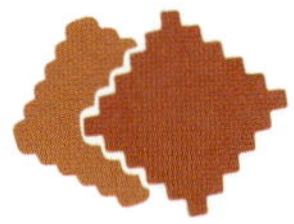
1 brewn
______

2 creem
______

3 oringe
______

4 yelow
______

5 perple
______

6 bleu
______

7 grean
______

Aa 5.5 MATCH THE PICTURES TO THE CORRECT WORDS

1 

2 

3 

4 

silk

paper

wool

fabric

glass

Aa 5.6 WRITE THE WORDS FROM THE PANEL NEXT TO THEIR OPPOSITES

	shallow	*deep*
1	______	far
2	______	dirty
3	tight	______
4	______	low
5	heavy	______
6	long	______

light clean high near
loose ~~deep~~ short

Aa 5.7 MARK THE CORRECT PICTURE FOR EACH WORD

narrow

A ☑ B ☐ C ☐

❸ cold

A ☐ B ☐ C ☐

❶ wide

A ☐ B ☐ C ☐

❹ heavy

A ☐ B ☐ C ☐

❷ loud

A ☐ B ☐ C ☐

❺ small

A ☐ B ☐ C ☐

5.8 LISTEN TO THE AUDIO, THEN NUMBER THE PICTURES IN THE ORDER YOU HEAR THEM

A ☐ B 1 C ☐ D ☐ E ☐ F ☐ G ☐ H ☐

06 Describing things: opinions

6.1 OPINION ADJECTIVES

nice

fun

lovely

delicious

exciting

thrilling

interesting

respectable

special

graceful

pleasant

useful

important

relaxing

harmless

frightening

shocking

irritating

annoying

horrible

nasty

old-fashioned

unpleasant

disastrous

useless

stunning

magnificent

pretty

beautiful

disgusting

boring

ugly

strange / odd

confusing

tiring

6.2 GOOD

remarkable

extraordinary

breathtaking

outstanding

wonderful

amazing

fantastic

great

superb

brilliant

incredible

6.3 BAD

awful

mediocre

terrible

disappointing

Aa 6.4 FILL IN THE GAPS, PUTTING THE WORDS FROM THE PANEL INTO THE CORRECT CATEGORIES

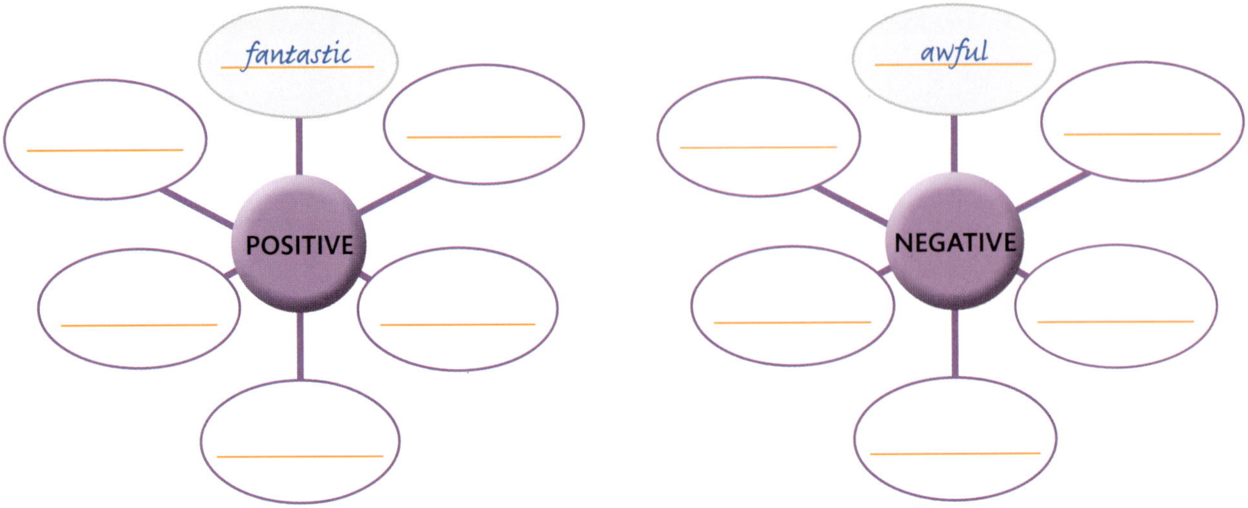

disastrous	breathtaking	incredible	annoying	fun	~~fantastic~~
nasty	amazing	exciting	disgusting	~~awful~~	terrible

Aa 6.5 MARK THE BEGINNING AND ENDING OF EACH WORD IN THE CHAIN OF LETTERS, THEN WRITE THE WORDS YOU FIND

horrible

1. ____________
2. ____________
3. ____________
4. ____________
5. ____________
6. ____________
7. ____________
8. ____________

Aa 6.6 WRITE THE CORRECT WORD UNDER EACH PICTURE

shocking

1 ______

2 ______

3 ______

4 ______

5 ______

6.7 LISTEN TO THE AUDIO AND WRITE THE WORD THAT IS SHOWN IN EACH PICTURE

confusing

1  ______

2  ______

3  ______

4  ______

5  ______

6  ______

Aa 6.8 FIND FIVE MORE WORDS IN THE GRID THAT MATCH THE PICTURES

D	E	L	I	C	I	O	U	S	J	A	H	A
S	T	U	N	N	I	N	G	V	T	Q	P	Q
A	E	D	E	M	J	S	L	D	A	T	E	M
P	O	T	N	T	E	R	Y	I	P	U	N	T
L	T	B	E	A	U	T	I	F	U	L	K	X
U	S	E	L	E	S	S	A	D	E	E	I	A
R	E	S	P	E	C	T	A	B	L	E	L	O

1 

2 

3 

4 

5 

07 Sharing information

7.1 CONTACT DETAILS

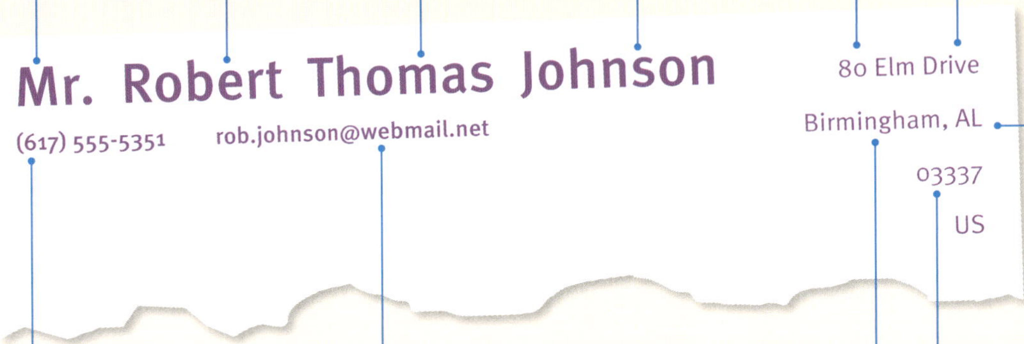

title

first name

middle name

last name

house number

street address

state

cell phone number (US)
mobile number (UK)

email address

city

zip code (US)
postcode (UK)

7.2 BUSINESS CARDS

name

job title

company name

website

business card

to introduce yourself

to exchange business cards

7.3 FORMS OF COMMUNICATION

letter

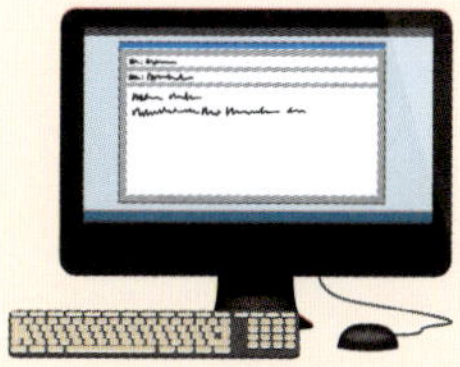
email

phone call

voicemail

text message

social networking

memo

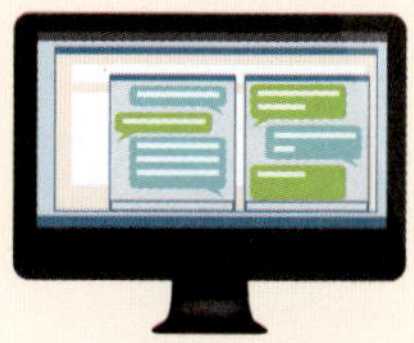
online chat

mail (US)
post (UK)

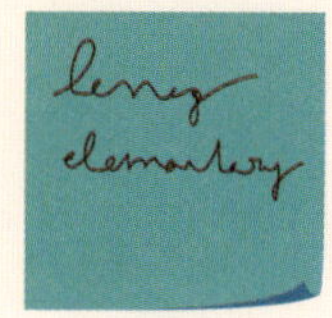
note

7.4 SENDING EMAILS

inbox

outbox

draft

junk mail / spam

trash

attachment

subject

contact

signature

to print

to reply

to reply all

to forward

to send

to delete

Aa 7.5 LOOK AT THE PICTURE AND WRITE THE CORRECT WORD FOR EACH LABEL

Aa 7.6 LOOK AT THE PICTURE AND WRITE THE CORRECT WORD FOR EACH LABEL

Aa 7.7 WRITE THE CORRECT WORD UNDER EACH PICTURE

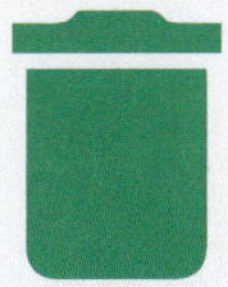

to delete

1 ______

2 ______

3 ______

4 ______

5 ______

6 ______

7 ______

8 ______

9 ______

7.8 LISTEN TO THE AUDIO AND CIRCLE THE WORDS YOU HEAR

	note	memo	title
1	attachment	trash	voicemail
2	spam	to send	subject
3	inbox	email	memo
4	mail	name	outbox
5	state	signature	phone call
6	draft	contact	to send
7	note	outbox	online chat
8	to reply	memo	website
9	draft	to delete	letter
10	voicemail	to forward	phone call
11	to print	trash	title

Aa 7.9 COMPLETE THE WORD FOR EACH PICTURE, FILLING IN THE MISSING LETTERS

v o i c e m a i l

1  t e _ _ m e _ _ a g _

2  p h _ n _ _ a l _

3  n _ t _

4 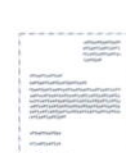 l _ t _ e _

5  _ m _ _ l

6  o _ l _ n _ c _ a t

08 Common English idioms

8.1 COMMON ENGLISH IDIOMS

Tamsin got cold feet about giving a presentation to the sales team.

to get cold feet
[to have a sudden loss of confidence]

Susan is feeling under the weather today. I think she should go home.

to feel under the weather
[to feel unwell, sick, or ill]

Ben and Rachel are head over heels in love with each other.

head over heels
[completely and utterly in love with someone]

You're so right about Jim. He's really lazy! You've hit the nail on the head.

to hit the nail on the head
[to describe exactly what is causing a situation or problem]

Can I lend a hand carrying those papers for you?

to lend a hand
[to help someone with something]

I'm so tired today! I'm really not on the ball.

on the ball
[alert, knowledgeable, or competent]

I heard on the grapevine that Neil and Amina are getting married.

to hear something on the grapevine
[to hear information or news through gossip or rumor]

Hamid is working against the clock to finish his report this week.

against the clock
[under time pressure to get something done]

Dylan is being so naughty today! He's a pain in the neck.

a pain in the neck
[a nuisance, annoying, or difficult]

I'm looking for someone to keep an eye on my house while I'm on vacation.

to keep an eye on
[to take care of or watch carefully]

Leo **has a heart of gold**. He always helps his grandma with her shopping.

to have a heart of gold
[to be kind and good-natured]

I don't know who to vote for yet. I'm still **on the fence**.

to be (US) / sit (UK) on the fence
[to be unwilling to commit or make a decision]

Miriam is a **teacher's pet**. She always arrives early and works very hard.

a teacher's pet
[someone who seeks and gets approval from a person in a position of authority]

If you **cut corners** to finish a project on time, the quality will suffer.

to cut corners
[to do something the easiest or shortest way, at the expense of high standards]

You can't believe all her stories. **Take** them **with a pinch of salt**.

to take something with a pinch of salt
[to not completely believe something or someone]

I have to **face the music** and tell Julia that I broke her new vase.

to face the music
[to confront the consequences of your actions]

I didn't mean to offend Luisa, but I think her reaction was **over the top**.

over the top
[an overreaction or a lack of restraint]

You two really **let your hair down** at Sunita's party last night.

to let your hair down
[to let yourself go or relax]

I haven't really won the lottery. I was just **pulling your leg**.

to pull someone's leg
[to tease or fool someone]

I'm planning a surprise party for Joe. Don't **let the cat out of the bag**.

to let the cat out of the bag
[to tell a secret to someone who shouldn't know about it]

Aa 8.2 MARK THE SENTENCES THAT ARE CORRECT

Can I lend an arm carrying those papers for you? ☐
Can I lend a hand carrying those papers for you? ☑

1 

Tamsin got cold legs about giving a presentation to the sales team. ☐
Tamsin got cold feet about giving a presentation to the sales team. ☐

2 

I'm so tired today! I'm really not on the ball. ☐
I'm so tired today! I'm really not off the ball. ☐

3 

Susan is feeling under the weather today. I think she should go home. ☐
Susan is feeling out of the weather today. I think she should go home. ☐

4 

I have to take the music and tell Julia that I broke her new vase. ☐
I have to face the music and tell Julia that I broke her new vase. ☐

Aa 8.3 MATCH THE PICTURES TO THE CORRECT SENTENCES

 → Miriam is a teacher's pet. She always arrives early and works very hard.

1 

2 

3 

4 

5 

- Hamid is working against the clock to finish his report this week.
- Leo has a heart of gold. He always helps his grandma with her shopping.
- Miriam is a teacher's pet. She always arrives early and works very hard.
- I didn't mean to offend Luisa, but I think her reaction was over the top.
- You two really let your hair down at Sunita's party last night.
- I don't know who to vote for yet. I'm still on the fence.

Aa 8.4 FILL IN THE GAPS, PUTTING THE WORDS IN THE CORRECT ORDER

grapevine | the | that | on

I heard *on* *the* *grapevine* *that* Neil and Amina are getting married.

the | hit | the | on | You've | nail

1 You're so right about Jim. He's really lazy! ______ ______ ______ ______ ______ ______ head.

of | cat | the | let | out

2 I'm planning a surprise party for Joe. Don't ______ ______ ______ ______ ______ the bag.

pinch | them | of | with | Take | a

3 You can't believe all her stories. ______ ______ ______ ______ ______ ______ salt.

corners | cut | to | you

4 If ______ ______ ______ ______ finish a project on time, the quality will suffer.

8.5 LISTEN TO THE AUDIO, THEN NUMBER THE SENTENCES IN THE ORDER YOU HEAR THEM

A  I haven't really won the lottery. I was just pulling your leg. ☐

B  Ben and Rachel are head over heels in love with each other. *1*

C  I'm looking for someone to keep an eye on my house while I'm on vacation. ☐

D  Dylan is being so naughty today! He's a pain in the neck. ☐

E  I have to face the music and tell Julia that I broke her new vase. ☐

09 Around the house

9.1 HOMES, ROOMS, AND FURNITURE

balcony

apartment block (US)
block of flats (UK)

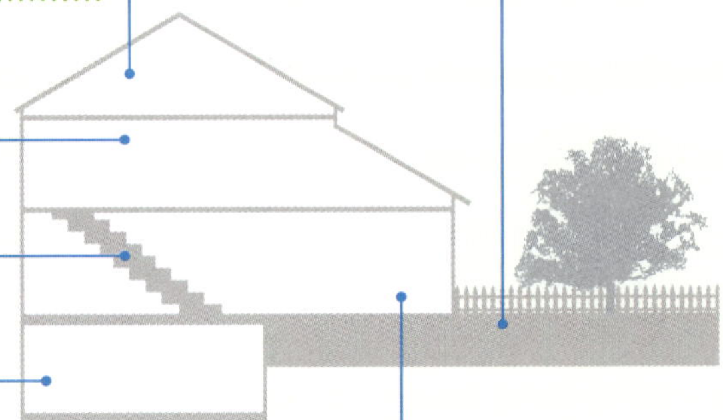

attic

yard (US)
garden (UK)

upstairs

stairs

basement

downstairs

door

roof

house

lawn

window

living room

armchair

couch (US)
sofa (UK)

television / TV

bedroom

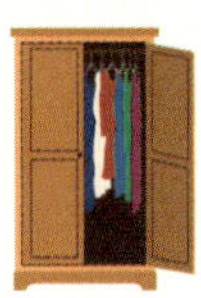

wardrobe

lamp

bed

dresser (US)
chest of drawers (UK)

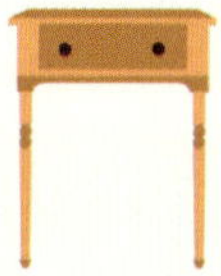
bedside table

cushion

rug

light

dining room

table

chair

study

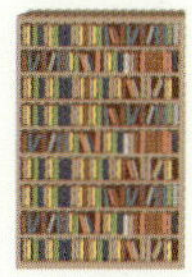
bookcase

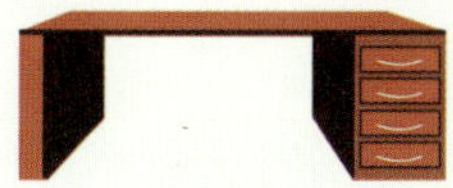
desk

bathroom

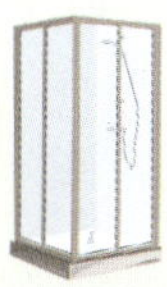
shower

towel

toilet

bathtub (US)
bath (UK)

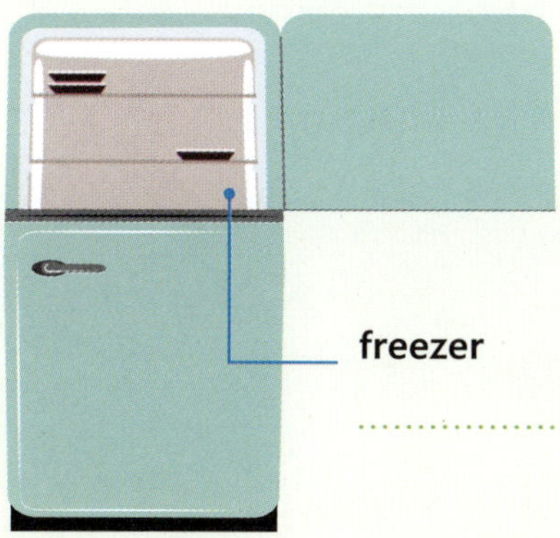

refrigerator /
fridge

kitchen

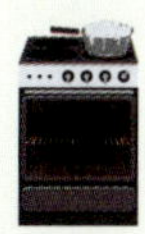
stove (US)
cooker (UK)

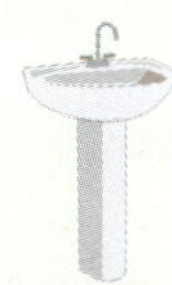
sink

dishwasher

cabinet (US)
cupboard (UK)

trash can (US)
bin (UK)

Aa 9.2 MATCH THE PICTURES TO THE CORRECT WORDS

1 

2 

3 

4 

5 

6 

7 

8 

- table
- cushion
- bedroom
- light
- dresser (US) chest of drawers (UK)
- rug
- shower
- window
- trash can (US) bin (UK)

Aa 9.3 CIRCLE THE WORD THAT DOES NOT BELONG IN EACH LIST

	shower	toilet	(stairs)
1	armchair	couch	cabinet
2	light	bed	lamp
3	table	upstairs	attic
4	bookcase	roof	desk
5	lawn	yard	kitchen
6	sink	window	door
7	study	bedroom	lamp
8	towel	living room	bathtub

Aa 9.4 LOOK AT THE PICTURE AND WRITE THE CORRECT WORD FOR EACH LABEL

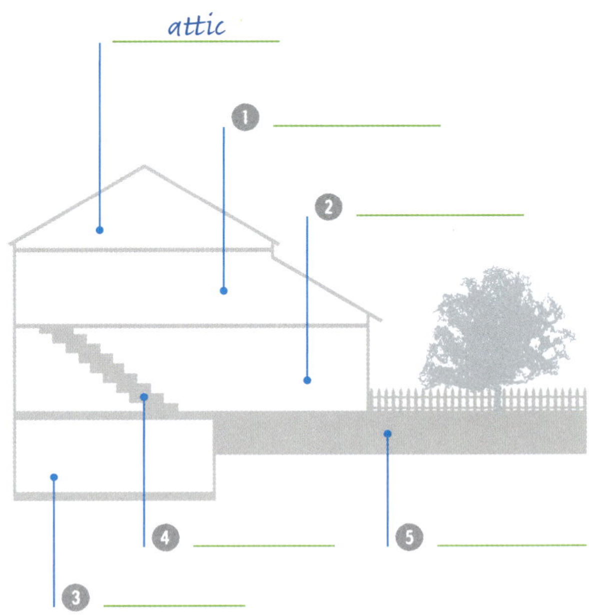

9.5 LISTEN TO THE AUDIO, THEN NUMBER THE PICTURES IN THE ORDER YOU HEAR THEM

A ☐

B 1

C ☐

D ☐

E ☐

F ☐

G ☐

H ☐

I ☐

J ☐

9.6 LOOK AT THE PICTURES BELOW, THEN WRITE THE NAME OF EACH OBJECT UNDER THE CORRECT ROOM

KITCHEN	BATHROOM	LIVING ROOM	BEDROOM
dishwasher			

10 Kitchen implements and toiletries

10.1 KITCHEN IMPLEMENTS

grater

peeler

whisk

cutting board (US)
chopping board (UK)

kitchen knife

scissors

can opener (US)
tin opener (UK)

bottle opener

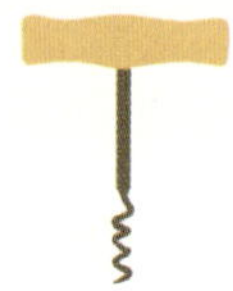
corkscrew

wooden spoon

spatula

ladle

toaster

microwave

kettle

dinnerware (US)
crockery (UK)

plate

bowl

cup

mug

silverware (US)
cutlery (UK)

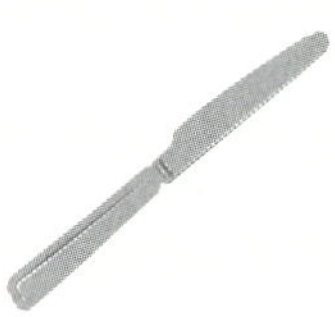
knife

fork

spoon

chopsticks

saucepan

frying pan

wok

colander

blender

rolling pin

mortar

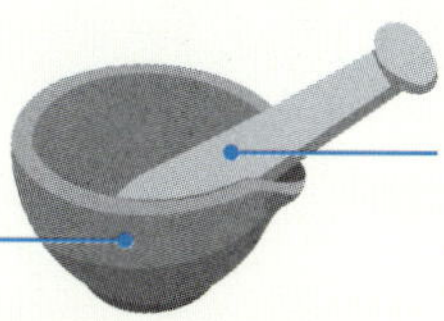

pestle

pestle and mortar

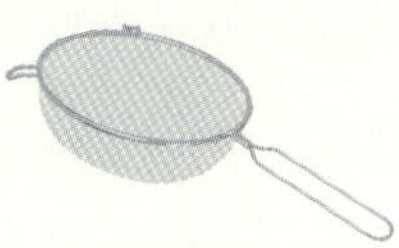

sieve

spatula (US)
fish slice (UK)

10.2 TOILETRIES AND BATHROOM EQUIPMENT

shampoo

conditioner

moisturizer

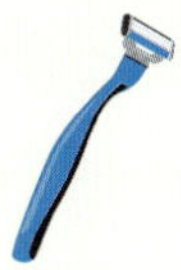

razor

shaving foam

shower gel

deodorant

soap

toothbrush

toothpaste

mouthwash

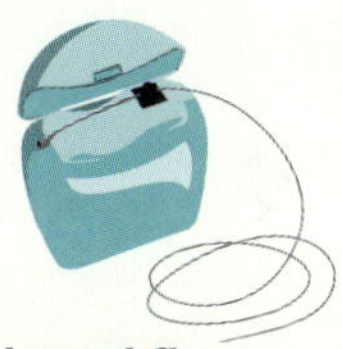

dental floss

sponge

face wash

toilet paper

Aa 10.3 FILL IN THE GAPS, PUTTING THE WORDS FROM THE PANEL INTO THE CORRECT ROOM

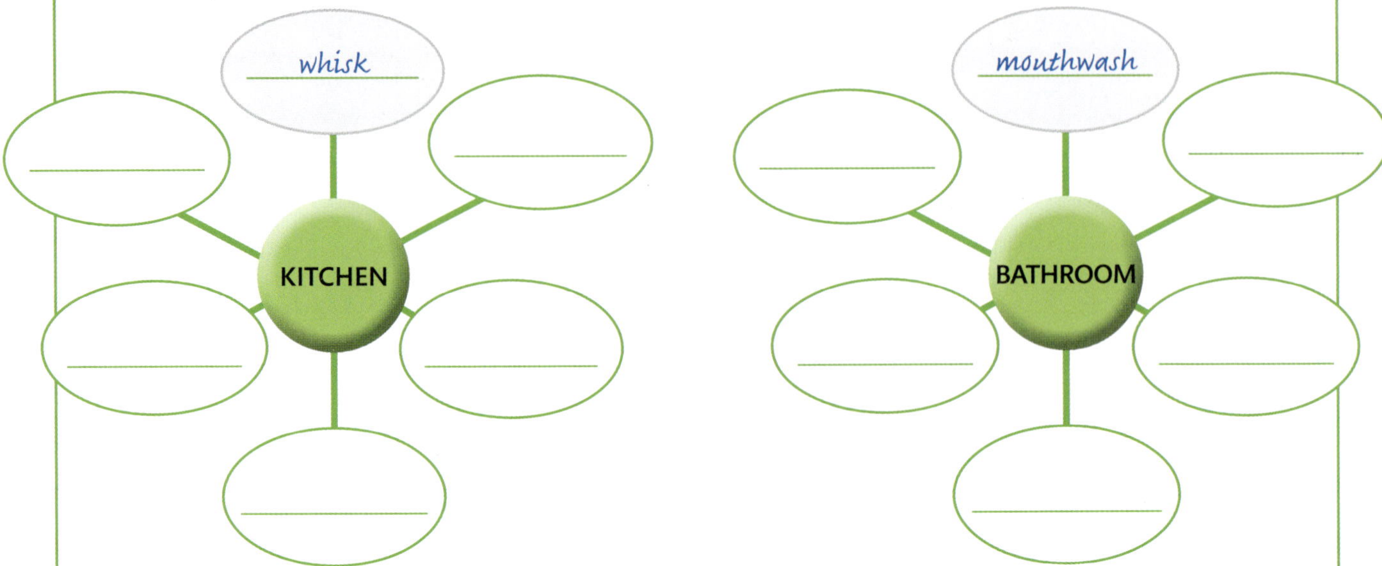

bowl	~~mouthwash~~	frying pan	toothbrush	knife	~~whisk~~
plate	soap	cup	shampoo	conditioner	sponge

Aa 10.4 MARK THE BEGINNING AND END OF EACH WORD IN THE CHAIN OF LETTERS, THEN WRITE THE WORDS YOU FIND

deodorant

1 ______

2 ______

3 ______

4 ______

5 ______

6 ______

7 ______

8 ______

10.5 WRITE THE CORRECT WORD UNDER EACH PICTURE

kettle

1 ______

2 ______

3 ______

4 ______

5 ______

6 ______

7 ______

8 ______

9 ______

10.6 LISTEN TO THE AUDIO AND MARK THE CORRECT PICTURE FOR EACH WORD YOU HEAR

A ☐

B ☐

C ☑

1 A ☐ B ☐ C ☐

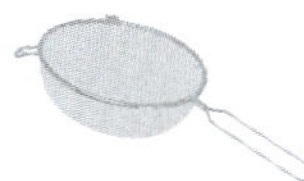

2 A ☐ B ☐ C ☐

3 A ☐ B ☐ C ☐

4 A ☐ B ☐ C ☐

5 A ☐ B ☐ C ☐

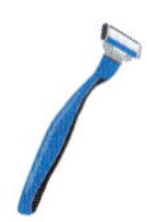

6 A ☐ B ☐ C ☐

7 A ☐ B ☐ C ☐

11 Chores and cleaning

11.1 HOUSEHOLD CHORES

to clean the windows

to sweep the floor

to scrub the floor

to mop the floor

to vacuum the carpet

to dust

to take out the trash (US) / rubbish (UK)

to clean up (US) to tidy (UK)

to go to the store (US) / shops (UK)

to clean the bathroom

to set the table

to clear the table

to do the dishes

to dry the dishes

to load the dishwasher

to unload the dishwasher

to do the laundry

to hang clothes

to do the ironing

to fold clothes

to make the bed

to change the sheets

to water the plants

to wash the car

to feed the pets

11.2 LAUNDRY AND CLEANING

washing machine

tumble dryer

laundry basket

laundry detergent

clothes line (US)
washing line (UK)

drying clip (US)
peg (UK)

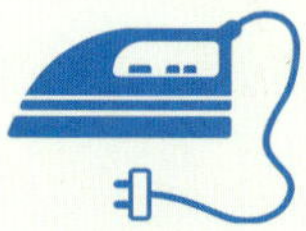
iron

ironing board

bucket

mop

dishwashing liquid (US)
washing up liquid (UK)

scouring pad

sponge

cloth

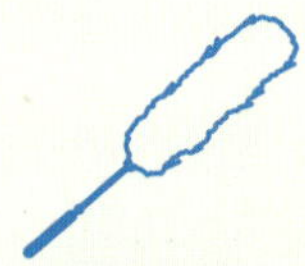
duster

polish

cleaning fluid

bleach

vacuum cleaner

dustpan

brush

broom

recycling bin

garbage bag (US)
bin liner (UK)

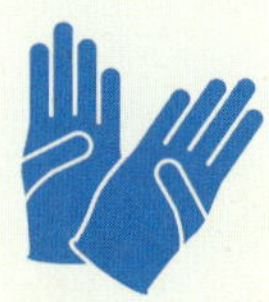
rubber gloves

Aa 11.3 FIND EIGHT MORE WORDS IN THE GRID THAT MATCH THE PICTURES

T	D	C	H	A	B	R	D	C	S	P
E	U	V	M	Q	U	K	U	V	T	O
K	S	D	O	M	C	S	S	D	A	L
F	T	I	P	T	K	R	T	I	P	I
U	E	B	C	X	E	D	P	B	L	S
B	R	O	O	M	T	Y	A	D	E	H
R	M	Z	L	O	L	A	N	Z	R	O
E	E	T	J	D	B	R	U	S	H	T
S	C	O	U	R	I	N	G	P	A	D
T	C	L	O	T	H	W	T	A	C	A

Aa 11.4 REWRITE THE WORDS OR EXPRESSIONS, CORRECTING THE SPELLINGS

to sweap the flour
to sweep the floor

1 landry detergint

____

2 spong

____

3 recicling bin

____

4 to scrab the floor

____

5 to clare the table

____

6 bleech

____

7 to lode the dishwasher

____

11.5 MATCH THE EXPRESSIONS TO THE CORRECT PICTURES

to water the plants

1. to do the ironing
2. to go to the store (US) / shops (UK)
3. to do the laundry
4. to feed the pets
5. to dry the dishes
6. to dust
7. to clean the bathroom
8. to change the sheets

A 

B 

C 

D 

E 

F 

G 

H 

11.6 LISTEN TO THE AUDIO AND WRITE THE EXPRESSION THAT IS SHOWN IN EACH PICTURE

 *vacuum cleaner*

1.  ____________________
2.  ____________________
3.  ____________________
4.  ____________________
5.  ____________________

11.7 COMPLETE THE EXPRESSION FOR EACH PICTURE, FILLING IN THE MISSING LETTERS

 *i* r *o* n *i* n g b *o* *a* r d

1.  c _ o _ _ e _ l _ n _
2.  r _ b _ e _ g _ o _ e s
3.  b _ c _ _ t
4. 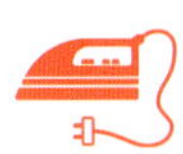 i _ o _

12 Tools and gardening

12.1 TOOLS AND HOME IMPROVEMENT

tape measure

hammer

vise (US)
vice (UK)

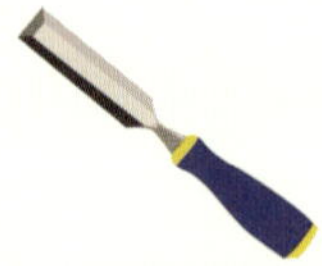
file

ladder

hacksaw

saw

screwdriver

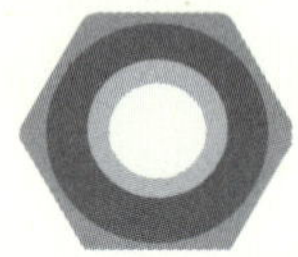
nut

tool box

bolt

screw

nail

drill

ax (US) / axe (UK)

pliers

monkey wrench

wrench (US)
spanner (UK)

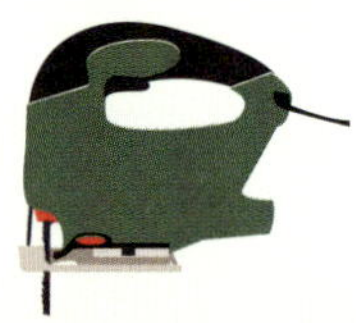
jigsaw

hex / Allen keys

level (US)
spirit level (UK)

paint

paintbrush

roller

plane

12.2 GARDENING EQUIPMENT

trowel

shears

spade

hoe

rake

fork

wheelbarrow

hose

sprinkler

lawn mower

12.3 HOME IMPROVEMENT VERBS

to paint the house

to paint a room

to plaster the walls

to tile the bathroom

to fit a carpet

to put up shelves

to make curtains

to unclog / unblock the sink

to change a lightbulb

12.4 GARDENING VERBS

to mow the lawn

to do the weeding

to plant bulbs

to prune trees

to trim a hedge

to water the flowers

Aa 12.5 MARK THE CORRECT VERB FOR THE ACTIVITY IN EACH PICTURE

- to tile the bathroom [x]
- to unblock the sink [ ]
- to fit a carpet [ ]

1

- to mow the lawn [ ]
- to plant bulbs [ ]
- to trim a hedge [ ]

2

- to put up shelves [ ]
- to prune trees [ ]
- to change a lightbulb [ ]

3

- to make curtains [ ]
- to fit a carpet [ ]
- to mow the lawn [ ]

4

- to prune trees [ ]
- to water the flowers [ ]
- to do the weeding [ ]

5

- to make curtains [ ]
- to plaster the walls [ ]
- to paint a room [ ]

6

- to plaster the walls [ ]
- to paint the house [ ]
- to put up shelves [ ]

7

- to fit a carpet [ ]
- to do the weeding [ ]
- to trim a hedge [ ]

Aa 12.6 WRITE THE CORRECT WORD UNDER EACH PICTURE

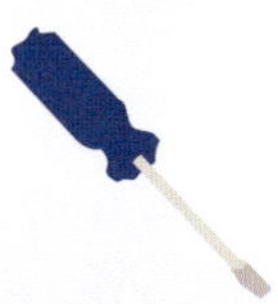

screwdriver

1 ______

2 ______

3 ______

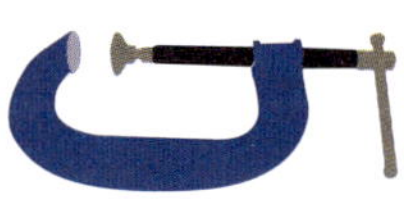

4 ______

5 ______

6 ______

7 ______

Aa 12.7 FILL IN THE GAPS, PUTTING THE WORDS FROM THE PANEL INTO THE CORRECT CATEGORIES

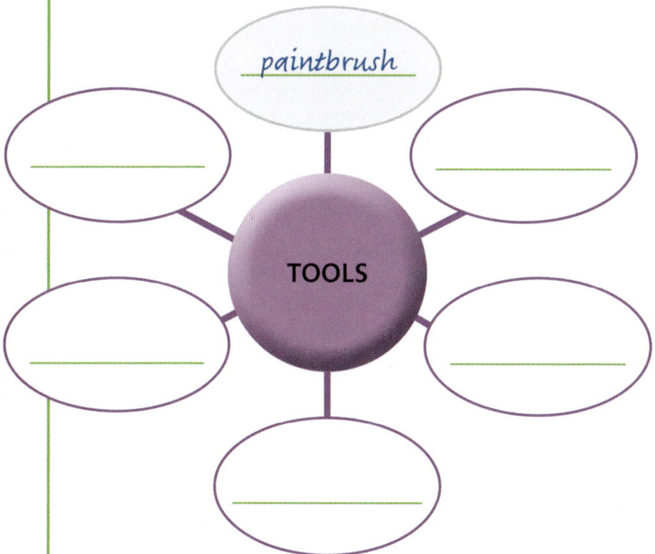

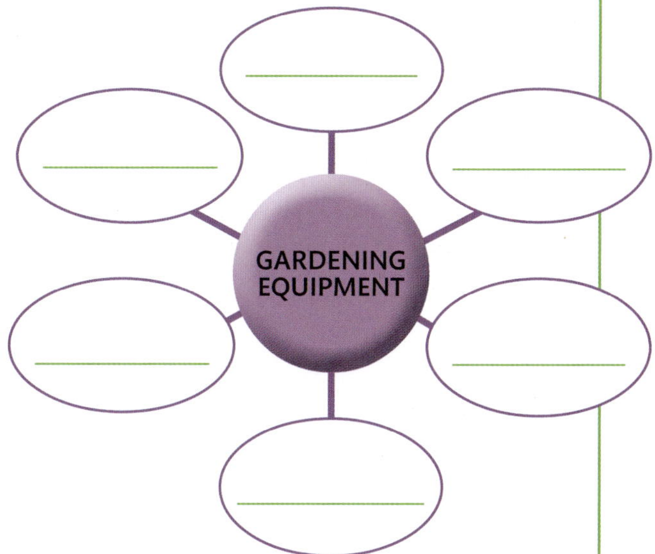

hose	hammer	file	sprinkler	wheelbarrow	plane
jigsaw	rake	hacksaw	hoe	trowel	~~paintbrush~~

12.8 LISTEN TO THE AUDIO AND MARK THE CORRECT PICTURE FOR EACH WORD YOU HEAR

A ☐

B ☐

C ☑

2

A ☐

B ☐

C ☐

1

A ☐

B ☐

C ☐

3
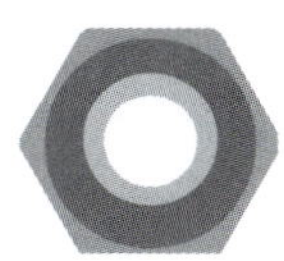
A ☐

B ☐

C ☐

13 Moving and renting

13.1 ACCOMMODATION, MOVING, AND RENTING

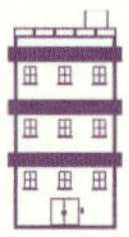
apartments (US)
flats (UK)

duplex (US)
semi-detached (UK)

detached houses

row (US) / terraced
houses (UK)

ranch house (US)
bungalow (UK)

cottage

furnished

unfurnished

open-plan

parking space

storage

realtor (US)
estate agent (UK)

moving truck (US)
removal van (UK)

boxes

keys

rent

bills

lease / tenancy
agreement (UK)

landlord

tenant

to view a house

to pack

to unpack

to move in

to move out

13.2 USEFUL EXPRESSIONS

I had to pay my landlord the equivalent of one month's rent as a deposit.

a deposit
[money that a tenant pays to a landlord before moving into a property]

My new landlord wants a reference from my previous landlord.

a reference
[a letter describing your character and ability to pay your rent]

We had a house-warming party to celebrate buying our new apartment.

a house-warming party
[an informal party that you give after moving into a new house or apartment]

The rent for my new apartment is $500, including utilities.

including utilities
[the rent covers the bills such as electricity, water, and gas]

Real estate is in high demand, so prices are increasing.

real estate (US) / property (UK)
[houses and apartments that are for sale or rented out]

We live in an attractive residential area with lots of parks.

a residential area
[a part of town where most buildings are houses or apartments]

The local stores sell a wide selection of food and drinks.

local
[belonging to the area where you live]

My roommate never does the dishes.

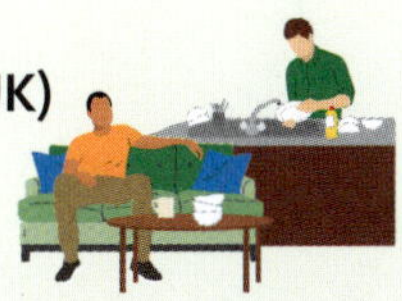

a roommate (US) / housemate (UK)
[a person you share your house or apartment with]

We have a roomer who lives in our spare bedroom.

a roomer (US) / a lodger (UK)
[a person who pays to live in your house]

We gave notice to our landlord two months before moving out.

to give notice
[to announce to your landlord that you wish to move out]

Aa 13.3 LOOK AT THE PICTURE CLUES AND WRITE THE ANSWERS IN THE CORRECT PLACES ON THE GRID

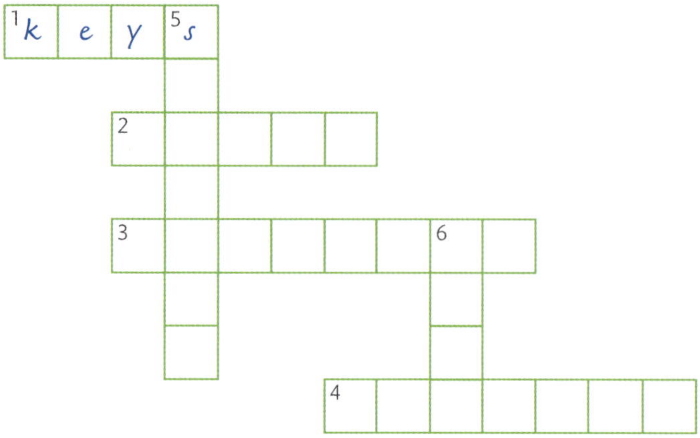

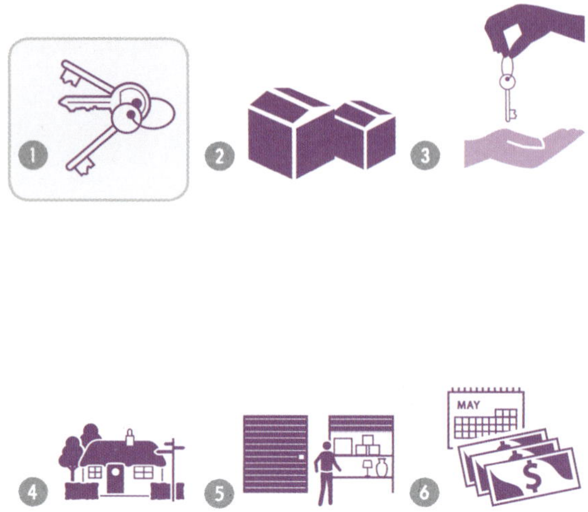

13.4 LISTEN TO THE AUDIO, THEN NUMBER THE PICTURES IN THE ORDER YOU HEAR THEM

A ☐ B ☐ C 1 D ☐

E ☐ F ☐ G ☐ H ☐

I ☐ J ☐ K ☐ L ☐

Aa 13.5 COMPLETE THE WORD FOR EACH PICTURE, FILLING IN THE MISSING LETTERS

p a r k i n g s p a c e

1  _ n f _ r n _ s h _ d

2  l _ n _ l _ r d

3  t _ n _ _ t

4  _ p _ r t _ _ n t s

5  s _ _ r _ g _

Aa 13.6 MATCH THE DEFINITIONS TO THE CORRECT PHRASES

a letter describing your character and ability to pay rent → a reference

1. houses and apartments that are for sale or rented out
2. a part of town where most buildings are houses or apartments
3. belonging to the area where you live
4. money that a tenant pays to a landlord before moving into a property
5. the rent covers the bills such as electricity, water, and gas

- a residential area
- a reference
- a deposit
- including utilities
- real estate (US) / property (UK)
- local

Aa 13.7 CROSS OUT THE INCORRECT WORD IN EACH SENTENCE

I had to pay my landlord the equivalent of one month's rent as a **deposit** / ~~notice~~.

1.  We had a **house-heating** / **house-warming** party to celebrate buying our new apartment.
2.  We have a **landlord** / **roomer** who lives in our spare bedroom.
3.  My **roommate** / **deposit** never does the dishes.
4.  We **took** / **gave** notice to our landlord two months before moving out.
5.  We live in an attractive **residence** / **residential** area with lots of parks.

14 The body

14.1 PARTS OF THE BODY

ear

eye

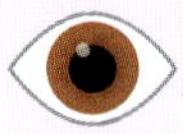

eyebrow

eyelashes

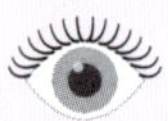

nose

nostrils

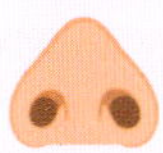

mouth

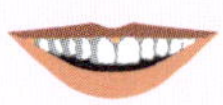

lips

teeth

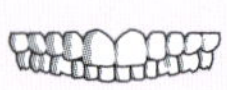

tooth

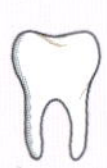

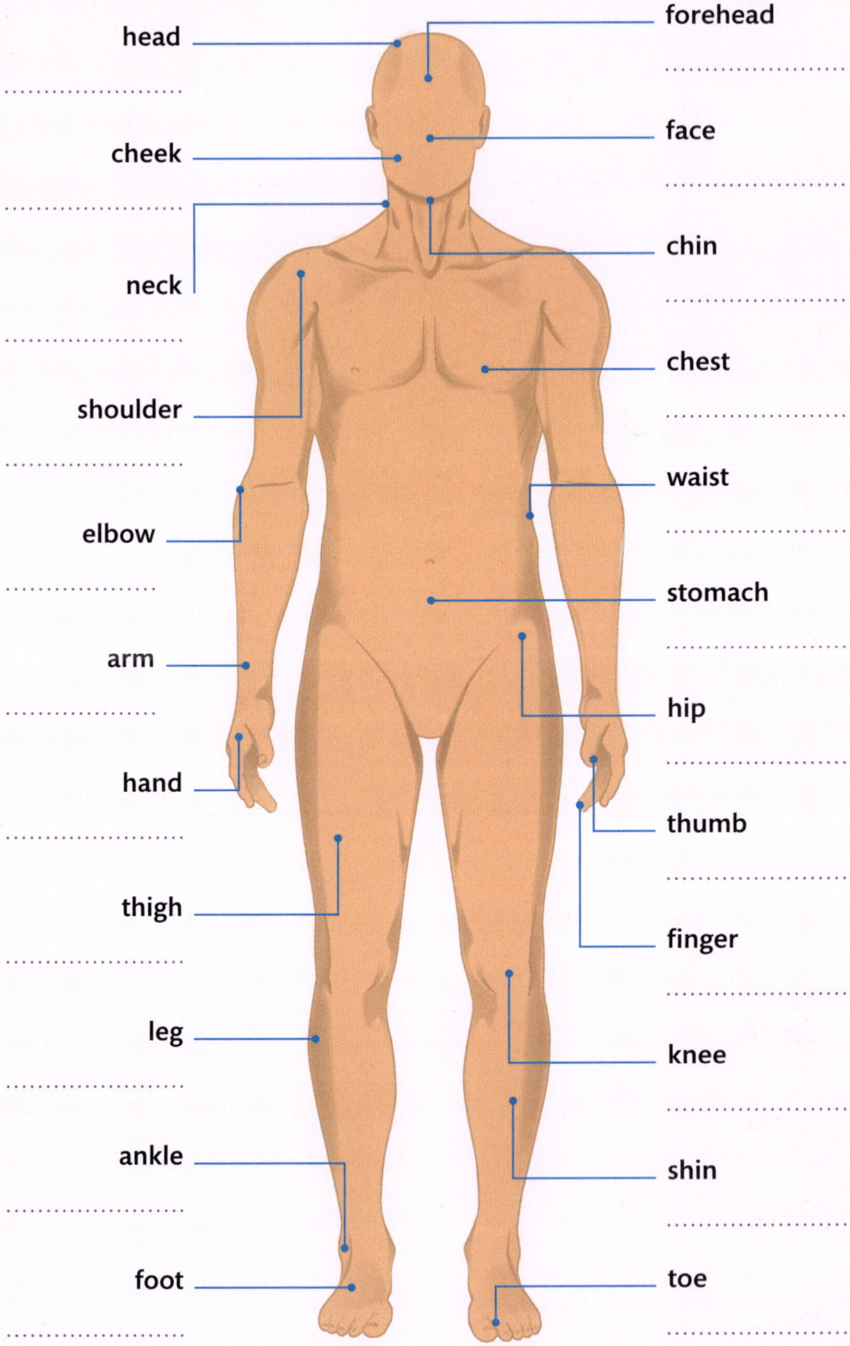

14.2 VERBS

to smile

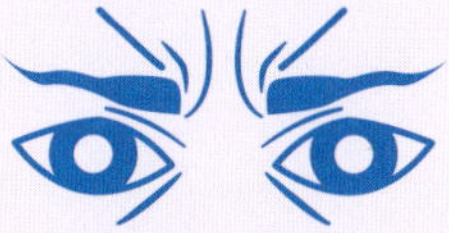
to frown

to grin

to laugh

to cry

to yawn

to cough

to sigh

to lick

to suck

to breathe

to hold your breath

to wink

to blink

to blush

to sweat / to perspire

to shiver

to snore

to sneeze

to wave

to clap

to shrug

to bow

to nod

to shake your head

Aa 14.3 LOOK AT THE PICTURE AND WRITE THE CORRECT WORD FROM THE PANEL FOR EACH LABEL

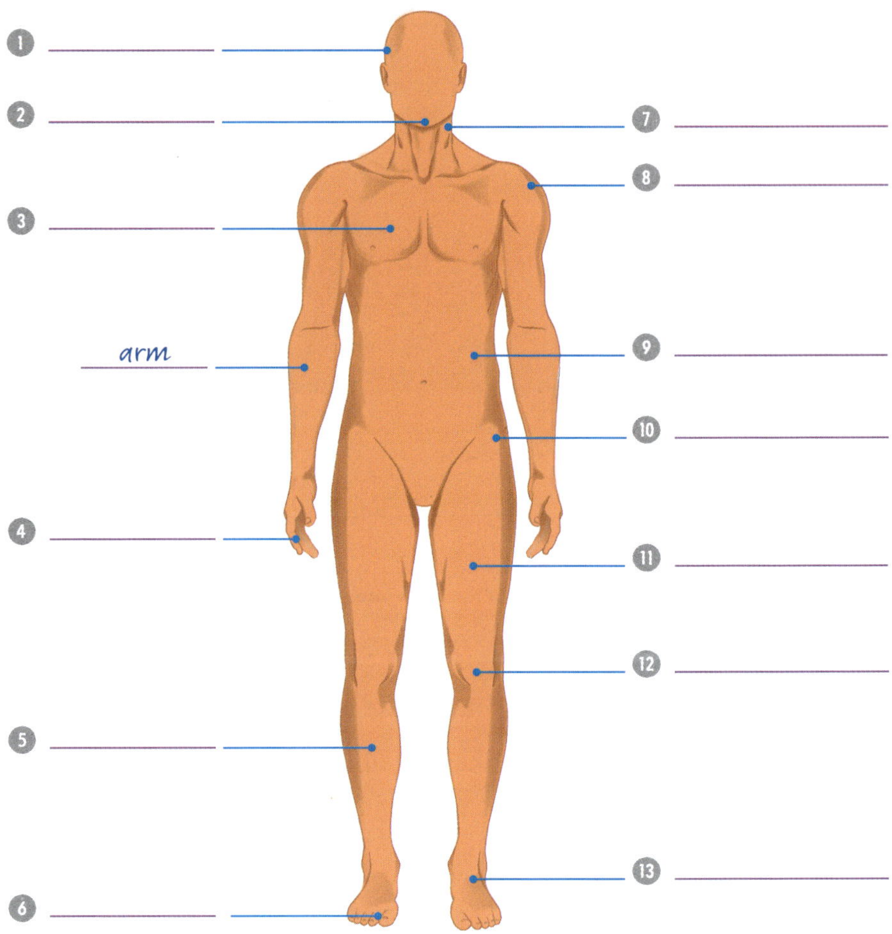

chest
waist
toe
shoulder
hip
~~arm~~
thigh
head
knee
chin
finger
foot
shin
neck

Aa 14.4 MARK THE BEGINNING AND ENDING OF EACH WORD IN THE CHAIN OF LETTERS

eyelashes/teethnosemoutheyebrownostrilsearanklelipsforeheadthighfingerstomachchinhip

Aa 14.5 MARK THE CORRECT VERB FOR THE ACTIVITY IN EACH PICTURE

to laugh ☑
to cry ☐
to blush ☐

1 

to grin ☐
to wave ☐
to clap ☐

2 

to shiver ☐
to sneeze ☐
to blink ☐

3 

to bow ☐
to shrug ☐
to wink ☐

4 

to yawn ☐
to frown ☐
to cry ☐

5 

to blush ☐
to breathe ☐
to sneeze ☐

6 

to lick ☐
to shiver ☐
to clap ☐

7 

to yawn ☐
to blink ☐
to frown ☐

8 

to smile ☐
to sigh ☐
to snore ☐

9 

to wink ☐
to suck ☐
to nod ☐

14.6 LISTEN TO THE AUDIO AND MARK THE CORRECT PICTURE FOR EACH WORD YOU HEAR

 A ☐
 B ☑
 C ☐

3  A ☐
 B ☐
 C ☐

1 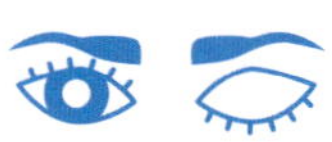 A ☐
 B ☐
 C ☐

4  A ☐
 B ☐
 C ☐

2  A ☐
 B ☐
 C ☐

5  A ☐
 B ☐
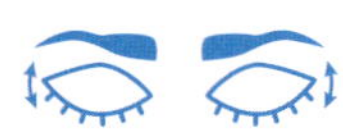 C ☐

15 Clothes

15.1 CLOTHES

shirt

t-shirt

blouse

suit

uniform

dress

skirt

pants (US)
trousers (UK)

jeans

jacket

raincoat

socks

shorts

tie

pajamas (US)
pyjamas (UK)

coat

sweater (US)
jumper (UK)

bra

panties (US)
knickers (UK)

bathrobe / dressing gown

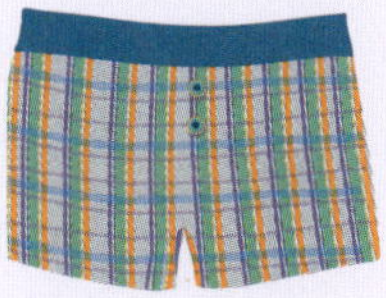

boxer shorts

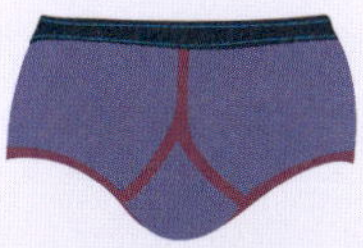

jockey shorts (US)
pants (UK)

pantyhose (US)
tights (UK)

leggings

15.2 VERBS

to wear

to suit (someone)

to fit

to put on

to take off

to do up / fasten

to undo / unfasten

to change / to get changed

15.3 DESCRIBING CLOTHES AND STYLES

leather

cotton

woolen (US)
woollen (UK)

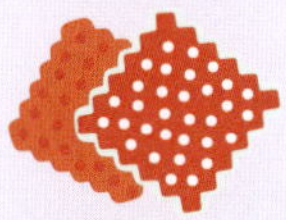

polka dot (US)
spotted (UK)

striped

checkered (US)
checked (UK)

plain

silk

denim

Aa 15.4 WRITE THE CORRECT WORD UNDER EACH PICTURE

jeans

1 ______

2 ______

3 ______

4 ______

5 ______

6 ______

7 ______

8 ______

9 ______

Aa 15.5 LOOK AT THE PICTURE AND WRITE THE CORRECT WORD FOR EACH LABEL

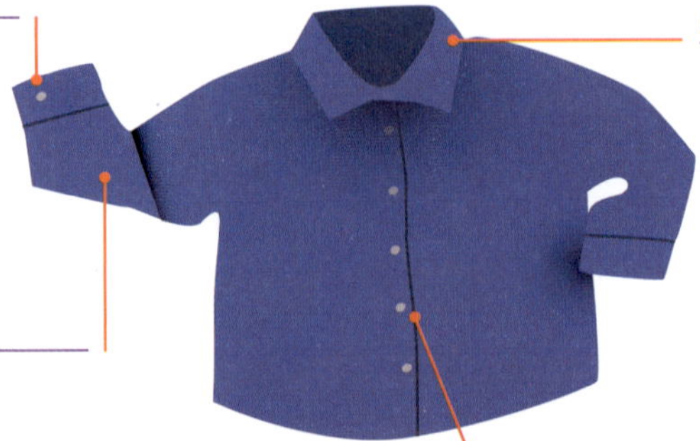

1 ______

2 ______

3 ______

Aa 15.6 REWRITE THE WORDS, CORRECTING THE SPELLINGS

legings

leggings

1  bathrob ______

2  cote ______

3  reincoat ______

4  shoorts ______

5  soks ______

6  tye ______

7  denem ______

8  siut ______

9  lether ______

10  brah ______

11  t-shert ______

15.7 LISTEN TO THE AUDIO, THEN NUMBER THE PICTURES IN THE ORDER YOU HEAR THEM

A ☐

B ☐

C ☐

D 1

E ☐

F ☐

G ☐

H ☐

I ☐

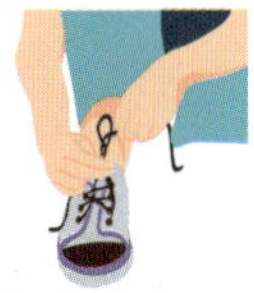
J ☐

15.8 FIND EIGHT MORE WORDS FOR DESCRIBING CLOTHES IN THE GRID THAT MATCH THE PICTURES

C	H	E	C	K	E	R	E	D	S	C
T	W	V	P	Q	H	K	Q	V	T	O
A	O	D	E	N	I	M	M	D	R	T
P	O	I	N	T	E	R	T	I	I	T
L	L	B	P	L	A	I	N	Z	P	O
E	E	D	I	H	T	U	A	D	E	N
A	N	Z	L	O	L	A	O	Z	D	O
T	A	S	D	C	E	B	Q	T	Z	T
H	Q	T	K	P	R	D	M	E	S	X
E	M	A	S	T	T	Z	T	M	I	A
R	T	P	R	A	E	S	X	A	L	O
P	O	L	K	A	D	O	T	Q	K	Q

1

2

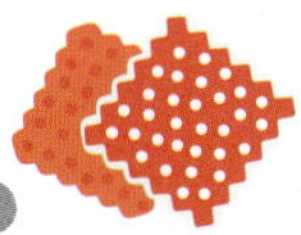
3

4

5

6

7

8

16 Accessories and beauty products

16.1 ACCESSORIES

scarf

hat

cap

gloves

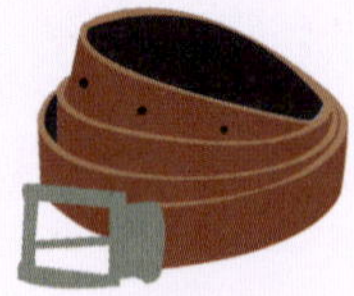
belt

purse (US)
handbag (UK)

briefcase

backpack /
rucksack (UK)

jewelry (US)
jewellery (UK)

necklace

bracelet

earrings

ring

brooch

pin (US)
badge (UK)

cufflinks

watch

handkerchief

bow tie

umbrella

hair band (US)
Alice band (UK)

glasses

sunglasses

wallet

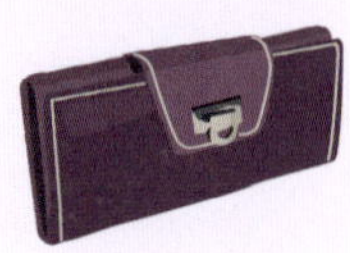
wallet (US)
purse (UK)

16.2 SHOES

high heels

sandals

boots

shoes

sneakers (US)
trainers (UK)

slippers

flip-flops

16.3 MAKE-UP AND BEAUTY PRODUCTS

lipstick

foundation

mascara

blush (US)
blusher (UK)

eyeliner

eyeshadow

hair dye

hair gel

hair spray

nail polish

perfume

aftershave

moisturizer

hairbrush

comb

Aa 16.4 COMPLETE THE WORD FOR EACH PICTURE, FILLING IN THE MISSING LETTERS

b r *i* *e* f c *a* s *e*

1  h a _ _ k _ r c _ _ e f

2  s _ n _ a l _

3  b _ c k _ a _ k

4  _ c a _ f

5  w _ l _ e _

Aa 16.5 CIRCLE THE WORD THAT DOES NOT BELONG IN EACH LIST

	sandals	high heels	(eyeliner)
1	earrings	necklace	shoes
2	mascara	belt	blush
3	hair band	boots	sneakers
4	hat	cap	eyeliner
5	handkerchief	hairbrush	comb
6	laces	scarf	buckle
7	moisturizer	perfume	umbrella

16.6 LISTEN TO THE AUDIO, THEN NUMBER THE PICTURES IN THE ORDER YOU HEAR THEM

A ☐

B ☐

C ☐

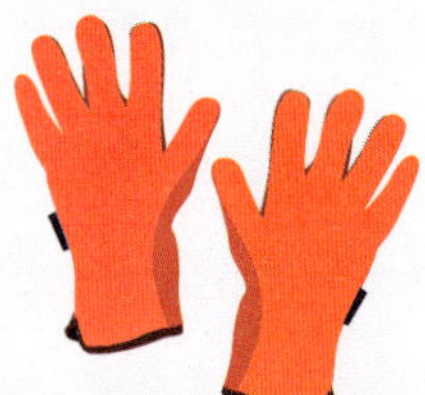

D *1*

E ☐

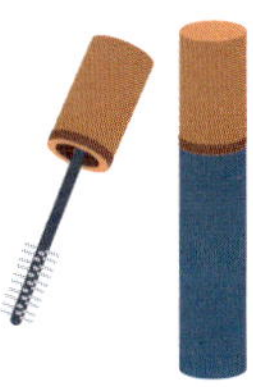

F ☐

G ☐

H ☐

I ☐

J ☐

Aa 16.7 MATCH THE PICTURES TO THE CORRECT WORDS

→ perfume

1 

2 

3 

4 

5 

6 

7 

8 

- high heels
- perfume
- lipstick
- nail polish
- bow tie
- purse (US) handbag (UK)
- hat
- flip-flops
- ring

Aa 16.8 REWRITE THE WORDS, CORRECTING THE SPELLINGS

breislet
bracelet

1 broach
____

2 earings
____

3 umbrela
____

4 combe
____

5 parfume
____

6 sunglases
____

7 neklace
____

17 Appearance

17.1 HAIR

long hair

short hair

shoulder-length hair

bald

straight hair

wavy hair

curly hair

frizzy hair

ponytail

black hair

brown hair

blond hair

red hair

gray hair (US)
grey hair (UK)

facial hair

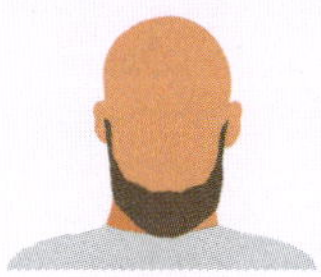
beard

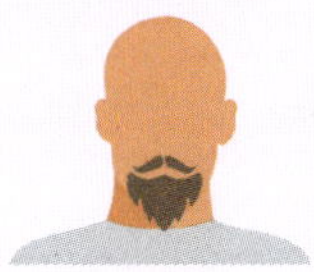
goatee

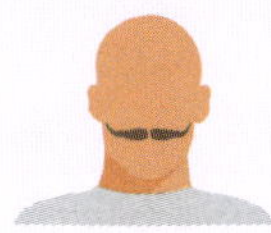
mustache (US)
moustache (UK)

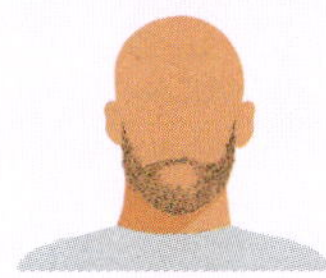
stubble

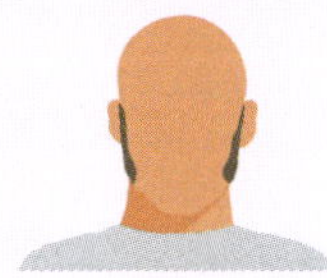
sideburns

17.2 VERBS

to style your hair

to have / get your hair cut

to tie your hair back

to shave

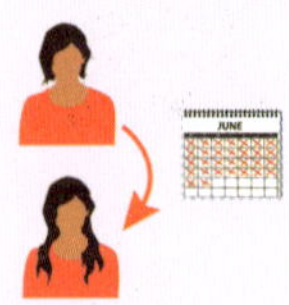
to grow your hair

17.3 EYES

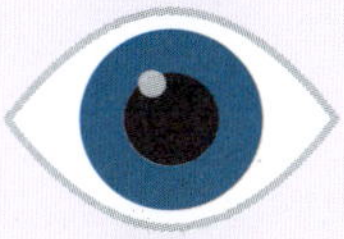
blue

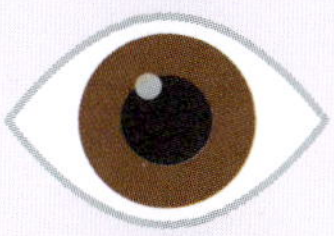
brown

green

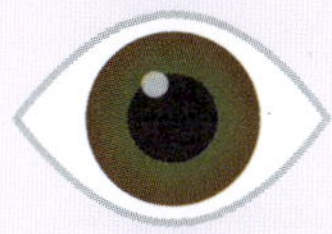
hazel

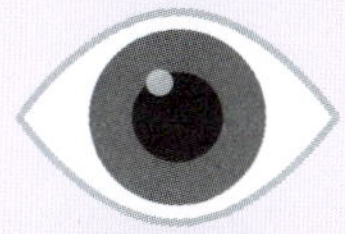
gray (US) / grey (UK)

17.4 APPEARANCE AND STYLE

short

medium height

tall

beautiful

handsome

young

middle-aged

old

formal (US)
smart (UK)

casual

elegant

glamorous

dark skin

tan skin (US)
tanned skin (UK)

olive skin

fair skin

pale skin

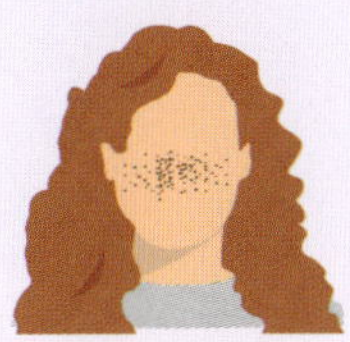
freckles

wrinkles

mole

Aa 17.5 MATCH THE WORDS TO THE CORRECT PICTURES

casual

1 ponytail

2 beautiful

3 gray hair (US) grey hair (UK)

4 goatee

5 wrinkles

6 handsome

7 hazel

8 mustache (US) moustache (UK)

9 dark skin

A 

B 

C 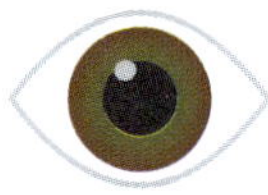

D 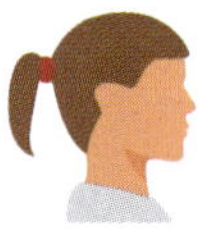

E 

F 

G 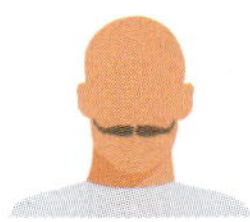

H 

I 

Aa 17.6 WRITE THE CORRECT WORDS UNDER EACH PICTURE

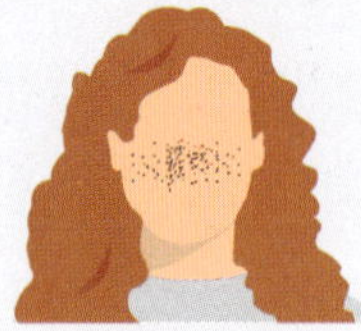

freckles

1 ____________

2 ____________

3 ____________

4 ____________

5 ____________

6 ____________

7 ____________

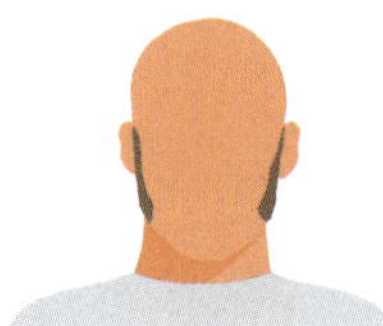

8 ____________

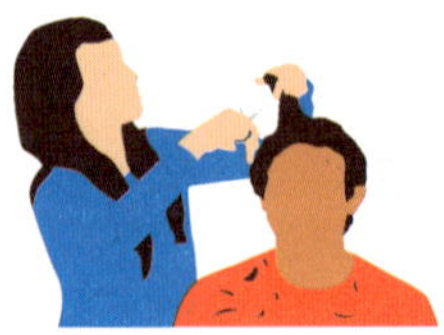

9 ____________

17.7 LISTEN TO THE AUDIO AND WRITE THE WORD THAT IS SHOWN IN EACH PICTURE

 elegant

1  ______

2  ______

3  ______

4  ______

5  ______

6 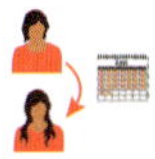 ______

7  ______

8  ______

9  ______

10  ______

11  ______

17.8 MARK THE CORRECT PICTURE FOR EACH WORD

young

A ☑ B ☐ C ☐

1 brown hair

A ☐ B ☐ C ☐

2 glamorous

A ☐ B ☐ C ☐

3 shoulder-length hair

A ☐ B ☐ C ☐

4 short

A ☐ B ☐ C ☐

5 brown

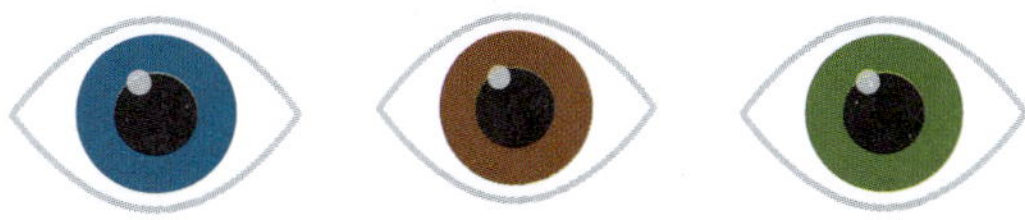

A ☐ B ☐ C ☐

18 Personality traits

18.1 DESCRIBING PERSONALITY

friendly

unfriendly

talkative

enthusiastic

serious

assertive

critical

caring

sensitive

insensitive

reasonable

unreasonable

kind

unkind

secretive

mature

immature

cautious

generous

mean

brave

funny

patient

impatient

lazy

laid-back

optimistic

outgoing

passionate

polite

rude

shy

intelligent

nervous

silly

selfish

eccentric

calm

confident

honest

dishonest

supportive

reliable

unreliable

talented

arrogant

considerate

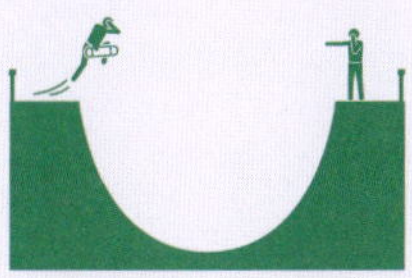
impulsive

approachable

unapproachable

Aa 18.2 CIRCLE THE WORD THAT DOES NOT BELONG IN EACH LIST

	calm	laid-back	~~(impulsive)~~
1	shy	assertive	nervous
2	rude	caring	supportive
3	friendly	impatient	approachable
4	unreliable	generous	kind
5	confident	outgoing	lazy
6	considerate	selfish	mean
7	dishonest	talented	unreliable
8	mean	rude	approachable
9	funny	insensitive	silly

Aa 18.3 COMPLETE THE WORD FOR EACH PICTURE, FILLING IN THE MISSING LETTERS

u n r *e* l *i* *a* b l *e*

1 
o _ t _ m i _ t _ c

2 
b _ a v _

3 
a _ r _ g a _ t

4 
l _ _ d - b _ c k

5 
_ s _ e r _ _ v e

6 
_ n s _ n s _ t _ v e

Aa 18.4 WRITE THE CORRECT WORD UNDER EACH PICTURE

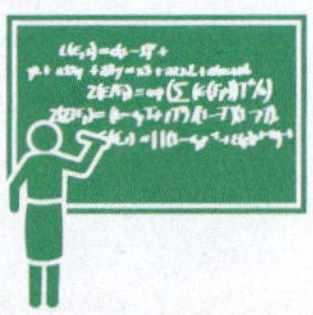
intelligent

1 ____________

2 ____________

3 ____________

4 ____________

5 ____________

6 ____________

7 ____________

8 ____________

9 ____________

18.5 LISTEN TO THE AUDIO AND MARK THE CORRECT PICTURE FOR EACH WORD YOU HEAR

A ☐ B ☑ C ☐

1 A ☐ B ☐ C ☐

2 A ☐ B ☐ C ☐

3 A ☐ B ☐ C ☐

4 A ☐ B ☐ C ☐

5 A ☐ B ☐ C ☐

6 A ☐ B ☐ C ☐

18.6 LOOK AT THE PICTURE CLUES AND WRITE THE ANSWERS IN THE CORRECT PLACES ON THE GRID

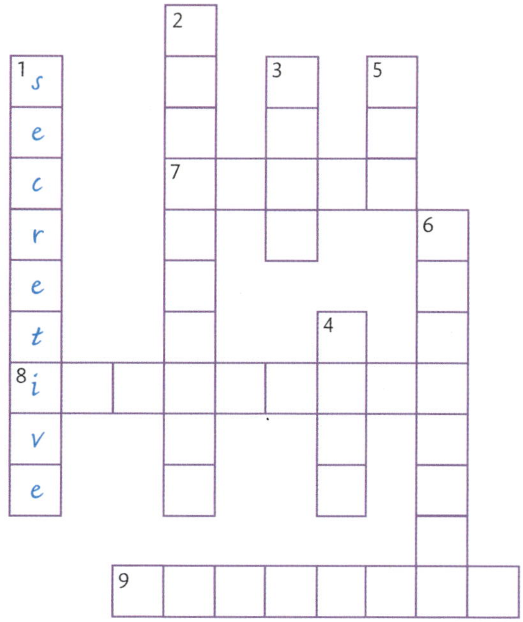

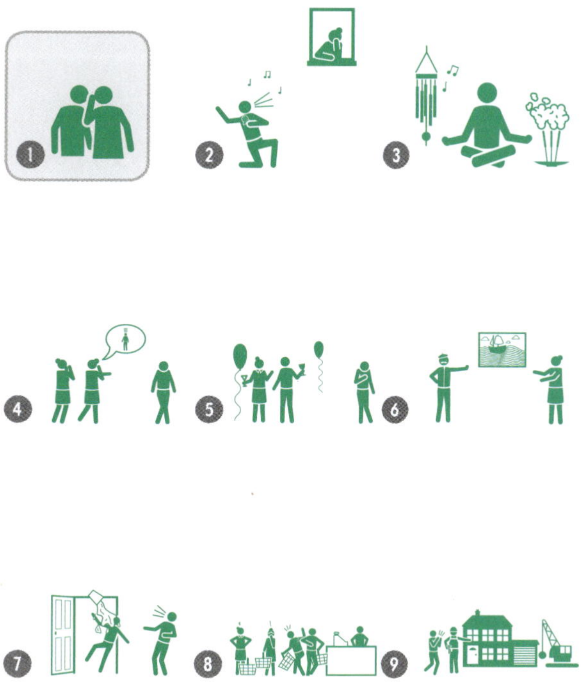

19 Feelings and moods

19.1 FEELINGS AND MOODS

calm

relaxed

pleased

cheerful

happy

delighted

ecstatic

grateful

lucky

amused

interested

curious

intrigued

surprised

shocked

excited

thrilled

amazed

confident

proud

sad

unhappy

upset

miserable

depressed

lonely

disappointed

unimpressed

unenthusiastic

disgusted

angry / mad (US)

furious

frustrated

annoyed

irritated

scared

frightened

terrified

worried

anxious

nervous

stressed

jealous

embarrassed

confused

tired

exhausted

bored

distracted

serious

Aa 19.2 WRITE THE CORRECT WORD UNDER EACH PICTURE

unimpressed

1 ______

2 ______

3 ______

4 ______

5 ______

6 ______

7 ______

8 ______

9 ______

10 ______

11 ______

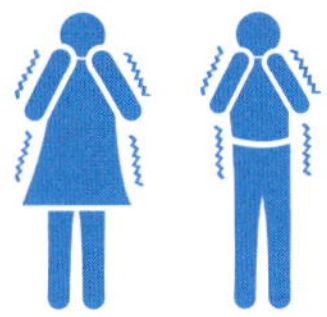

12 ______

13 ______

14 ______

15 ______

16 ______

17 ______

18 ______

19 ______

Aa 19.3 MARK THE BEGINNING AND ENDING OF EACH WORD IN THE CHAIN OF LETTERS

delighted/annoyedgratefulembarrassedecstaticworriedcuriousunenthusiasticjealousconfused

Aa 19.4 CIRCLE THE WORD THAT DOES NOT BELONG IN EACH LIST

	unhappy	(amused)	miserable
1	disgusted	happy	cheerful
2	angry	furious	grateful
3	amazed	unimpressed	unenthusiastic
4	calm	scared	relaxed
5	frightened	terrified	interested
6	disappointed	curious	intrigued
7	happy	pleased	depressed
8	tired	annoyed	exhausted
9	bored	thrilled	excited
10	anxious	worried	proud
11	relaxed	irritated	annoyed
12	happy	miserable	ecstatic

Aa 19.5 WRITE THE WORDS FROM THE PANEL NEXT TO THEIR OPPOSITES

	relaxed	*stressed*
1	unhappy	______
2	bored	______
3	confident	______
4	anxious	______
5	cheerful	______
6	disappointed	______
7	serious	______

proud ~~stressed~~ amused interested
nervous miserable happy calm

19.6 LISTEN TO THE AUDIO, THEN NUMBER THE PICTURES IN THE ORDER YOU HEAR THEM

A ☐

B 1

C ☐

D ☐

E ☐

F ☐

G ☐

H ☐

I ☐

J ☐

K ☐

L ☐

M ☐

N ☐

O ☐

P ☐

20 Family tree

20.1 JAMAL'S FAMILY

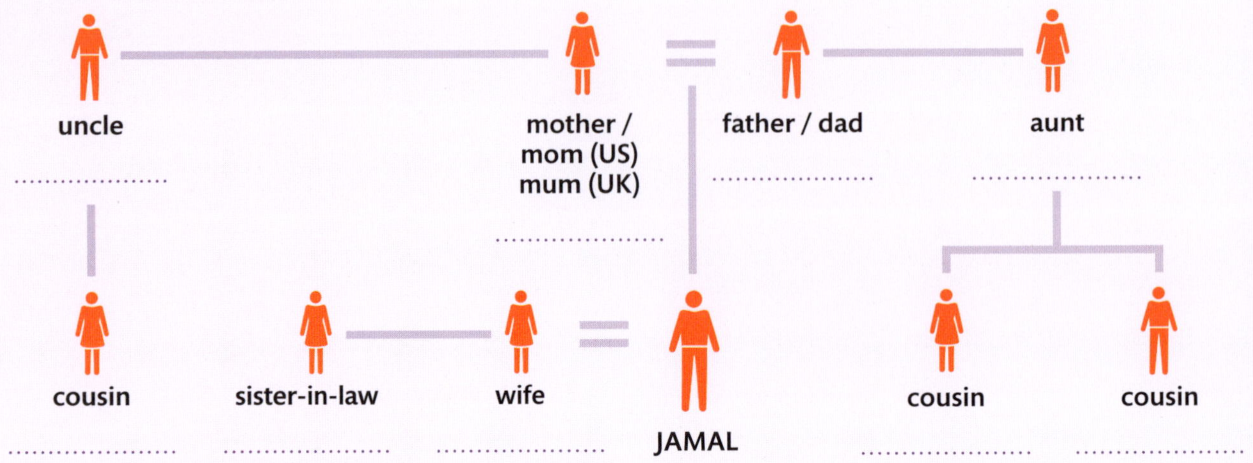

20.2 DEBBIE'S FAMILY

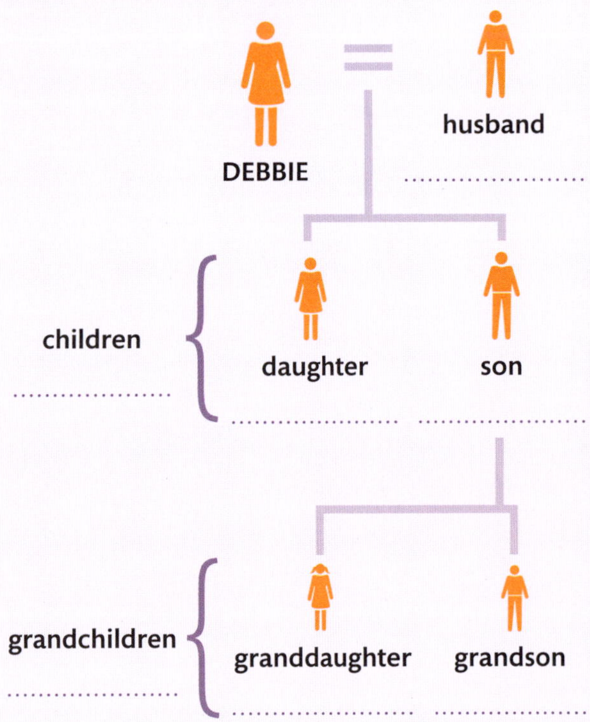

20.3 ANA'S FAMILY

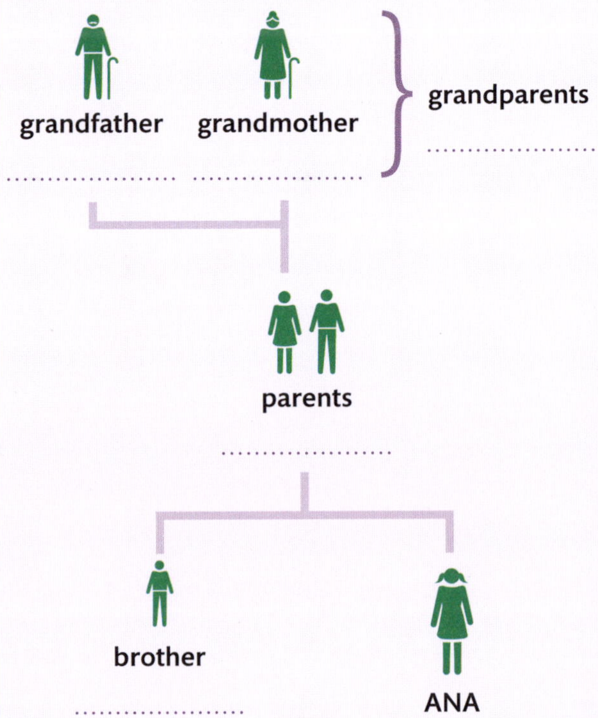

20.4 GROWING UP

20.5 ROGER'S FAMILY

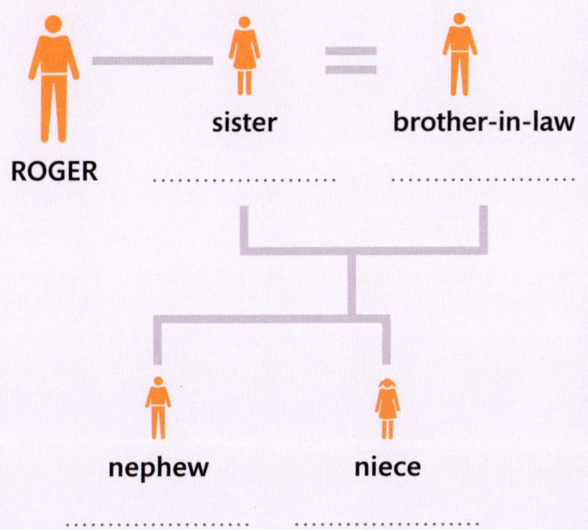

20.6 LOGAN'S FAMILY

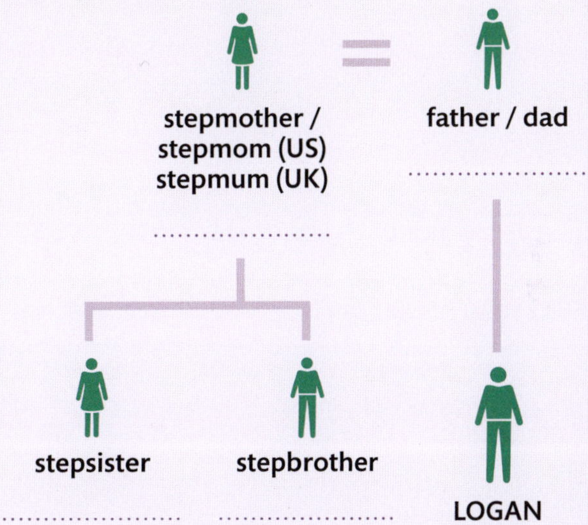

20.7 RELATIONSHIPS

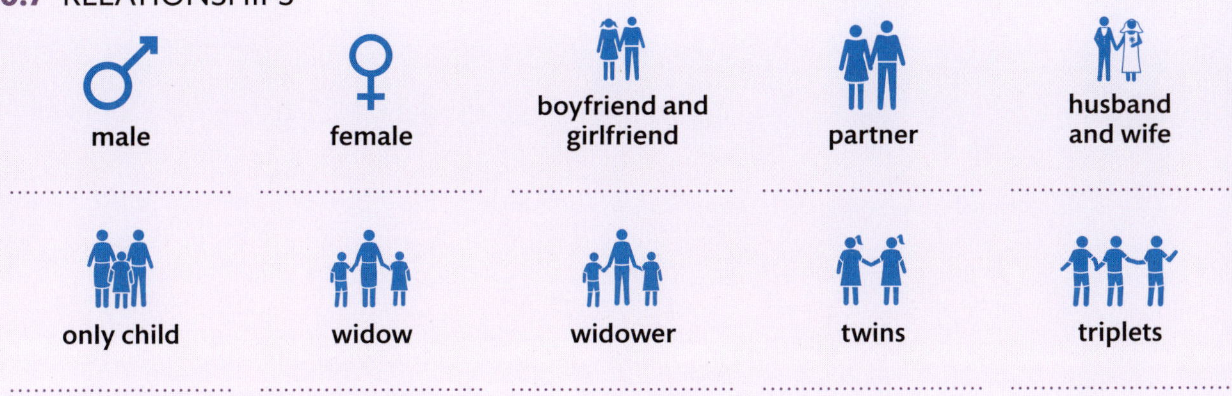

Aa 20.8 FILL IN THE GAPS ON JAMAL'S FAMILY TREE

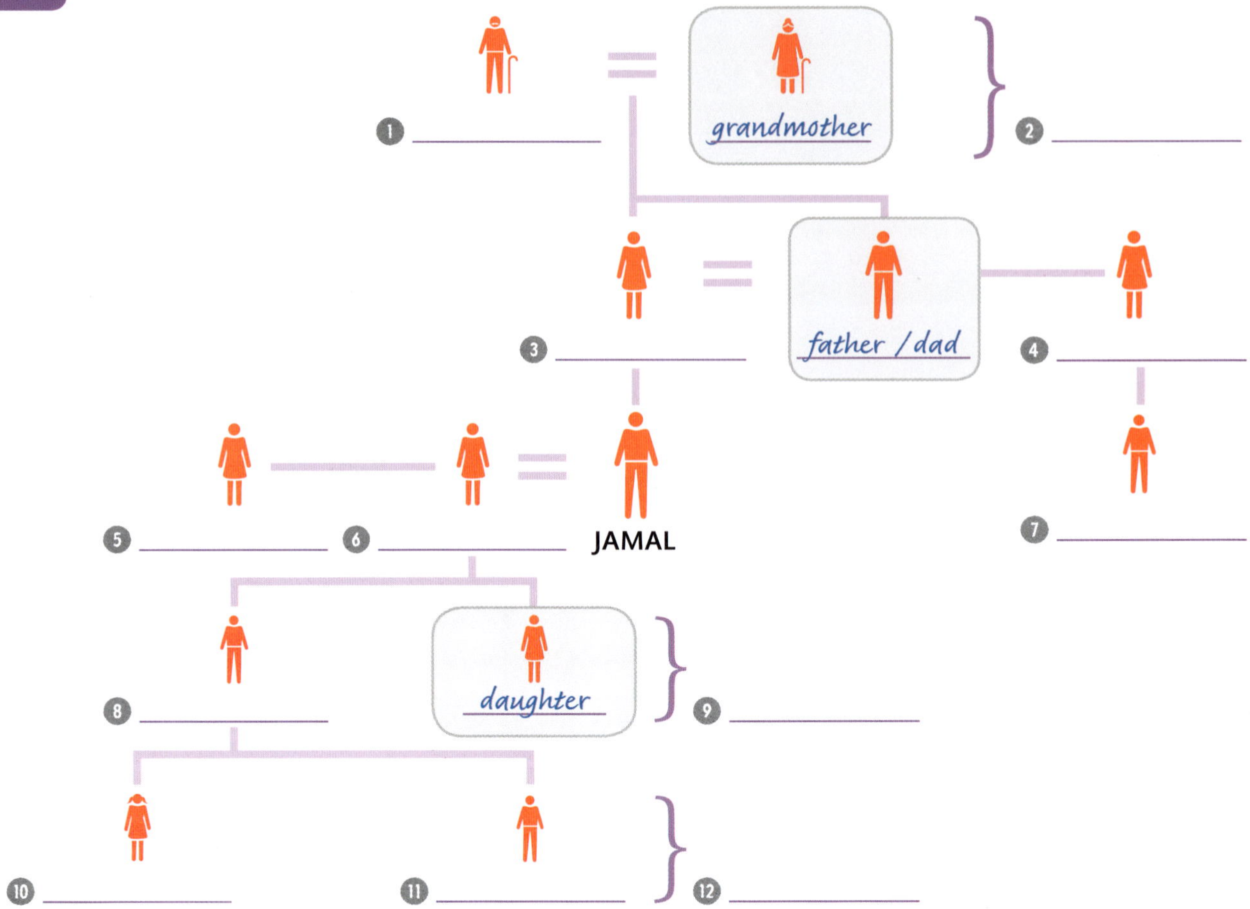

Aa 20.9 MATCH THE PICTURES TO THE CORRECT WORDS

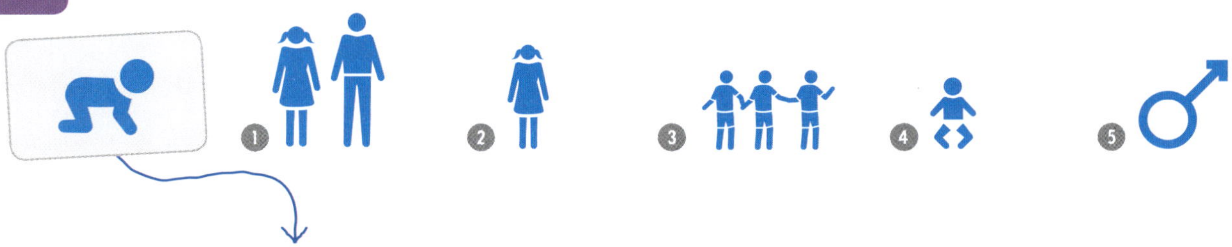

toddler

adults

triplets

girl

baby

male

20.10 LISTEN TO THE AUDIO AND WRITE THE WORD THAT IS SHOWN IN EACH PICTURE

parents

1 ______

2 ______

3 ______

4 ______

5 ______

20.11 FILL IN THE GAPS ON LOGAN'S FAMILY TREE

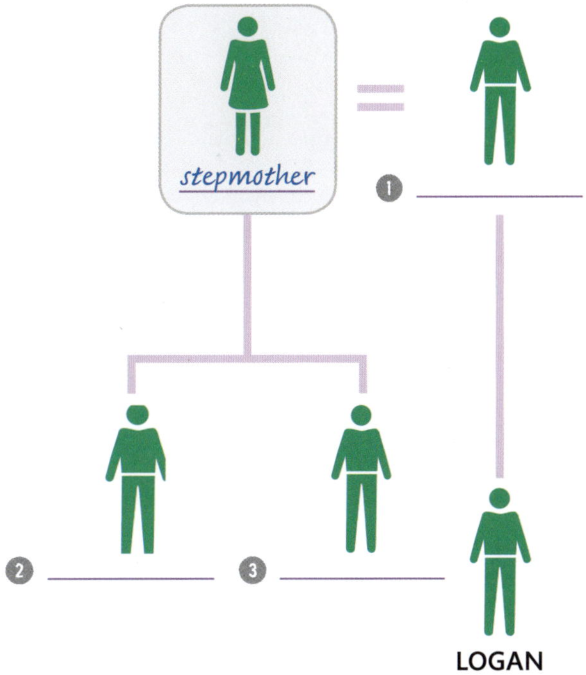

20.12 REWRITE THE WORDS, CORRECTING THE SPELLINGS

neice
niece

1 femeil ______

2 partener ______

3 nehpew ______

4 dauhgter ______

5 husbend ______

6 widou ______

7 girlfreind ______

21 Family and relationships

21.1 USEFUL EXPRESSIONS

Caroline looks up to her eldest brother.

to look up to someone
[to have respect and admiration for someone]

Sadie takes after her mother. They are both very kind.

to take after someone
[to have characteristics of a parent or relative]

We're bringing up our children to work hard at school.

to bring up someone / bring someone up
[to care for a child and teach them how to behave]

I hope my grandson will grow up to enjoy books.

to grow up
[to develop from a child to an adult]

Jo gets along with her boss.

to get along / get on with someone
[to have a good relationship with someone]

My siblings are always falling out with each other.

to fall out with someone
[to stop being friends with someone, often after an argument]

I fell in love with him while we were backpacking in India.

to fall in love with someone
[to begin to love someone]

We broke up because I didn't love him any more.

to break up with someone
[to end a romantic relationship]

They stopped working together last year, so they have drifted apart.

to drift apart
[to slowly become less friendly or close to someone]

I made friends with Miguel after he moved to my town.

to make friends with someone
[to become friendly with a person]

We've been close friends since we shared an apartment.

a close friend
[a friend who you know very well]

My cousin gave birth to a baby boy last year.

to give birth to someone
[to have a child]

We see eye to eye about most important issues.

to see eye to eye with someone
[to agree with or have similar opinions to someone]

We often bump into Mary at the local store.

to bump into someone
[to meet someone unexpectedly]

I stick up for my friends if people are mean to them.

to stick up for someone
[to speak out in support of someone]

Everyone says how much my wife and I have in common.

to have something in common
[to share an interest or opinion]

My sisters and I all have curly hair. It runs in the family.

to run in the family
[to be a common feature of a family]

Jared was really friendly, and I clicked with him immediately.

to click with someone
[to like someone quickly and easily]

I always put my foot down if my son is naughty.

to put your foot down
[to be strict about something]

I love playing with my grandson. I think the world of him.

to think the world of someone
[to have a very high opinion of someone]

21.2 MATCH THE PICTURES TO THE CORRECT SENTENCES

1 

2 

3 

4 

- I love playing with my grandson. I think the world of him.
- We're bringing up our children to work hard at school.
- We see eye to eye about most important issues.
- My siblings are always falling out with each other.
- We often bump into Mary at the local store.

21.3 CROSS OUT THE INCORRECT WORDS IN EACH SENTENCE

I always put my foot ~~up~~ / ~~on~~ / **down** if my son is naughty.

1 

Caroline **sees** / **looks** / **takes** up to her eldest brother.

2 

Sadie takes **onto** / **after** / **into** her mother. They are both very kind.

3 

My cousin **had** / **made** / **gave** birth to a baby boy last year.

4 

I stick **up** / **in** / **through** for my friends if people are mean to them.

5 

I **made** / **took** / **put** friends with Miguel after he moved to my town.

21.4 LISTEN TO THE AUDIO, THEN NUMBER THE SENTENCES IN THE ORDER YOU HEAR THEM

A  I fell in love with him while we were backpacking in India. ☐

B  I hope my grandson will grow up to enjoy books. ☐

C  My sisters and I all have curly hair. It runs in the family. ☐

D  They stopped working together last year, so they have drifted apart. ☐

E  Jared was really friendly, and I clicked with him immediately. *1*

F  Everyone says how much my wife and I have in common. ☐

21.5 REWRITE THE SENTENCES, CORRECTING THE ERRORS

We **see eyes to eyes** about most important issues.
We see eye to eye about most important issues.

1. Jo **takes along with** her boss.

____

2. We've been **near friends** since we shared an apartment.

____

3. I love playing with my grandson. I **think the earth of** him.

____

4. We **broke in** because I didn't love him any more.

____

5. My siblings are always **falling apart with** each other.

____

22 Baby equipment and toys

22.1 EQUIPMENT AND CLOTHES

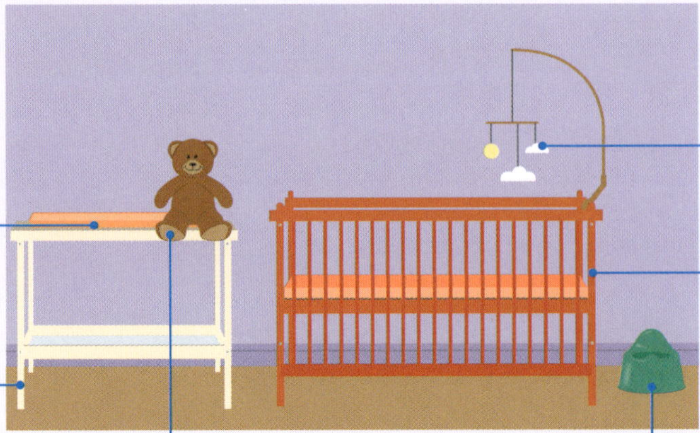

changing mat

changing table

teddy bear

nursery

potty

mobile

crib (US)
cot (UK)

diaper (US)
nappy (UK)

high chair

pacifier (US)
dummy (UK)

stroller (US)
buggy (UK)

baby carriage (US)
pram (UK)

bottle

wet wipe

Moses basket

playpen

stair gate

baby monitor

romper suit

snowsuit

bib

booties

bodysuit (US)
babygro (UK)

rattle

22.2 TOYS AND GAMES

toy

stuffed animal (US)
soft toy (UK)

doll

board game

playing cards

dollhouse (US)
doll's house (UK)

building blocks / bricks

ball

spinning top

yo-yo

jump rope (US)
skipping rope (UK)

jigsaw puzzle

train set

puppet

kite

playground

balloon

marbles

Aa 22.3 MATCH THE WORDS TO THE CORRECT PICTURES

bottle → 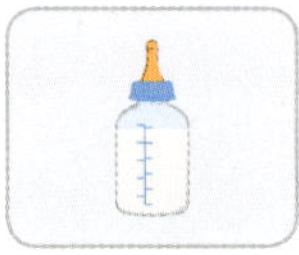

1 booties

2 puppet

3 rattle

4 doll

5 jigsaw puzzle

6 Moses basket

A 

B 

C 

D 

E 

F 

22.4 LISTEN TO THE AUDIO, THEN NUMBER THE PICTURES IN THE ORDER YOU HEAR THEM

A ☐

B ☐

C ☐

D 1

E ☐

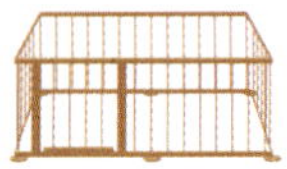
F ☐

G ☐

H ☐

I ☐

J ☐

K ☐

L ☐

M ☐

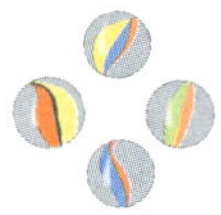
N ☐

O ☐

P ☐

Aa 22.5 MARK THE BEGINNING AND ENDING OF EACH WORD IN THE CHAIN OF LETTERS

booties/nurserytoysandboxswingstrainsetdollmarblesbottlekitepuppetchangingtablerattle

22.6 FILL IN THE GAPS, PUTTING THE WORDS FROM THE PANEL INTO THE CORRECT CATEGORIES

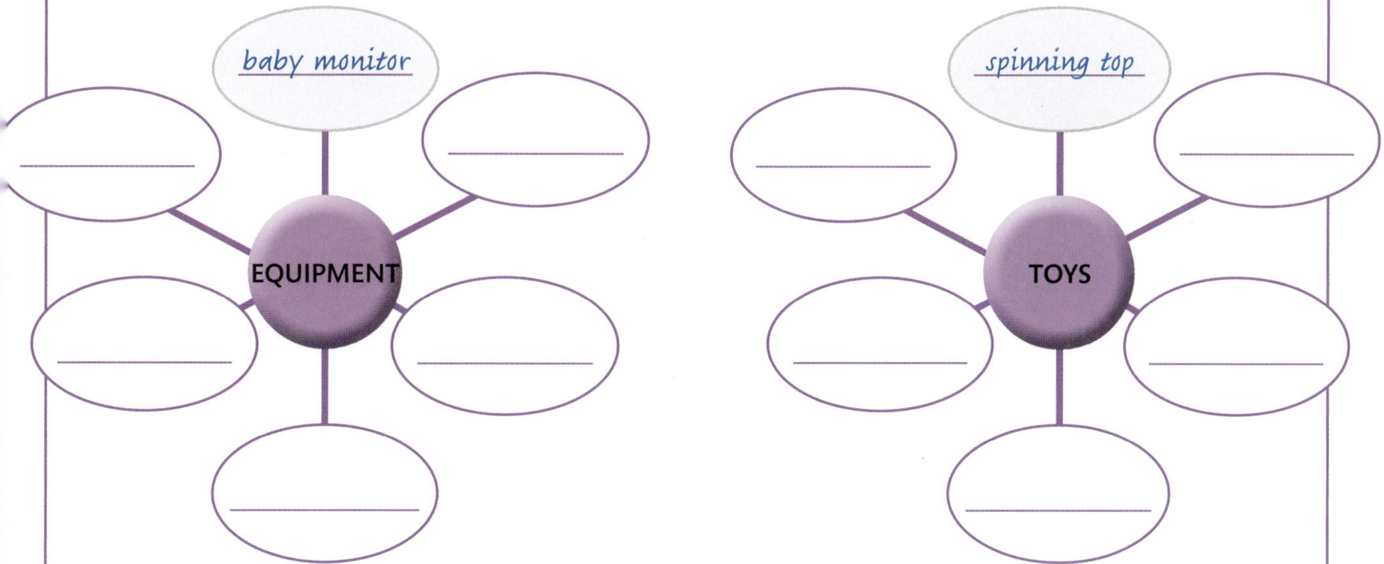

~~baby monitor~~ building blocks wet wipe slide potty bib
puppet bottle kite high chair playing cards ~~spinning top~~

22.7 LOOK AT THE PICTURE CLUES AND WRITE THE ANSWERS IN THE CORRECT PLACES ON THE GRID

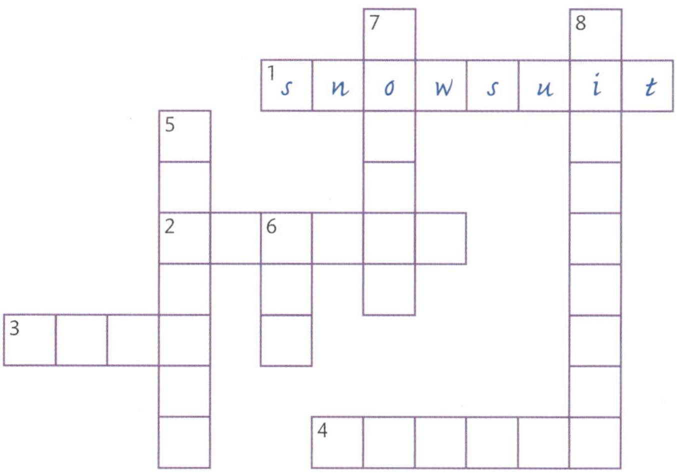

23 Education

23.1 SUBJECTS

- English
- art
- history
- geography
- science
- biology
- physics
- chemistry
- math (US)
maths (UK)
- medicine
- economics
- law
- business studies
- engineering
- architecture
- psychology
- philosophy
- music
- drama
- languages
- design and technology
- information technology
- physical education
- veterinary medicine
- geology

23.2 STUDYING AND EXAMS (NOUNS)

school

college (US)
university (UK)

library

classroom

laboratory

class

exam

essay

homework

exercise book

textbook

thesis

lecture

test

diploma (US)
qualification (UK)

degree

teacher

professor / lecturer

student

graduate

23.3 STUDYING AND EXAMS (VERBS)

to study a subject

to review (US)
to revise (UK)

to sit an exam

to pass

to fail

to resit

Aa 23.4 MARK THE CORRECT PICTURE FOR EACH WORD

to review (US) / to revise (UK)

A ☐ B ☑ C ☐

❸ diploma (US) / qualification (UK)

A ☐ B ☐ C ☐

❶ economics

A ☐ B ☐ C ☐

❹ to pass

A ☐ B ☐ C ☐

❷ homework

A ☐ B ☐ C ☐

❺ philosophy

A ☐ B ☐ C ☐

Aa 23.5 MATCH THE PICTURES TO THE CORRECT WORDS

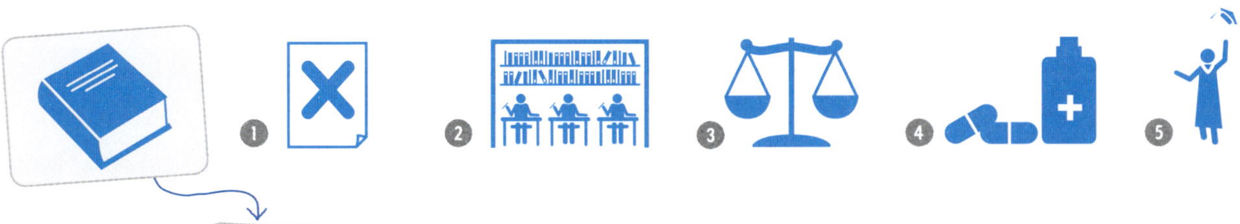

textbook

to fail

law

classroom

medicine

degree

23.6 LISTEN TO THE AUDIO AND WRITE THE WORD THAT IS SHOWN IN EACH PICTURE

chemistry

1  ______

2  ______

3  ______

4  ______

5  ______

6  ______

7  ______

8  ______

9  ______

10  ______

11  ______

12  ______

13  ______

Aa 23.7 WRITE THE CORRECT WORD UNDER EACH PICTURE

library

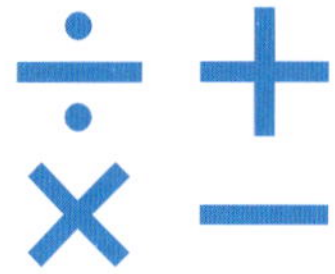
1 ______

2 ______

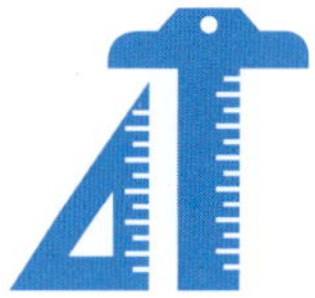
3 ______

4 ______

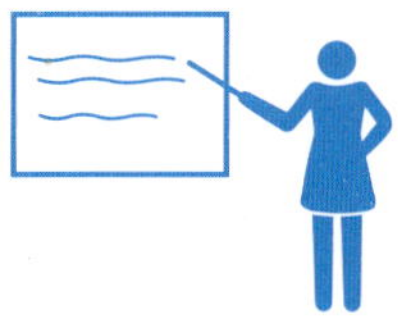
5 ______

6 ______

7 ______

8 ______

9 ______

24 Studying

24.1 USEFUL EXPRESSIONS

Rowena is taking a year off before she starts college.

to take a year off (US) / take a year out (UK)
[to have a year away from education or work]

Matt enrolled in a computer science course last month.

to enroll in (US) / enrol on (UK)
[to register to start something]

Many undergraduates live in a dormitory in their first year of college.

an undergraduate
[someone studying for a first degree at college or university]

Amira is studying for a graduate degree in chemistry.

graduate (US) / postgraduate (UK)
[study carried out following graduation from a first degree]

When Gavin was a freshman, he was very nervous about starting college.

a freshman (US) / fresher (UK)
[a student in their first year at college or university]

I have to write five essays this semester, so I'm doing lots of research.

a semester (US) / term (UK)
[a period of time in an academic calendar, during which classes are held]

Millie's parents were really proud when she got a degree.

to get a degree
[to be awarded a diploma / qualification after college or university]

I expect my students to attend classes every week.

to attend classes
[to go to lessons or lectures]

Emma took her driving test last week, and she passed.

to take a test / take an exam
[to answer questions or perform actions to show how much you know about something]

It's important to give students regular feedback on their work.

to give someone feedback on something
[to provide comments and advice on how somebody is doing something]

Tyson is working all day to **meet the deadline** for his essay.

to meet a deadline

[to finish something within a given time]

Boris almost **missed the deadline** for his research project.

to miss a deadline

[to fail to finish something within a given time]

I like **continuous assessment** more than just taking final exams.

continuous assessment

[grading based on work done over a long period]

Chris **passed** his final college exams **with flying colors**.

to pass with flying colors (US) / colours (UK)

[to perform excellently on a test]

I've finished the **first draft** of my essay, but I'm sure that I'll have to make lots of changes to it.

a first draft

[a first, rough version of a piece of written work]

I'd like you to **compare and contrast** these two pictures.

to compare and contrast

[to consider and describe the similarities and differences between things]

Their views on teaching a class are **polar opposites**.

polar opposites

[completely different]

There is a **clear distinction** between these two experiments.

a clear distinction

[an obvious difference]

Kate and Helen take **strikingly different** after-school classes.

strikingly different

[surprisingly not alike]

Practicing for her class presentation made **a world of difference**.

a world of difference

[a significant level of difference]

Aa 24.2 MARK THE SENTENCES THAT ARE CORRECT

Tyson is working all day to meet the deadline for his essay. ☑
Tyson is working all day to reach the deadline for his essay. ☐

1 

Rowena is taking a year off before she starts college. ☐
Rowena is taking a year away before she starts college. ☐

2 

Practicing for her class presentation made a mountain of difference. ☐
Practicing for her class presentation made a world of difference. ☐

3 

I expect my students to appear in classes every week. ☐
I expect my students to attend classes every week. ☐

4 

Their views on teaching a class are polar opposites. ☐
Their views on teaching a class are Arctic opposites. ☐

5 

Chris passed his final college exams with burning colors. ☐
Chris passed his final college exams with flying colors. ☐

Aa 24.3 FILL IN THE GAPS USING THE WORDS IN THE PANEL

Kate and Helen take *strikingly different* after-school classes.

1. When Gavin was a ______________, he was very nervous about starting college.
2. There is a ______________ between these two experiments.
3. Emma ______________ last week, and she passed.
4. It's important to give students ______________ on their work.
5. Amira is studying for a ______________ in chemistry.
6. Boris almost ______________ for his research project.

freshman	took her driving test	graduate degree	clear distinction
missed the deadline	regular feedback	~~strikingly different~~	

24.4 WRITE THE CORRECT PHRASE NEXT TO ITS DEFINITION

to fail to finish something within a given time = *to miss a deadline*

1. someone studying for a first degree at college or university = ____________
2. a first, rough version of a piece of written work = ____________
3. a student in their first year at college or university = ____________
4. grading based on work done over a long period = ____________
5. to perform excellently on a test = ____________

24.5 LISTEN TO THE AUDIO AND COMPLETE THE SENTENCES THAT DESCRIBE EACH PICTURE

Millie's parents were really proud when she *got a degree* .

3. Matt ____________ a computer science course last month.

1. I like ____________ ____________ more than just taking final exams.

4. I'd like you to ____________ ____________ these two pictures.

2. I've finished the ____________ ____________ of my essay, but I'm sure that I'll have to make lots of changes to it.

5. Many ____________ live in a dormitory in their first year of college.

25 Speaking a foreign language

25.1 USEFUL EXPRESSIONS

I speak conversational German, but my grammar is awful.

conversational
[language that is not technically perfect, but clear enough for basic communication]

Maria's strong accent is impossible to understand.

an accent
[the way in which people from a country or region pronounce a word]

My uncle is fluent in five different languages.

fluent in
[able to use a language easily, without making many mistakes]

Juan finds the pronunciation of the word "squirrel" impossible.

pronunciation
[the way a specific word is spoken]

I was taught French by a native speaker from Marseille.

a native speaker
[a person who speaks a language as their first language]

Dan's spoken Mandarin isn't bad, but he needs to improve his grammar.

grammar
[the way in which you make sentences from separate words]

My wife is bilingual; she speaks English and Japanese.

bilingual
[able to speak two languages fluently]

I bought a dictionary to improve my Spanish vocabulary.

vocabulary
[the set of words that make up a language]

Zara's Portuguese is a bit rusty. She hasn't spoken it in years.

rusty
[not as fluent in a language as you used to be]

Watching French TV helps you improve your listening skills.

listening
[the ability to understand spoken language]

The best way to improve your speaking skills is to talk to native speakers.

speaking
[the ability to communicate using spoken language]

The language barrier stopped me from talking to Wen.

the language barrier
[difficulty communicating with someone who speaks another language]

Looking at American websites can help you improve your English reading skills.

reading
[the ability to understand written materials]

After only a few weeks living in Italy, I was able to make myself understood.

to make yourself understood
[to be able to express basic information and ideas to people]

I understand some Hebrew, but find the writing impossible.

writing
[the ability to communicate using written words]

Although Pedro has a strong accent, he does speak accurately.

to speak accurately
[to speak without making mistakes]

English acts as a lingua franca for the people at the conference.

a lingua franca
[a shared language that allows people from various countries to understand each other]

Living in Cairo, I managed to pick up Arabic quickly.

to pick something up quickly
[to be able to learn something in little time]

The translation of the contract was full of mistakes.

a translation
[a piece of writing that has been changed from one language to another]

I have a good ear for languages. I learned Swahili in six months.

to have a good ear for languages
[to be able to understand languages without difficulty]

Aa 25.2 CROSS OUT THE INCORRECT WORD IN EACH SENTENCE

Living in Cairo, I managed to pick ~~on~~ / up Arabic quickly.

1 After only a few weeks living in Italy, I was able to **make** / **take** myself understood.

2 I have a good **ear** / **nose** for languages. I learned Swahili in six months.

3 The language **wall** / **barrier** stopped me from talking to Wen.

4 My uncle is fluent **of** / **in** five different languages.

5 I speak **conversational** / **conversing** German, but my grammar is awful.

6 Juan finds the **pronounce** / **pronunciation** of the word "squirrel" impossible.

Aa 25.3 WRITE THE CORRECT EXPRESSION NEXT TO ITS DEFINITION

the way in which you make sentences from separate words = *grammar*

1 the way people from a country or region pronounce a word = ______

2 able to speak two languages fluently = ______

3 a person who speaks a language as their first language = ______

4 the ability to communicate using spoken language = ______

5 to speak without making mistakes = ______

6 the set of words that make up a language = ______

7 able to use a language easily, without making many mistakes = ______

Aa 25.4 FILL IN THE GAPS, PUTTING THE WORDS IN THE CORRECT ORDER

your | improve | reading | English

Looking at American websites can help you *improve* *your* *English* *reading* skills.

speaker | a | by | from | native

1 I was taught French ______ ______ ______ ______ ______ Marseilles.

as | for | a | franca | acts | lingua

2 English ______ ______ ______ ______ ______ ______ the people at the conference.

writing | the | find | but

3 I understand some Hebrew, ______ ______ ______ ______ impossible.

accent, | a | he | speak | strong | does

4 Although Pedro has ______ ______ ______ ______ ______ ______ accurately.

25.5 LISTEN TO THE AUDIO, THEN NUMBER THE SENTENCES IN THE ORDER YOU HEAR THEM

A 
The translation of the contract was full of mistakes. ☐

D 
Maria's strong accent is impossible to understand. ☐

B 
I bought a dictionary to improve my Spanish vocabulary. ☐

E 
My wife is bilingual; she speaks English and Japanese. *1*

C 
Watching French TV helps you improve your listening skills. ☐

F 
The best way to improve your speaking skills is to talk to native speakers. ☐

26 Communication and beliefs

26.1 USEFUL EXPRESSIONS

Jenna **told a white lie** and said she liked Barry's new suit.

to tell a white lie
[to say something that is not true to avoid upsetting someone]

Tara is **dropping a hint** that she would like new shoes for her birthday.

to drop a hint
[to say something indirectly]

Farah **started a rumor** that Kerry stole a car.

to start / spread a rumor (US)
to start / spread a rumour (UK)
[to say things that may not be true]

Martin loves to **gossip** about other people's relationships.

to gossip
[to talk about other people, often in a negative way]

We **have a sneaking suspicion** that Tim won't come to the party with us.

to have a sneaking suspicion
[to have an idea about something with little evidence]

Do you really **believe in** ghosts?

to believe in something
[to think that something exists or is true]

I have never lost my keys. **Knock on wood**!

to knock on wood (US)
to touch wood (UK)
[to wish for good luck, or avoid bad luck]

Make a wish when you cut your birthday cake!

to make a wish
[to hope for something to happen]

I **have serious misgivings** about accepting this job offer.

to have serious misgivings / doubts
[to have a strong feeling that something is not right]

You shouldn't be a **tattletale** at school.

a tattletale (US) / telltale (UK)
[somebody who tells an authority figure when another person has done something wrong]

I often find out about new products by **word of mouth**.

word of mouth

[information or news transmitted by people telling other people]

I really enjoy reading **fairy tales** to my grandchildren.

a fairy tale

[a traditional story with magic, usually written for children]

I don't think the park is haunted. That's just an **urban myth**.

an urban myth

[a modern story that is untrue, but believed by many]

To some people, a black cat is a **good omen**; to others, a **bad omen**.

a good / bad omen

[a positive / negative sign about something that will happen]

It was such a **stroke of luck** to win that new car.

a stroke of luck

[a single piece of good fortune]

I've never played this game, so I'm hoping for **beginner's luck**.

beginner's luck

[good fortune the first time you do something]

Anyone can win this game. It's a game of **pure luck**.

pure luck

[good fortune with no skill involved]

That book about Chinese **folklore** was really interesting.

folklore

[stories, sayings, and traditions from a certain area or culture]

He has a very old-fashioned **set of beliefs**.

a set of beliefs

[a group of values]

Rosa has an **unshakable belief** in the importance of being kind.

an unshakable belief

[a firm and unchangeable conviction]

26.2 FILL IN THE GAPS, PUTTING THE WORDS IN THE CORRECT ORDER

about | have | misgivings | serious

I *have* *serious* *misgivings* *about* accepting this job offer.

ghosts | in | believe | really

1. Do you ______ ______ ______ ______ ?

tales | my | reading | to | fairy

2. I really enjoy ______ ______ ______ ______ ______ grandchildren.

a | that | suspicion | have | sneaking

3. We ______ ______ ______ ______ ______ Tim won't come to the party with us.

rumor | a | started

4. Farah ______ ______ ______ that Kerry stole a car.

26.3 CROSS OUT THE INCORRECT WORDS IN EACH SENTENCE

It was such a **stroke** / ~~strike~~ / ~~stoke~~ of luck to win that new car.

1. Tara is **falling** / **throwing** / **dropping** a hint that she would like new shoes for her birthday.

2. Jenna told a **clean** / **white** / **kind** lie and said she liked Barry's new suit.

3. I've never played this game, so I'm hoping for **beginner's** / **starter's** / **opener's** luck.

4. He has a very old-fashioned **set** / **collection** / **box** of beliefs.

Aa 26.4 WRITE THE CORRECT PHRASE NEXT TO ITS DEFINITION, FILLING IN THE MISSING LETTERS

to wish for good luck, or avoid bad luck = t o k *n o c k* *o* n w *o o d*

1. to hope for something to happen = t _ m _ _ _ a w _ _ _ h
2. good fortune with no skill involved = _ u r _ l _ _ k
3. a modern story that is untrue, but believed by many = a _ u _ b _ _ m _ _ h
4. stories, sayings, and traditions from a certain area or culture = f _ l _ _ o _ _
5. to talk about other people, often in a negative way = t _ g _ s _ _ _

26.5 LISTEN TO THE AUDIO AND COMPLETE THE SENTENCES THAT DESCRIBE EACH PICTURE

Rosa has an *unshakable* *belief* in the importance of being kind.

3 You shouldn't be a ______________ at school.

1 I often find out about new products ______________ .

4 To some people, a black cat is a ______________ ; to others, a ______________ .

2 Anyone can win this game. It's a game of ______________ .

5 Martin loves ______________ about other people's relationships.

27 Crime and the law

27.1 CRIME

robbery

burglary

mugging

car theft

shoplifting

pickpocketing

vandalism

graffiti

fraud

hacking

hooliganism

drug dealing

smuggling

speeding

bribery

27.2 PUNISHMENT AND THE LAW

police

law court

judge

lawyer

jury

trial

witness

fine

prison

criminal record

27.3 USEFUL EXPRESSIONS

The burglar wouldn't admit he had **committed a crime**.

to commit a crime

[to break the law]

Austin **served a sentence** of two years before he was released from prison.

to serve a sentence

[to spend time in prison]

The police officer **arrested** Tina for shoplifting.

to arrest somebody

[to use the power of the law to take and question somebody]

It's a police officer's job to **enforce the law**.

to enforce the law

[to make people obey a rule or a law]

After discussing all the evidence, the jury **reached a verdict**.

to reach a verdict

[to come to a decision about somebody's guilt or innocence]

The recent **crime wave** in my home town is very worrying.

a crime wave

[a lot of crimes happening suddenly in the same area]

The jury **found** Colin **guilty** of car theft.

to find somebody (not) guilty

[to decide officially that someone has (not) broken the law]

Street crime, such as mugging, can be a problem in our cities.

street crime

[crime committed in a public place]

Paula was **sentenced** to 100 hours of community service.

to sentence somebody to something

[to decide on a punishment in accordance with the law]

André is trained to deal with **white-collar crime**, such as fraud.

white-collar crime

[financial, nonviolent crime]

27.4 WRITE THE CORRECT WORD UNDER EACH PICTURE

graffiti

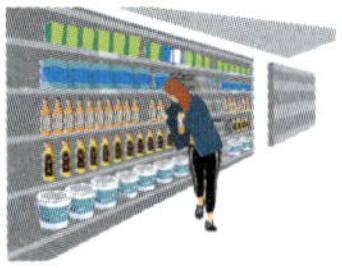
1 ______________

2 ______________

3 ______________

4 ______________

5 ______________

27.5 MATCH THE PICTURES TO THE CORRECT WORDS

1 

2 

3 

judge

prison

trial

law court

27.6 LISTEN TO THE AUDIO AND MARK THE CORRECT PICTURE FOR EACH WORD YOU HEAR

 A ☐
 B ☐
 C ☑

1
 A ☐
 B ☐
 C ☐

2
 A ☐
 B ☐
 C ☐

3
 A ☐
 B ☐
 C ☐

4
 A ☐
 B ☐
 C ☐

5
 A ☐
 B ☐
 C ☐

Aa 27.7 MARK THE SENTENCES THAT ARE CORRECT

Street crime, such as mugging, can be a problem in our cities. ☑

Street criminal, such as mugging, can be a problem in our cities. ☐

1 

The recent crime wave in my home town is very worrying. ☐

The recent crime flood in my home town is very worrying. ☐

2 

The jury revealed Colin guilty of car theft. ☐

The jury found Colin guilty of car theft. ☐

3 

The burglar wouldn't admit he had performed a crime. ☐

The burglar wouldn't admit he had committed a crime. ☐

4 

After discussing all the evidence, the jury reached a verdict. ☐

After discussing all the evidence, the jury touched a verdict. ☐

5 

It's a police officer's job to enforce the law. ☐

It's a police officer's job to cause the law. ☐

Aa 27.8 FILL IN THE GAPS USING THE WORDS IN THE PANEL

Austin served a _sentence_ of two years before he was released from prison.

1. The police officer ______________ Tina for shoplifting.
2. It's a police officer's job to ______________ the law.
3. ______________, such as mugging, can be a problem in our cities.
4. Paula was ______________ to 100 hours of community service.
5. André is trained to deal with ______________, such as fraud.

enforce | white-collar crime | Street crime | arrested | sentenced | ~~sentence~~

28 Meat, fish, dairy, and snacks

28.1 MEAT

meat

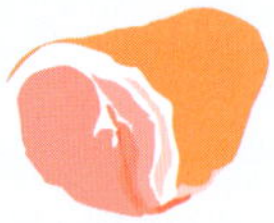

pork

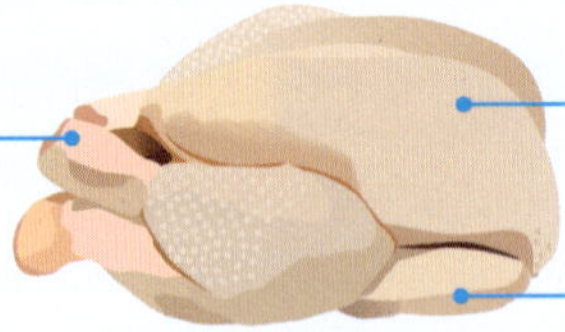

chicken

lamb

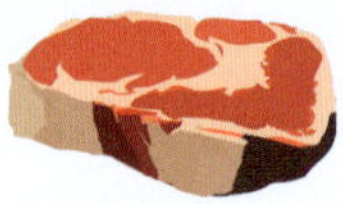

beef

sausages

bacon

ham

28.2 FISH AND SEAFOOD

fish

salmon

lobster

octopus

scallops

mackerel

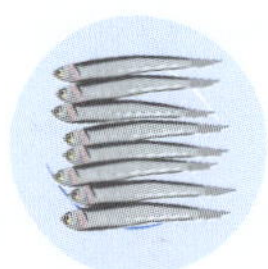

sardines

seafood platter

cod

sushi

28.3 DAIRY

milk

cheese

butter

margarine

yogurt

cream

fried egg

scrambled eggs

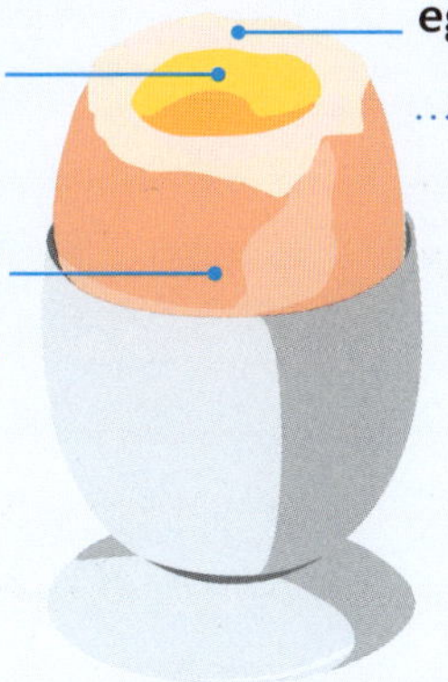

boiled egg

poached egg

omelet (US)
omelette (UK)

cottage cheese

28.4 FAST FOOD AND LIGHT SNACKS

burger

fries (US)
chips (UK)

hot dog

kebab

pizza

wrap

soup

sandwich

salad

chips (US)
crisps (UK)

28.5 LOOK AT THE PICTURES BELOW, THEN WRITE THE ANSWERS UNDER THE CORRECT HEADING

MEAT	SEAFOOD	DAIRY	FAST FOOD
sausages			

28.6 FIND FIVE MORE WORDS IN THE GRID THAT MATCH THE PICTURES

S G C R E A M A C B
T A M A C K E R E L
O C T O P U S M D K
P S X O J E R T I B
L O B C X W G V S E
E U D W Q R H A D E
R P B A C O N O Z F

Aa 28.7 MATCH THE PICTURES TO THE CORRECT WORDS

1 

2 

3 

4 

5 

6 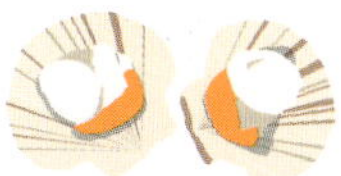

7 

8 

- soup
- sandwich
- wrap
- scrambled eggs
- cottage cheese
- salad
- chips (US) crisps (UK)
- burger
- scallops

28.8 LISTEN TO THE AUDIO, THEN NUMBER THE PICTURES IN THE ORDER YOU HEAR THEM

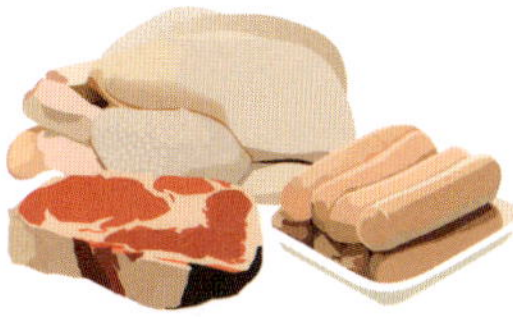

A ☐

B ☐

C 1

D ☐

E ☐

F ☐

G ☐

H ☐

I ☐

J ☐

29 Fruit and nuts

29.1 FRUIT

apple

orange

banana

strawberries

mango

pineapple

lemon

melon

raspberries

peach

pear

grapes

mandarin

grapefruit

lime

nectarine

apricot

plum

cherries

blackberries

blueberries

cranberries

blackcurrants

watermelon

papaya

guava | starfruit | lychees | coconut | passion fruit

pomegranate | kiwi fruit | redcurrants | gooseberries | quince

29.2 NUTS AND DRIED FRUIT

29.3 WRITE THE CORRECT WORD UNDER EACH PICTURE

strawberries

1 ______

2 ______

3 ______

4 ______

5 ______

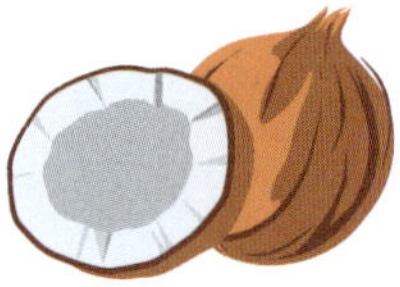

6 ______

7 ______

8 ______

9 ______

10 ______

11 ______

12 ______

13 ______

14 ______

29.4 LOOK AT THE PICTURE AND WRITE THE CORRECT WORD FOR EACH LABEL

1 ______

2 ______

3 ______

4 ______

5 ______

6 ______

7 ______

8 ______

9 ______

cashew nut

Aa 29.5 CIRCLE THE WORD THAT DOES NOT BELONG IN EACH LIST

walnut	(pork)	cashew nut

1. fries blackcurrants cranberries
2. hazelnut quince peanut
3. guava gooseberries salmon
4. pistachio pomegranate redcurrants
5. pineapple peach yolk
6. soup plum watermelon
7. lamb fig date
8. raisin pizza currant

29.6 LISTEN TO THE AUDIO, THEN NUMBER THE PICTURES IN THE ORDER YOU HEAR THEM

A ☐

B ☐

C ☐

D ☐

E [1]

F ☐

G ☐

H ☐

I ☐

Aa 29.7 COMPLETE THE WORD FOR EACH PICTURE, FILLING IN THE MISSING LETTERS

b a n a n a

1.  w _ t e _ m _ l _ n
2.  m a _ g _
3.  w _ l _ u t
4.  p _ p _ y _
5.  p _ _ r
6.  p _ s _ i _ n _ f r _ _ t

30 Vegetables

30.1 VEGETABLES

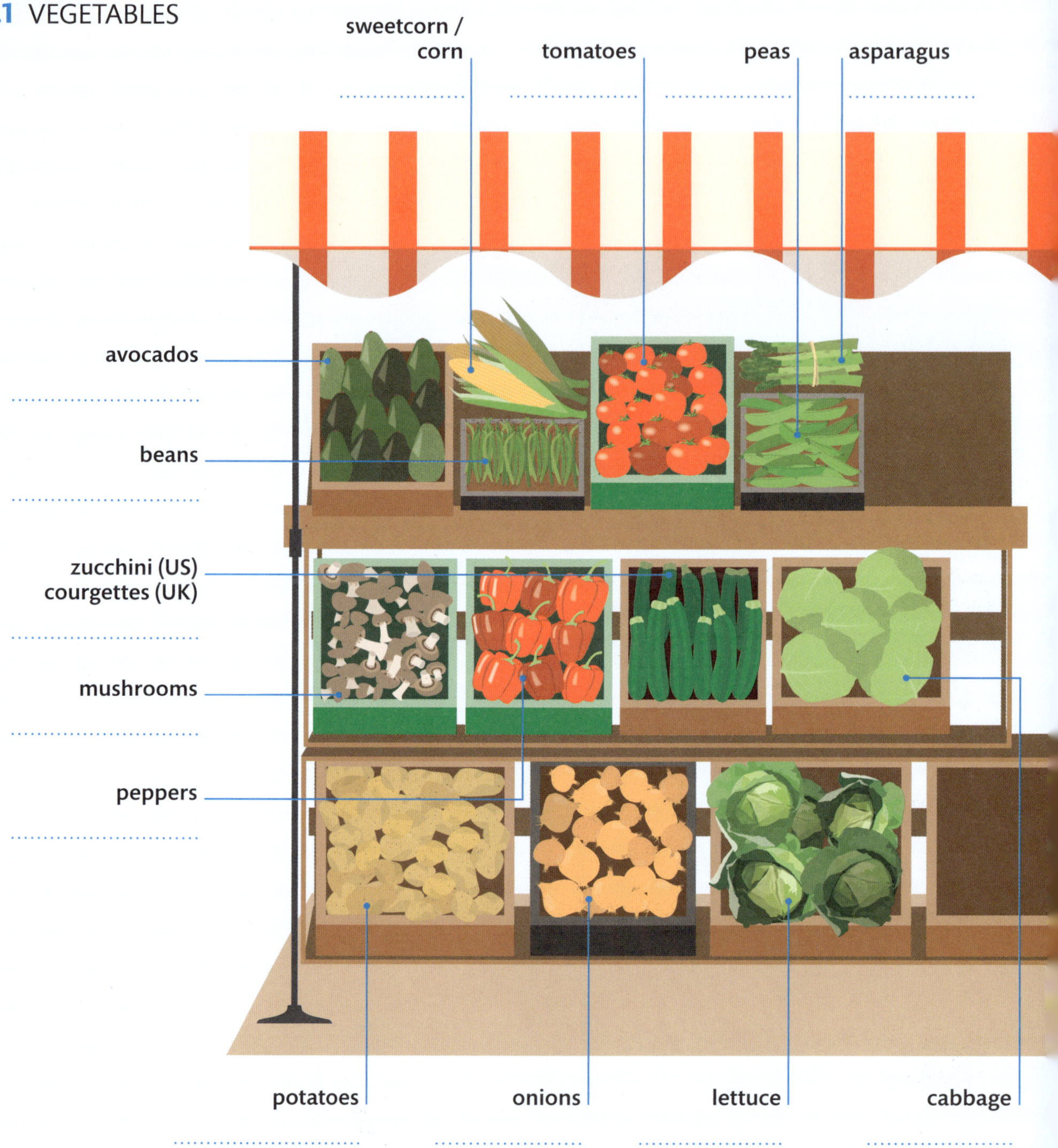

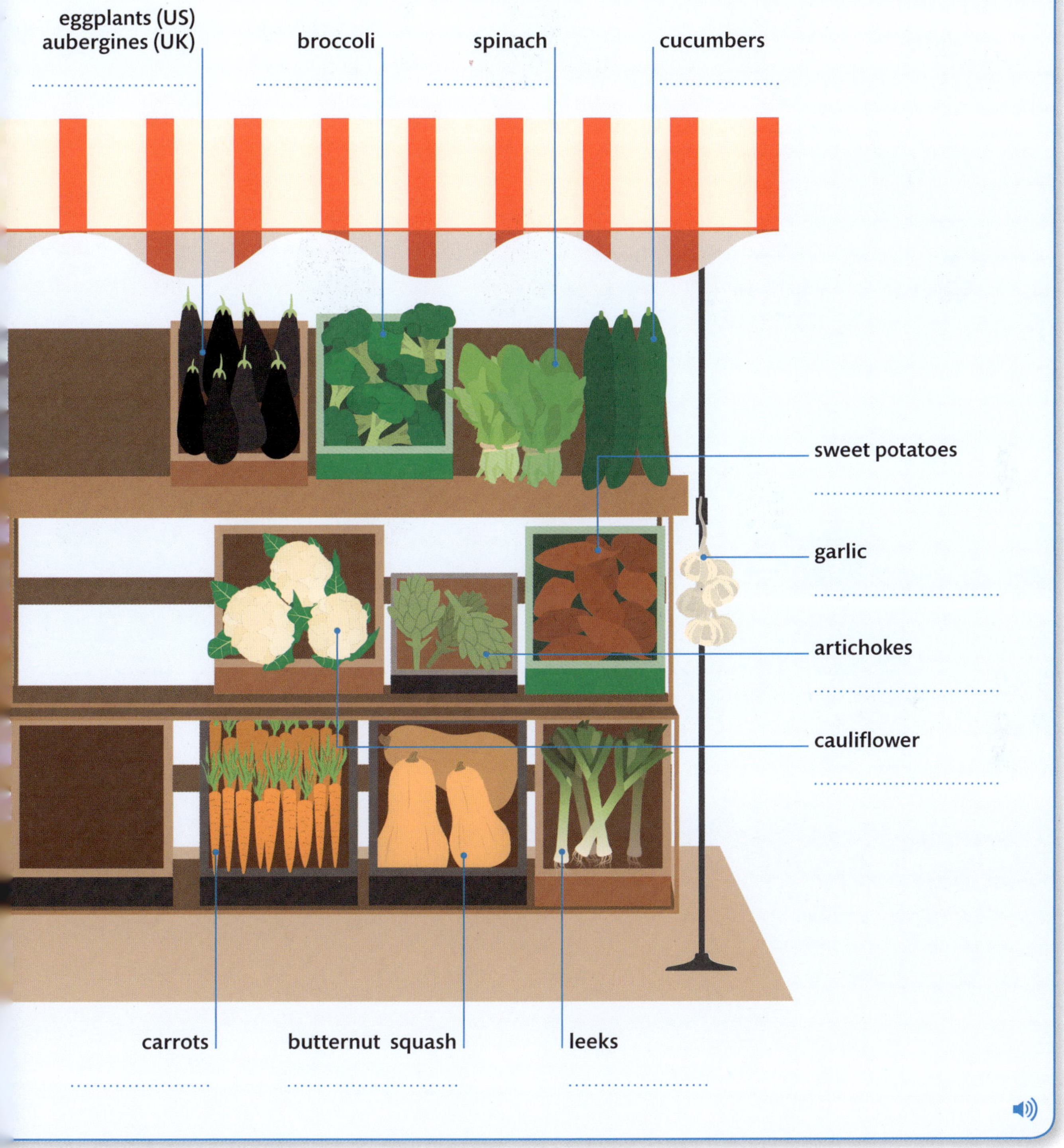
eggplants (US)
aubergines (UK)
broccoli
spinach
cucumbers
sweet potatoes
garlic
artichokes
cauliflower
carrots
butternut squash
leeks

Aa 30.2 WRITE THE CORRECT WORD UNDER EACH PICTURE

peas

1 ______

2 ______

3 ______

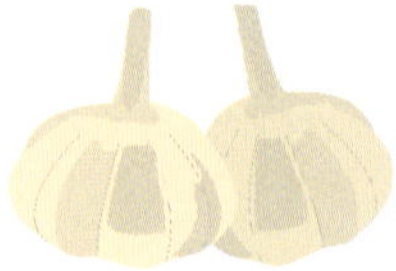

4 ______

5 ______

6 ______

7 ______

8 ______

9 ______

10 ______

11 ______

12 ______

13 ______

14 ______

Aa 30.3 MARK THE BEGINNING AND ENDING OF EACH WORD IN THE CHAIN OF LETTERS, THEN WRITE THE WORDS YOU FIND

garlic|artichokesspinachmushroomscauliflowercucumberseggplantsasparagussweetcorn

garlic

1 ______

2 ______

3 ______

4 ______

5 ______

6 ______

7 ______

8 ______

30.4 LISTEN TO THE AUDIO AND MARK THE CORRECT PICTURE FOR EACH WORD YOU HEAR

A ☐ B ☑ C ☐

3 A ☐ B ☐ C ☐

1 A ☐ B ☐ C ☐

4 A ☐ B ☐ C ☐

2 A ☐ B ☐ C ☐

5 A ☐ B ☐ C ☐

30.5 COMPLETE THE WORD FOR EACH PICTURE, FILLING IN THE MISSING LETTERS

 p o t a t o e s

5  _ _ t _ _ r n _ t s _ _ a _ h

1  c _ _ b _ g _

6  m _ s h _ _ o _ _

2  _ o m _ _ o _ _

7  _ p _ _ a _ h

3  l _ _ k _

8  a _ _ _ c h _ k _ _

4  c _ _ u _ b _ r _

9  s _ e _ t _ o t _ _ o _ _

31 Bread, desserts, and condiments

31.1 BREAD, PASTA, AND DESSERTS

bread

bagel

roll

croissant

toast

pasta

spaghetti

rice

noodles

dumplings

cookie (US)
biscuit (UK)

chocolate

cereal

flour

cupcake

pancakes

candy (US)
sweets (UK)

31.2 FLAVORINGS AND CONDIMENTS

sugar

salt

pepper

oil

vinegar

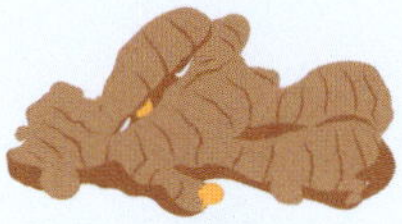
ginger

jam

marmalade

honey

mayonnaise

ketchup

mustard

chutney

peanut butter

chili flakes (US)
chilli flakes (UK)

spices

herbs

parsley

basil

mint

soy sauce

cilantro (US)
coriander (UK)

chives

dill

lemongrass

31.3 MARK THE CORRECT PICTURE FOR EACH WORD

croissant

A ☑ B ☐ C ☐

1 toast

A ☐ B ☐ C ☐

2 fruit salad

A ☐ B ☐ C ☐

3 pasta

A ☐ B ☐ C ☐

4 ginger

A ☐ B ☐ C ☐

5 vinegar

A ☐ B ☐ C ☐

31.4 MATCH THE PICTURES TO THE CORRECT WORDS

1 

2 

3 

4 

5 

ice cream

flour

pancakes

noodles

dumplings

chocolate

31.5 LISTEN TO THE AUDIO AND WRITE THE WORD THAT IS SHOWN IN EACH PICTURE

 *cookie*

1  ______

2  ______

3  ______

4  ______

5  ______

6  ______

7  ______

8  ______

9  ______

10  ______

11  ______

12  ______

13  ______

14  ______

15  ______

16  ______

17  ______

31.6 REWRITE THE WORDS, CORRECTING THE SPELLINGS

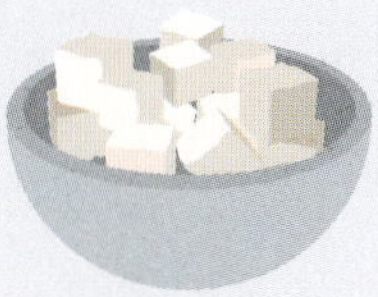
suger
sugar

1 marmelaid ______

2 spageti ______

3 role ______

4 mayonais ______

5 cuppcake ______

6 cheelie flakes ______

7 merange ______

32 Drinking and eating

32.1 DRINKS

coffee

tea

hot chocolate

herbal tea

juice

water

ice tea

lemonade

orangeade

cola

beer

wine

milkshake

smoothie

sports drink / energy drink

32.2 FOOD AND DRINK CONTAINERS

bottle

bag

glass

carton

jar

packet

box

can (US) / tin (UK)

hot drink container (US) / flask (UK)

bowl

32.3 FOOD AND DRINK: ADJECTIVES

sweet

savory (US)
savoury (UK)

tasty

iced / chilled

salty

bitter

spicy / hot

fresh

off / gone off

strong

sour

carbonated /
sparkling

non-carbonated /
still

delicious

disgusting

32.4 EATING AND DRINKING

to eat

to dine

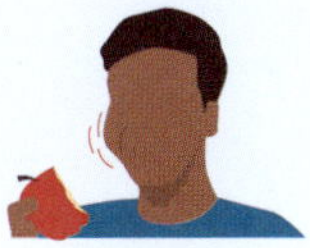
to chew

to taste

to nibble

to bite

to swallow

to drink

to sip

to gulp

32.5 MATCH THE WORDS TO THE CORRECT PICTURES

lemonade → 

1 wine

2 ice tea

3 smoothie

4 hot chocolate

5 cola

6 coffee

7 tea

8 water

9 herbal tea

A 

B 

C 

D 

E 

F 

G 

H 

I 

32.6 FILL IN THE MISSING LETTERS FOR EACH WORD

 s a l t y

1  s _ r _ n _

2  _ o n _ _ f _

3  s _ _ r

4  f _ _ s _

5  i _ _ d

6  s w _ _ t

7  t _ s _ _

8  d _ l _ c _ _ _ s

9  s _ v _ r _

10  _ i _ _ e _

11  d _ _ g _ s _ _ n _

12  _ p _ c _

32.7 LISTEN TO THE AUDIO AND MARK THE CORRECT PICTURE FOR EACH WORD YOU HEAR

A ☐ B ☑ C ☐

1 A ☐ B ☐ C ☐

2 A ☐ B ☐ C ☐

3 A ☐ B ☐ C ☐

4 A ☐ B ☐ C ☐

5 A ☐ B ☐ C ☐

6 A ☐ B ☐ C ☐

7 A ☐ B ☐ C ☐

32.8 WRITE THE CORRECT VERB UNDER EACH PICTURE

to sip

1 ______

2 ______

3 ______

4 ______

5 ______

6 ______

7 ______

8 ______

9 ______

33 Eating in and eating out

33.1 MEALS

breakfast

brunch

lunch

dinner

snack

33.2 FOOD PREPARATION

to broil (US)
to grill (UK)

to bake

to roast

to boil

to fry

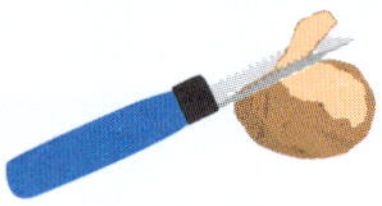
to peel

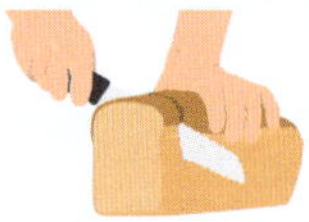
to slice

to grate

to pour

to mix

to add

to whisk

to roll

to stir

to simmer

to poach

to mash

to chop

to cut

to mince

33.3 EATING OUT: NOUNS

café

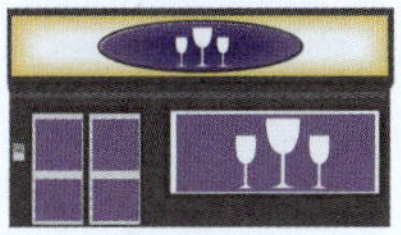
bar

restaurant

food stall

napkin

fast food

chef

waiter

waitress

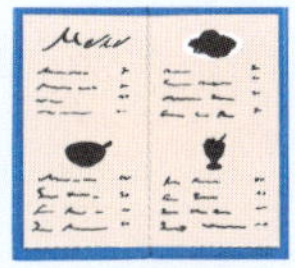
menu

appetizer (US)
starter (UK)

entrée (US)
main course (UK)

dessert /
pudding (UK)

buffet

fixed menu (US)
set menu (UK)

side / side order

specials

check (US)
bill (UK)

service charge

tip

33.4 EATING OUT: VERBS

to make a
reservation

to order

to take out (US)
to take away (UK)

to pay separately

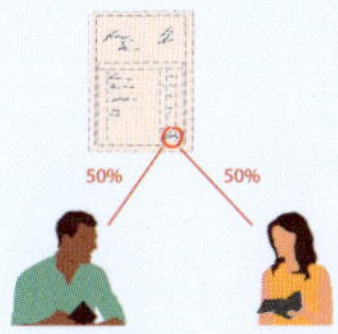

to split the check
(US) / bill (UK)

Aa 33.5 MARK THE CORRECT VERB FOR THE ACTIVITY IN EACH PICTURE

- to cut ☐
- to fry ☐
- to boil ☑

1

- to peel ☐
- to whisk ☐
- to simmer ☐

2

- to roast ☐
- to bake ☐
- to mince ☐

3

- to roll ☐
- to poach ☐
- to simmer ☐

4

- to mash ☐
- to chop ☐
- to stir ☐

5

- to slice ☐
- to grate ☐
- to add ☐

6

- to broil ☐
- to chop ☐
- to bake ☐

7

- to mix ☐
- to fry ☐
- to add ☐

8

- to peel ☐
- to pour ☐
- to mix ☐

9

- to roll ☐
- to whisk ☐
- to cut ☐

Aa 33.6 LOOK AT THE PICTURE CLUES AND WRITE THE ANSWERS IN THE CORRECT PLACES ON THE GRID

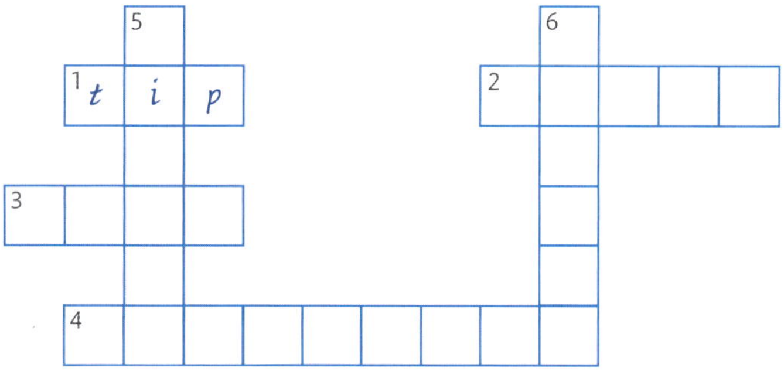

1
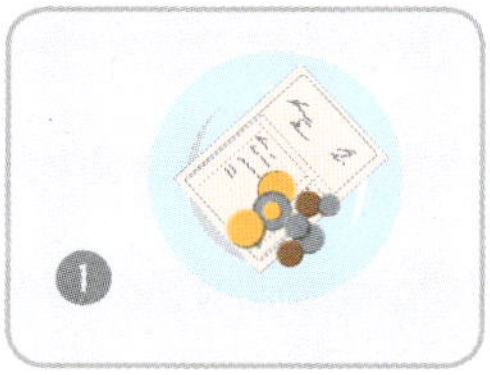

2

3

4

5

6

Aa 33.7 WRITE THE CORRECT WORD UNDER EACH PICTURE

waiter

1 ______

2 ______

3 ______

4 ______

5 ______

6 ______

7 ______

8 ______

9 ______

10 ______

11 ______

12 ______

13 ______

14 ______

33.8 LISTEN TO THE AUDIO, THEN NUMBER THE PICTURES IN THE ORDER YOU HEAR THEM

A ☐

B ☐

C 1

D ☐

E ☐

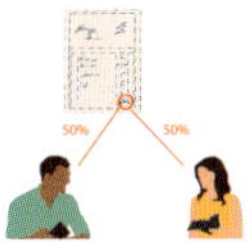
F ☐

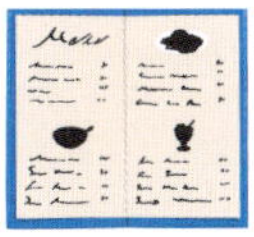
G ☐

H ☐

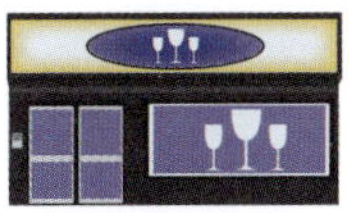
I ☐

J ☐

K ☐

L ☐

M ☐

N ☐

O ☐

34 Jobs

34.1 JOBS

waiter

waitress

chef

butcher

farmer

scientist

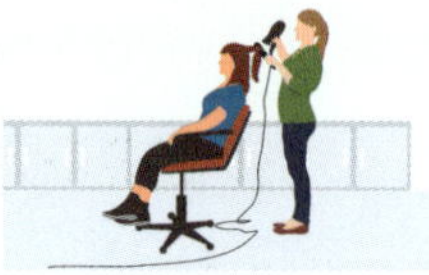
hairdresser / stylist

gardener

cleaner / janitor

train driver

taxi driver

librarian

lawyer

teacher

judge

police officer

firefighter

security guard

driver

electrician

construction worker

plumber

engineer

architect

mechanic

businessman

businesswoman

sales assistant

receptionist

personal assistant / PA

surgeon

doctor

nurse

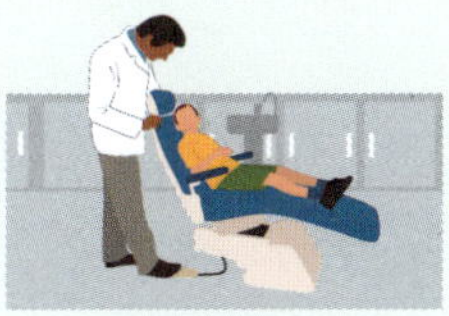
dentist

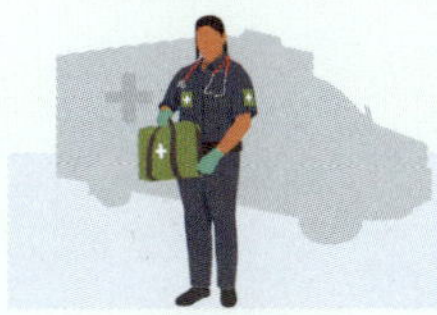
paramedic

psychologist

child-care provider

vet

pilot

flight attendant

travel agent

tour guide

journalist

writer

designer

photographer

actor

artist

musician

fashion designer

Aa 34.2 MARK THE CORRECT JOB FOR THE PERSON IN EACH PICTURE

- teacher ☑
- firefighter ☐
- gardener ☐

1 

- artist ☐
- writer ☐
- waiter ☐

2 

- mechanic ☐
- surgeon ☐
- architect ☐

3 

- butcher ☐
- plumber ☐
- librarian ☐

4 

- gardener ☐
- musician ☐
- pilot ☐

5 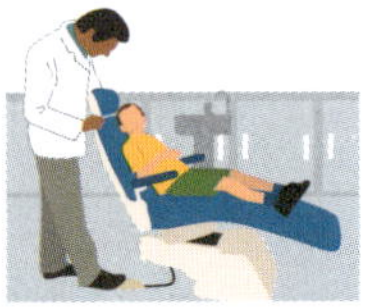

- dentist ☐
- nurse ☐
- lawyer ☐

6 

- actor ☐
- artist ☐
- librarian ☐

7 

- firefighter ☐
- mechanic ☐
- plumber ☐

8 

- judge ☐
- scientist ☐
- electrician ☐

9 

- farmer ☐
- cleaner / janitor ☐
- tour guide ☐

10 

- lawyer ☐
- doctor ☐
- psychologist ☐

11 

- travel agent ☐
- sales assistant ☐
- vet ☐

12 

- train driver ☐
- chef ☐
- waitress ☐

13 

- actor ☐
- fashion designer ☐
- doctor ☐

14 

- stylist ☐
- designer ☐
- gardener ☐

Aa 34.3 MARK THE BEGINNING AND ENDING OF EACH WORD IN THE CHAIN OF LETTERS

psychologist | judgedriverphotographerparamedicbusinessmanjournalistengineerscientist

Aa 34.4 MATCH THE WORDS TO THE CORRECT PICTURES

doctor

1. firefighter
2. chef
3. police officer
4. security guard
5. journalist

A 

B 

C 

D 

E 

Aa 34.5 CIRCLE THE WORD THAT DOES NOT BELONG IN EACH LIST

	journalist	dentist	writer
1	flight attendant	pilot	lawyer
2	doctor	teacher	paramedic
3	musician	actor	scientist
4	artist	plumber	mechanic
5	farmer	gardener	train driver
6	police officer	butcher	firefighter
7	scientist	engineer	librarian
8	mechanic	travel agent	tour guide
9	chef	surgeon	nurse
10	sales assistant	psychologist	butcher
11	waitress	designer	chef
12	doctor	vet	architect

34.6 LISTEN TO THE AUDIO AND CIRCLE THE WORDS YOU HEAR

	actor	artist	architect
1	vet	chef	judge
2	businessman	nurse	gardener
3	doctor	dentist	driver
4	surgeon	scientist	psychologist
5	writer	waitress	waiter
6	nurse	musician	judge
7	teacher	taxi driver	designer
8	artist	architect	actor
9	plumber	photographer	psychologist
10	lawyer	farmer	librarian
11	firefighter	taxi driver	train driver

35 Working conditions

35.1 EMPLOYMENT

company

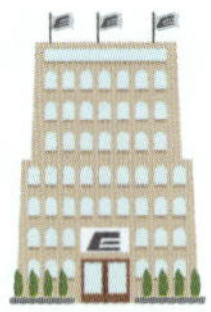
headquarters

staff

employer

employee

manager

permanent

temporary

co-worker / colleague

assistant

intern

apprentice

annual vacation (US) / leave (UK)

nine-to-five job

client

35.2 VERBS

to work part-time

to work full-time

to work from home

to work shifts

to have a day off

to retire

to get fired

to earn

to call in sick

to go on maternity leave

35.3 PAY AND CONDITIONS

The store pays its staff an **hourly rate** of $15.

an hourly rate
[an amount of money paid per hour]

Benefits include gym membership and health insurance.

benefits
[extras given to employees in addition to their usual pay]

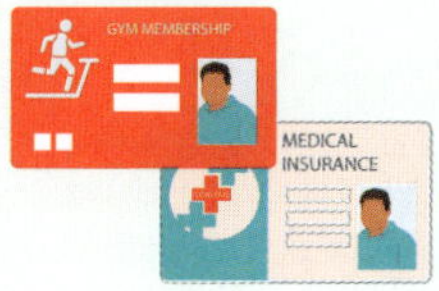

My new job is much more interesting, but I had to take a **pay cut**.

a pay cut
[a reduction in pay]

Our profits are up, so your **wages** will increase by $100 per week.

wages
[an amount of money paid per week or month]

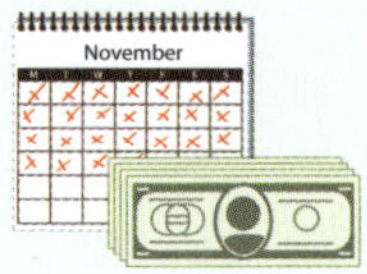

My boss is really pleased with my work, so I'm hoping to get a **raise** next year.

a raise (US) / a pay rise (UK)
[an increase in pay]

I'm looking for a job with a **salary** of at least $25,000.

a salary
[a fixed, regular payment, often expressed as an annual sum]

My **bonus** this year was $1,000, so I'm going to go on vacation.

a bonus
[money added to a person's salary as a reward for good performance]

I got a **promotion** after working for the company for only six months.

a promotion
[a new job at the same company that is more senior or better paid]

We will pay **overtime** to all staff who are willing to work weekends.

overtime
[additional pay for extra hours worked]

I had to find a new job last year because I **was laid off**.

to be laid off (US) / made redundant (UK)
[to lose your job because it is no longer necessary]

Aa 35.4 FIND SEVEN MORE WORDS IN THE GRID THAT MATCH THE PICTURES

```
S D M Y U I R A C S A H A
T A P P R E N T I C E P Q
Y S T I M T A O T A A E T
B L I N T E R N E P S N E
C O L L E A G U E L S C M
L E Y E P A O C A R I I P
I M A N A G E R Q B S S L
E Y Q A B F R S T H T V O
N M P L N Y T T A P A D Y
T J S X S M T A E E N I E
P R Z W T B M F U L T S E
L F E R G A V F I M F W X
```

1 

2 

3 

4 

5 

6 

7 

Aa 35.5 WRITE THE CORRECT VERB UNDER EACH PICTURE

to retire

1 ______________

2 ______________

3 ______________

4 ______________

5 ______________

6 ______________

7 ______________

8 ______________

9 ______________

35.6 LISTEN TO THE AUDIO AND COMPLETE THE SENTENCES THAT DESCRIBE EACH PICTURE

My boss is really pleased with my work, so I'm hoping to get a *raise* next year.

1 The store pays its staff an ______________ of $15.

2 We will pay ______________ to all staff who are willing to work weekends.

3 I'm looking for a job with a ______________ of at least $25,000.

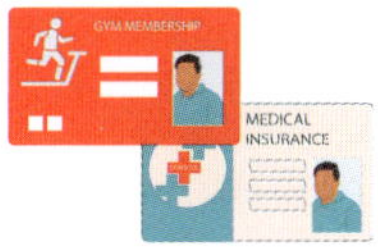

4 ______________ include gym membership and health insurance.

5 My ______________ this year was $1,000, so I'm going to go on vacation.

6 I had to find a new job last year because I ______________.

7 I got a ______________ after working for the company for only six months.

35.7 WRITE THE CORRECT WORD OR PHRASE NEXT TO ITS DEFINITION, FILLING IN THE MISSING LETTERS

additional pay for extra hours worked = o *v e r t i m e*

1 extras given to employees in addition to their usual pay = b _ n _ f _ _ s

2 an amount of money paid per week or month = w _ _ _ s

3 a reduction in pay = a p _ _ c _ _

4 an increase in pay = a r _ _ s _

5 an amount of money paid per hour = a n h _ _ _ _ _ _ _ _ t _

36 Industries and departments

36.1 INDUSTRIES

education

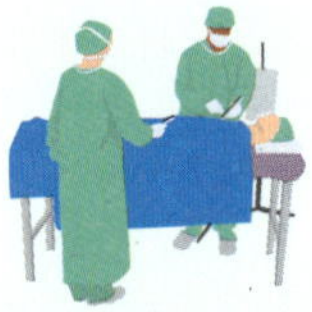
healthcare

catering / food

chemical

construction

agriculture / farming

energy

electronics

entertainment

fashion

finance

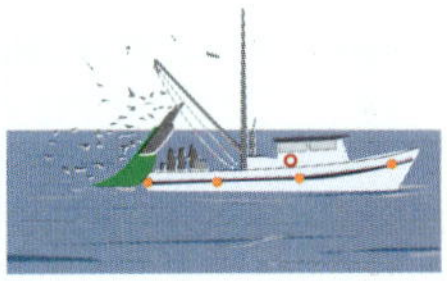
fishing

hospitality

journalism

manufacturing

advertising

mining

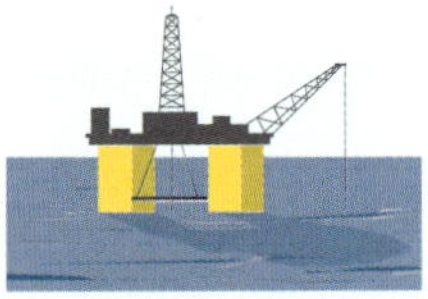
petroleum engineering

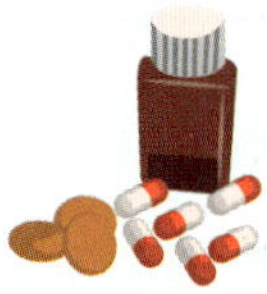
pharmaceutical

real estate (US) property (UK)

recycling

shipping

tourism

transportation

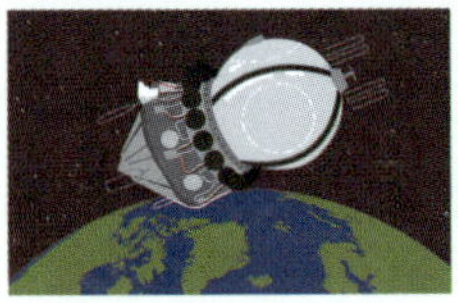
aerospace

36.2 DEPARTMENTS

Administration

[deals with organization and internal and external communication]

Production

[ensures that all manufacturing stages run smoothly]

Research and Development (R&D)

[researches and develops future products for a company]

Purchasing

[buys goods and raw materials for manufacturers and other companies]

Human Resources (HR)

[deals with employee relations and matters such as hiring staff]

Sales

[sells products to buyers and outside markets]

Accounts / Finance

[deals with money matters, from paying bills to projecting sales]

Facilities / Office Services

[carries out cleaning, maintenance, and building operation services]

Marketing

[promotes products for companies to the market]

Legal

[ensures that all contracts and company activities are legal]

Public Relations (PR)

[presents and maintains a positive public image for a company]

Information Technology (IT)

[sets up and maintains all technological systems in an organization]

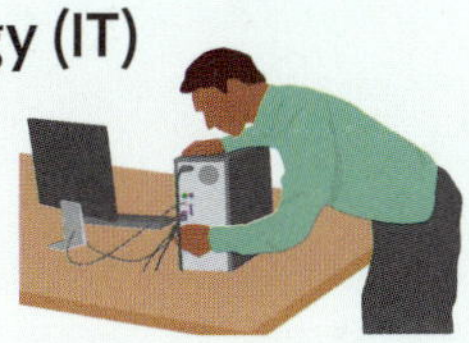

Aa 36.3 MATCH THE WORDS TO THE CORRECT PICTURES

fishing → 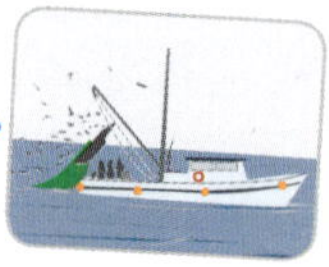

1 fashion

2 recycling

3 chemical

4 hospitality

5 real estate

6 education

7 mining

8 catering / food

9 pharmaceutical

A 

B 

C 

D 

E 

F 

G 

H 

I 

Aa 36.4 COMPLETE THE WORD FOR EACH PICTURE, FILLING IN THE MISSING LETTERS

 e l e c t r o n i c s

1 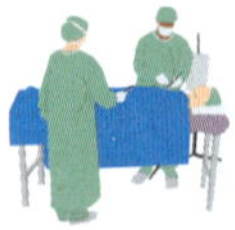 h _ _ l t h c _ r _

2  _ g r _ c _ l t _ r _

3  f _ n _ n c _

4  s h _ p p _ n g

5  _ n _ r g y

6  _ d v _ r t _ s _ n g

7  j _ _ r n _ l _ s m

8  t _ _ r _ s m

9  _ _ r _ s p _ c _

36.5 LISTEN TO THE AUDIO, THEN NUMBER THE PICTURES IN THE ORDER THEY ARE MENTIONED

A ☐

B ☐

C ☐

D ☐

E ☐

F 1

G ☐

H ☐

I ☐

J ☐

K ☐

L ☐

36.6 WRITE THE NAME OF THE DEPARTMENT NEXT TO ITS DEFINITION

ensures that all manufacturing stages run smoothly = *Production*

1. deals with employee relations and matters such as hiring staff = ______
2. deals with money matters, from paying bills to projecting sales = ______
3. ensures that all contracts and company activities are legal = ______
4. deals with organization and internal and external communication = ______
5. presents and maintains a positive public image for a company = ______
6. sells products to buyers and outside markets = ______
7. promotes products for companies to the market = ______

37 Office equipment

37.1 IN THE OFFICE

37.2 EQUIPMENT

photocopier

telephone / phone

printer

projector

shredder

scanner

computer

laptop

cell phone (US)
mobile phone (UK)

headset

37.3 STATIONERY

letter

envelope

calendar

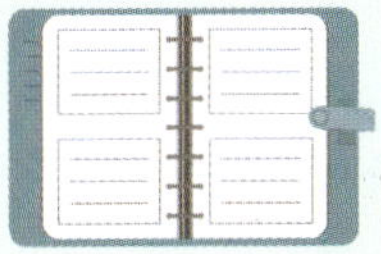
planner (US)
diary (UK)

clipboard

files / folders

hole punch

stapler

staples

pencil sharpener

pencil

pen

highlighter

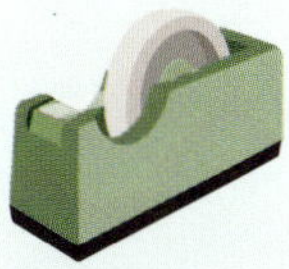
adhesive tape

notepad

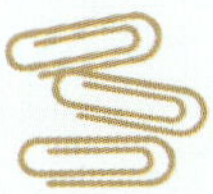
paper clips

eraser (US)
rubber (UK)

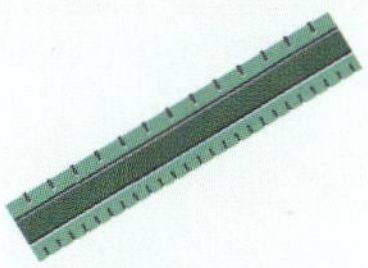
ruler

paper

correction fluid

sticky notes

rubber bands

binder clip

thumbtack (US)
drawing pin (UK)

scissors

Aa 37.4 LOOK AT THE PICTURE AND WRITE THE CORRECT WORD FOR EACH LABEL

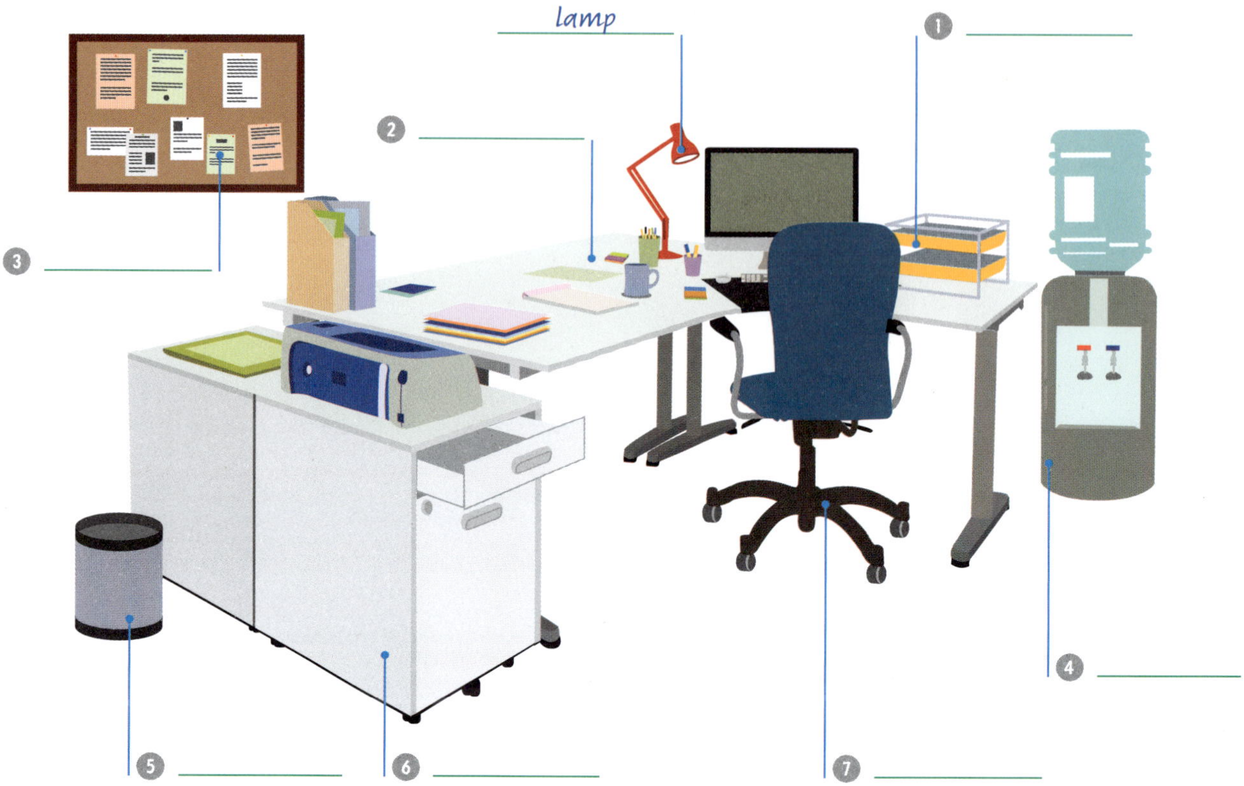

Aa 37.5 LOOK AT THE PICTURE CLUES AND WRITE THE ANSWERS IN THE CORRECT PLACES ON THE GRID

37.6 LISTEN TO THE AUDIO AND MARK THE CORRECT PICTURE FOR EACH WORD YOU HEAR

A ☐ B ☑ C ☐

1 A ☐ B ☐ C ☐

2 A ☐ B ☐ C ☐

3 A ☐ B ☐ C ☐

4 A ☐ B ☐ C ☐

5 A ☐ B ☐ C ☐

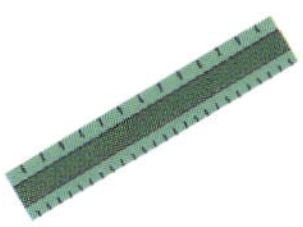  

6 A ☐ B ☐ C ☐

37.7 COMPLETE THE WORD FOR EACH PICTURE, FILLING IN THE MISSING LETTERS

 p r o j e c t o r

1  c _ l _ n d _ r

2  s _ _ s _ _ r _

3  p h _ t _ c _ p _ _ r

4  r _ b b _ r b _ n d s

5  c l _ p b _ _ r d

6  l _ p t _ p

7  s _ r _ d _ _ r

8  p _ p _ r c l _ p s

9  _ c _ n _ _ r

10  h _ g h l _ g h t _ r

11  _ n v _ l _ p _

12  h _ l _ p _ n c h

38 Money and finance

38.1 MONEY

bills (US)
notes (UK)

coins

wallet

wallet (US)
purse (UK)

credit card

debit card

cash machine / ATM

bank

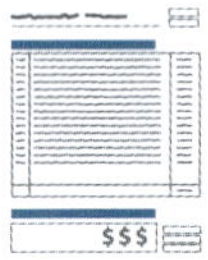

bank statement

online banking

mobile banking

receipt

currency

cash register (US)
till (UK)

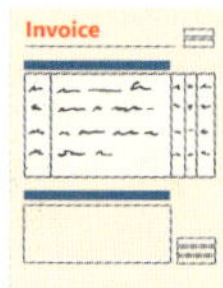

invoice

check (US)
cheque (UK)

mortgage

bank loan

PIN

stock exchange

interest rate

to withdraw money

to change money

to transfer money

to save

38.2 FINANCE

Our income fell after we lost an important client.

income

[money coming into a business]

If we can't sell more products, we will get into debt.

to get into debt

[to get into a situation where you owe people money]

We have a large marketing budget, so there's no excuse for poor sales.

a budget

[the amount of money that is available to spend on something]

We've made a loss because we haven't sold any pineapples.

to make a loss

[to lose money by spending more than you earn]

The bank charges $10 per month for overdrafts.

an overdraft

[extra money the bank allows you to spend]

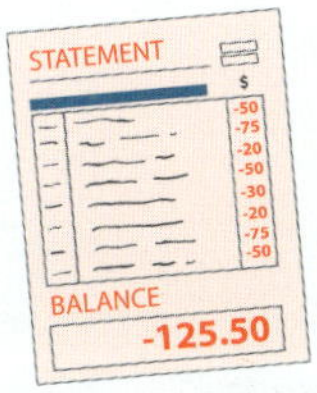

The exchange rate has made trips to some countries more expensive.

the exchange rate

[the amount of one currency that you get when you change it for another]

We have to sell these cars if we're going to break even.

to break even

[to earn just enough to cover the costs of producing a product]

The store has gone out of business because most people download movies now.

to go out of business

[to no longer be able to exist as a business]

The expenditure on these laptops was huge, but now we can work from home.

expenditure / outlay

[an amount of money spent]

We might lose our jobs because of the economic downturn.

an economic downturn

[a major decline in economic activity]

Aa 38.3 MARK THE CORRECT WORD FOR EACH PICTURE

- receipt ☑
- PIN ☐
- bank ☐

1
- currency ☐
- mortgage ☐
- purse ☐

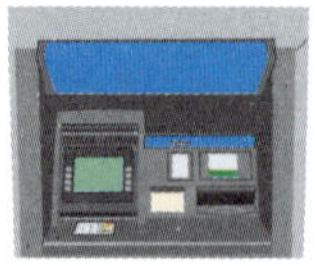

2
- online banking ☐
- cash machine ☐
- invoice ☐

3
- bank loan ☐
- stock exchange ☐
- coins ☐

4
- credit card ☐
- bank ☐
- check ☐

5
- stock exchange ☐
- interest rate ☐
- bills ☐

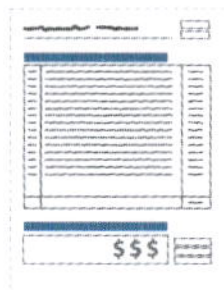

6
- mortgage ☐
- bank statement ☐
- receipt ☐

7
- interest rate ☐
- to change money ☐
- currency ☐

8
- to save ☐
- mobile banking ☐
- bank loan ☐

9
- mobile banking ☐
- stock exchange ☐
- PIN ☐

10
- mobile banking ☐
- credit card ☐
- cash register ☐

11
- wallet ☐
- invoice ☐
- coins ☐

12
- mortgage ☐
- stock exchange ☐
- bank ☐

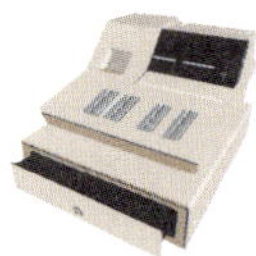

13
- bank loan ☐
- credit card ☐
- cash register ☐

14
- coins ☐
- invoice ☐
- bills ☐

Aa 38.4 MARK THE BEGINNING AND ENDING OF EACH WORD IN THE CHAIN OF LETTERS

mortgage/cashmachineinvoicewalletcoinsbankreceiptcheckmobilebankingstockexchange

Aa 38.5 MARK THE SENTENCES THAT ARE CORRECT

We've made a loss because we haven't sold any pineapples. ☑
We've made a lose because we haven't sold any pineapples. ☐

1 
The store has gone out for business because most people download movies now. ☐
The store has gone out of business because most people download movies now. ☐

2 
The bank charges $10 per month for underdrafts. ☐
The bank charges $10 per month for overdrafts. ☐

3 

The exchange rate has made trips to some countries more expensive. ☐
The exchange rata has made trips to some countries more expensive. ☐

4 
If we can't sell more products, we will get into debit. ☐
If we can't sell more products, we will get into debt. ☐

5 
Our income fell after we lost an important client. ☐
Our incomings fell after we lost an important client. ☐

38.6 LISTEN TO THE AUDIO AND MARK THE CORRECT PICTURE FOR EACH WORD YOU HEAR

A ☑

B ☐

C ☐

1

A ☐

B ☐

C ☐

2

A ☐

B ☐

C ☐

3
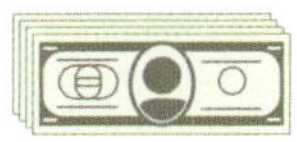
A ☐

B ☐

C ☐

4

A ☐

B ☐

C ☐

5
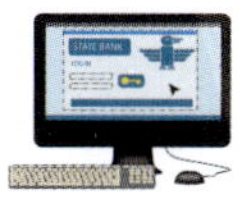
A ☐

B ☐
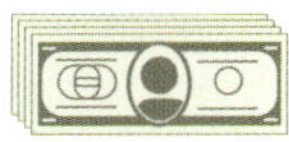
C ☐

39 Working

39.1 USEFUL EXPRESSIONS

I don't work a nine-to-five job because I have two young children.

a nine-to-five

[a job with regular hours]

It's very important to create a positive working environment.

a working environment

[the conditions in which you work]

All our employees are fully trained and have hands-on experience.

hands-on experience

[knowledge and skill gained through doing something yourself]

Elena's chosen career path involves a lot of travel.

a career path

[progression within a profession, in a job, or through a series of jobs]

Bruno's career took off after he won an important new client.

to take off

[to suddenly become more successful]

I have held a position in management for five years.

to hold a position

[to have a job]

My boss started working here at the bottom of the career ladder.

the bottom of the career ladder

[a position with the lowest level of responsibility or pay]

Lucas has been stuck in a dead-end job for two years.

a dead-end job

[a position without many prospects for promotion]

Gavin was fired because he was caught stealing from the warehouse.

to be fired

[to be forced to leave your job for doing something wrong]

Some of the factory workers were laid off after our profits fell.

to be laid off / made redundant (UK)

[to lose your job because the company can no longer give you work]

I'm stepping down from this job because I need more training.

to step down

[to stop doing a job voluntarily]

We've set our sights on winning more industry awards.

to set your sights on something

[to aim to achieve a particular goal]

We've taken on three new employees for the busy summer months.

to take someone on / to take on someone

[to employ someone]

People who work in childcare have their hands full all day.

to have your hands full

[to be busy with a task or many tasks]

Clive always goes the extra mile to deliver our products on time.

to go the extra mile

[to do more than you are required to do]

I need to tackle this problem head-on or it will get worse.

to tackle something head-on

[to deal with something directly]

If they don't stop arguing, they'll never get ahead in this company.

to get ahead

[to make more progress than others]

Can I call you back later? I'm snowed under right now.

snowed under

[very busy with too much work]

Don't disturb Harry today! He's up to his eyeballs with work.

up to your eyeballs / ears (UK)

[extremely busy]

Working well with clients involves a lot of give and take.

give and take

[compromise]

Aa 39.2 WRITE THE CORRECT PHRASE NEXT TO ITS DEFINITION, FILLING IN THE MISSING LETTERS

a job with regular hours	=	a n *i n e*-t *o*-f *i v e*
1 to make more progress than others	=	t _ g _ _ a _ _ _ _
2 to suddenly become more successful	=	t _ t _ _ _ o _ _
3 to employ someone	=	t _ t _ _ _ s _ _ _ _ _ _ o _
4 compromise	=	g _ _ _ a _ _ t _ _ _
5 to stop doing a job voluntarily	=	t _ s _ _ _ d _ _ _

39.3 LISTEN TO THE AUDIO AND COMPLETE THE SENTENCES THAT DESCRIBE EACH PICTURE

It's very important to create a positive *working environment*.

1 All our employees are fully trained and have ____________.

2 Gavin ____________ because he was caught stealing from the warehouse.

3 Bruno's career ____________ after he won an important new client.

4 People who work in childcare ____________ ____________ all day.

5 We've ____________ ____________ winning more industry awards.

6 I need to ____________ ____________ or it will get worse.

7 Working well with clients involves a lot of ____________.

Aa 39.4 FILL IN THE GAPS, PUTTING THE WORDS IN THE CORRECT ORDER

position | held | in | a

I have *held* *a* *position* *in* management for five years.

of | career | the | at | bottom | the

1 My boss started working here ______ ______ ______ ______ ______ ______ ladder.

a | in | job | dead | -end | stuck

2 Lucas has been ______ ______ ______ ______ ______ ______ for two years.

job | five | -to- | nine | a

3 I don't work ______ ______ ______ ______ ______ because I have two young children.

job | down | stepping | this | from

4 I'm ______ ______ ______ ______ ______ because I need more training.

Aa 39.5 CROSS OUT THE INCORRECT WORD IN EACH SENTENCE

Don't disturb Harry today! He's up to his **eyeballs** / ~~**nose**~~ with work.

1  Elena's chosen career **path** / **route** involves a lot of travel.

2  Can I call you back later? I'm **rained** / **snowed** under right now.

3  Clive always goes the extra **inch** / **mile** to deliver our products on time.

4  Some of the factory workers were laid **off** / **up** after our profits fell.

40 Meeting and presenting

40.1 USEFUL EXPRESSIONS

Carla will attend the team meeting tomorrow afternoon.

to attend a meeting
[to go to a meeting]

Emir is giving a presentation on his team's latest research.

to give a presentation
[to present a formal talk to an audience]

Our poor sales figures will be on the agenda today.

on the agenda
[included in a list of things to discuss]

Stefan is on vacation and will be absent from this meeting.

absent
[not present]

We're having a conference call with our clients in Japan this morning.

a conference call
[a telephone call with a number of people at the same time]

Deepak has been promoted, so now he's on the board of directors.

the board of directors
[a group of people who manage a business or organization]

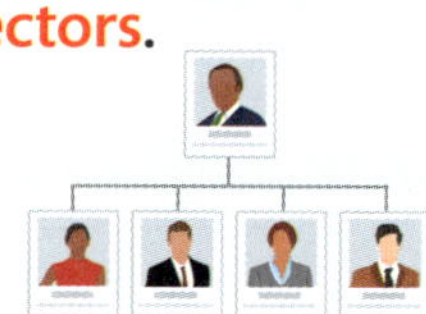

Let me see a show of hands. How many of you agree with my proposal?

a show of hands
[a vote made by raising hands in the air to show agreement]

We reached a unanimous agreement on the budget.

a unanimous agreement
[when everyone agrees]

I'll talk through the report and then I'll take questions.

to take questions
[to answer questions]

Cameron is going to take minutes during our finance meeting.

to take minutes
[to write a record of what is said during a meeting]

We easily **reached a consensus** on the best poster design.

to reach a consensus
[to come to an agreement about an issue]

We've gone through the agenda. Is there **any other business**?

any other business (AOB)
[any matter discussed in a meeting that is not on the agenda]

The main objective of this meeting is to discuss product ideas.

the main objective
[the primary aim]

This is my **strategy** for selling more products overseas.

a strategy
[a plan for achieving a particular goal]

There were three clear **action points** arising from today's meeting.

action points
[proposals for specific action to be taken]

To sum up, sales of our older products have fallen this year.

to sum up
[to give a brief summary]

Ellen has **reviewed the minutes** from our meeting last week.

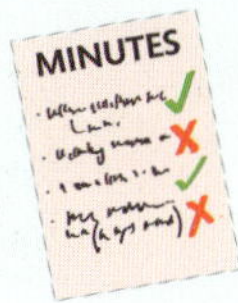

to review the minutes
[to look again at the written record of a past meeting]

Let's **wrap up** this meeting. It's almost one o'clock.

to wrap up
[to conclude or finish something]

I'm sorry to **interrupt**, but your client is waiting in reception.

to interrupt
[to disturb a meeting or say something before someone else has finished speaking]

We can't discuss the new computer system because we've **run out of time**.

to run out of time
[to have no time left for something]

Aa 40.2 MATCH THE PICTURES TO THE CORRECT SENTENCES

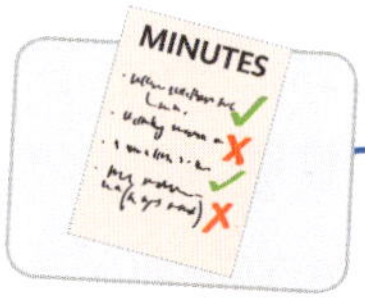

1 

2 

3 

4 

- We easily reached a consensus on the best poster design.
- Ellen has reviewed the minutes from our meeting last week.
- I'm sorry to interrupt, but your client is waiting in reception.
- Our poor sales figures will be on the agenda today.
- Stefan is on vacation and will be absent from this meeting.

40.3 LISTEN TO THE AUDIO, THEN NUMBER THE SENTENCES IN THE ORDER YOU HEAR THEM

A  Let me see a show of hands. How many of you agree with my proposal? ☐

B  We reached a unanimous agreement on the budget. ☐

C  The main objective of this meeting is to discuss product ideas. 1

D  Let's wrap up this meeting. It's almost one o'clock. ☐

E  Cameron is going to take minutes during our finance meeting. ☐

Aa 40.4 MATCH THE DEFINITIONS TO THE CORRECT PHRASES

	a plan for achieving a particular goal → a strategy	to sum up
1	included in a list of things to discuss	to attend a meeting
2	to give a brief summary	a strategy
3	to go to a meeting	to reach a consensus
4	the primary aim	on the agenda
5	to come to an agreement about an issue	to give a presentation
6	not present	the main objective
7	to have no time left for something	absent
8	to present a formal talk to an audience	action points
9	proposals for specific action to be taken	to run out of time

Aa 40.5 MARK THE SENTENCES THAT ARE CORRECT

Emir is taking a presentation on his team's latest research. ☐
Emir is giving a presentation on his team's latest research. ☑

1 

To sum up, sales of our older products have fallen this year. ☐
To add up, sales of our older products have fallen this year. ☐

2 

Stefan is on vacation and will be absence from this meeting. ☐
Stefan is on vacation and will be absent from this meeting. ☐

3 

I'll talk through the report and then I'll hear questions. ☐
I'll talk through the report and then I'll take questions. ☐

4 

Our poor sales figures will be on the agenda today. ☐
Our poor sales figures will be in the agenda today. ☐

5 

Let's tie up this meeting. It's almost one o'clock. ☐
Let's wrap up this meeting. It's almost one o'clock. ☐

41 Work and business idioms

41.1 WORKPLACE IDIOMS

The store was closed for remodeling, but it's business as usual now.

business as usual
[the normal daily routine at a company]

Health and safety in the warehouse involves a lot of red tape.

red tape
[administration, paperwork, or rules and regulations]

We're in the red after losing three of our clients this year.

in the red
[owing money or making a loss]

This is the best deal we can offer. The ball is in your court now.

the ball is in your court
[it is your turn to do or say something]

Let's get the ball rolling. What do you all think of this logo design?

to get the ball rolling
[to start something]

This product will never sell. We're throwing money down the drain.

to throw money down the drain
[to waste money]

The client loves our cars and we've agreed on a great price. It's a win-win situation.

a win-win situation
[a situation with no negative outcome]

You need to think outside the box to come up with good designs.

to think outside the box
[to think about something in an original way]

This client will never be satisfied because he keeps moving the goalposts.

to move the goalposts
[to change the desired end result]

Let's get down to business. I have to leave by 5 o'clock.

to get down to business
[to start work on something that needs doing]

41.2 BUSINESS IDIOMS

We're really **ahead of the game** with these great new products.

ahead of the game
[ahead of your competitors in a certain field]

We don't know the exact costs, but here's a **ballpark figure**.

a ballpark figure
[a rough estimate]

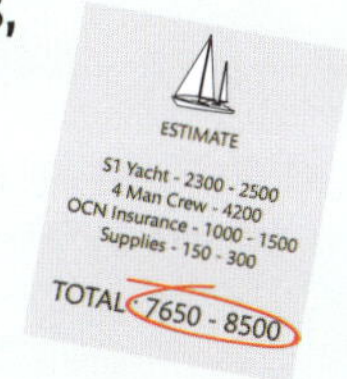

Great! We're all **on the same page** about this marketing campaign.

on the same page
[in agreement about something]

They've **cornered the market** with their new range of sports shoes.

to corner the market
[to dominate a particular market]

This is a difficult job. Make sure you **do everything by the book**.

to do something by the book
[to do something strictly according to the rules]

We expected a **change of pace** after we received several large orders.

a change of pace
[an increase or decrease in speed from what is normal]

Could I **touch base** with you for a quick update on this project?

to touch base
[to talk to someone briefly in order to catch up or get an update]

We're losing money, so we need a **game plan** for increasing sales.

a game plan
[a strategy worked out beforehand]

Rohit **clinched the deal** after offering the clients a discount.

to clinch the deal
[to confirm or settle an agreement or contract]

I'm so busy today. Please tell me the facts **in a nutshell**.

in a nutshell
[simply and quickly]

Aa 41.3 REWRITE THE SENTENCES, CORRECTING THE ERRORS

The store was closed for remodeling, but it's **business like usual** now.

The store was closed for remodeling, but it's business as usual now.

1. This is a difficult job. Make sure you **do everything by the instructions**.

2. Great! We're all **on the same chapter** about this marketing campaign.

3. This client will never be satisfied because he keeps **moving the net**.

4. Health and safety in the warehouse involves a lot of **red papers**.

Aa 41.4 MATCH THE PICTURES TO THE CORRECT SENTENCES

1. 

2. 

3. 

4. 

We're losing money, so we need a game plan for increasing sales.

We're really ahead of the game with these great new products.

Could I touch base with you for a quick update on this project?

We don't know the exact costs, but here's a ballpark figure.

Rohit clinched the deal after offering the clients a discount.

Aa 41.5 MATCH THE BEGINNINGS OF THE SENTENCES TO THE CORRECT ENDINGS

I'm so busy today. Please tell me → the facts in a nutshell.

1. We expected a change of pace
2. This product will never sell. We're
3. This client will never be satisfied because
4. They've cornered the
5. This is a difficult job. Make

- throwing money down the drain.
- market with their new range of shoes.
- the facts in a nutshell.
- sure you do everything by the book.
- after we received several large orders.
- he keeps moving the goalposts.

41.6 LISTEN TO THE AUDIO, THEN NUMBER THE SENTENCES IN THE ORDER YOU HEAR THEM

A  Let's get down to business. I have to leave by 5 o'clock. ☐

B  The store was closed for remodeling, but it's business as usual now. ☐

C  We're in the red after losing three of our clients this year. [1]

D  Let's get the ball rolling. What do you all think of this logo design? ☐

E  You need to think outside the box to come up with good designs. ☐

F  This is the best deal we can offer. The ball is in your court now. ☐

G  The client loves our cars and we've agreed on a great price. It's a win-win situation. ☐

H  Health and safety in the warehouse involves a lot of red tape. ☐

42 Applying for a job

42.1 RÉSUMÉ HEADINGS

Adriana Pires

275 Main Street, Minneapolis, MN 55401
addi123@pires456.com · 612-555-1746

PERSONAL STATEMENT
A highly motivated individual, with a proven track record in hotel reception and front-of-house work.

PROFESSIONAL ACHIEVEMENTS
Won an award for the Best Hotel Receptionist in the Midwestern Region.

CAREER SUMMARY
Hotel Deluxe Cite
FRONT DESK MANAGER • May 2014–Present
- Working in a service-oriented environment.
- Gained in-depth knowledge of the hospitality industry, and hands-on experience in customer service.

EDUCATION
- BA in Tourism and Hospitality
- Minor in Spanish

KEY SKILLS
- Fluent in Portuguese, Spanish, and English
- Proficient in IT use, including most types of reservation systems

INTERESTS
Cooking, traveling, paragliding, scuba diving

REFERENCES
Available upon request

résumé (US)
CV (UK)

job ad (US) / advert (UK)

application form

portfolio

cover letter (US)
covering letter (UK)

recruitment agency

42.2 VERBS

to apply for a job

to fill out a form

to have an interview

to manage

to negotiate

to coordinate

to collaborate

to volunteer

to organize

to supervise

42.3 USEFUL EXPRESSIONS

I have a **proven track record** in the catering industry.

a proven track record
[a long list of achievements]

I am **proficient in** all major types of accounting software.

proficient in
[highly skilled at something]

As an ex-car salesman, I have a **service-oriented** background.

service-oriented
[having a lot of contact with customers]

All our staff are fully **trained in** first aid.

trained in
[taught how to do something]

I have an **in-depth knowledge** of hair-coloring techniques.

an in-depth knowledge
[an expert understanding of something]

I am **responsible for** six other staff members.

responsible for
[having control over someone or something]

Aa 42.4 LOOK AT THE RÉSUMÉ AND WRITE THE CORRECT WORD FROM THE PANEL FOR EACH LABEL

Adriana Pires

275 Main Street, Minneapolis, MN 55401
addi123@pires456.com · 612-555-1746

Personal statement
A highly motivated individual, with a proven track record in hotel reception and front-of-house work.

1 ______________

Won an award for the Best Hotel Receptionist in the Midwestern Region.

2 ______________

Hotel Deluxe Cite
FRONT DESK MANAGER • May 2014–Present
• Working in a service-oriented environment.
• Gained in-depth knowledge of the hospitality industry, and hands-on experience in customer service.

3 ______________

• BA in Tourism and Hospitality
• Minor in Spanish

4 ______________

• Fluent in Portuguese, Spanish, and English
• Proficient in IT use, including most types of reservation systems

5 ______________

Cooking, traveling, paragliding, scuba diving

6 ______________

Available upon request

Career summary
Key skills
~~Personal statement~~
Interests
References
Professional achievements
Education

Aa 42.5 WRITE THE CORRECT WORD UNDER EACH PICTURE

application form

1 ______________

2 ______________

3 ______________

4 ______________

Aa 42.6 WRITE THE CORRECT WORD UNDER EACH PICTURE

to volunteer

1 ______________

2 ______________

3 ______________

4 ______________

5 ______________

6 ______________

7 ______________

8 ______________

9 ______________

42.7 LISTEN TO THE AUDIO AND COMPLETE THE SENTENCES THAT DESCRIBE EACH PICTURE

All our staff are fully *trained in* first aid.

3 I have a ______________ in the catering industry.

1 I am ______________ six other staff members.

4 As an ex-car salesman, I have a ______________ background.

2 I have an ______________ of hair-coloring techniques.

5 I am ______________ all major types of accounting software.

43 Workplace skills and abilities

43.1 PROFESSIONAL ATTRIBUTES

organized

patient

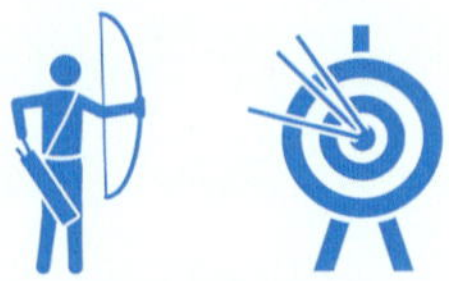
accurate

creative

honest

practical

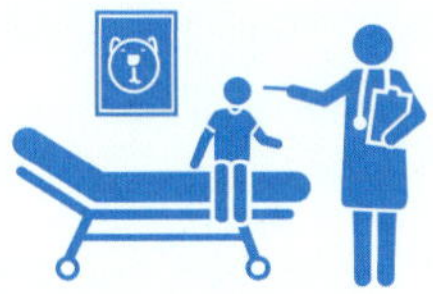
professional

adaptable

ambitious

calm

confident

punctual

reliable

customer-focused

independent

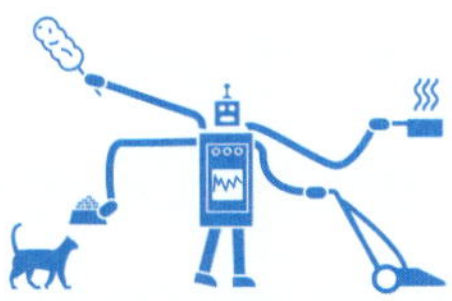
efficient

energetic

flexible

hardworking

responsible

innovative

motivated

determined

team player

competitive

43.2 FOR THE WORKPLACE

organization

IT / computing

administration

problem-solving

data analysis

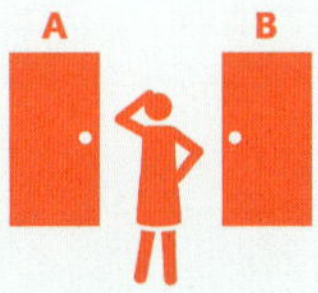

decision-making

teamwork

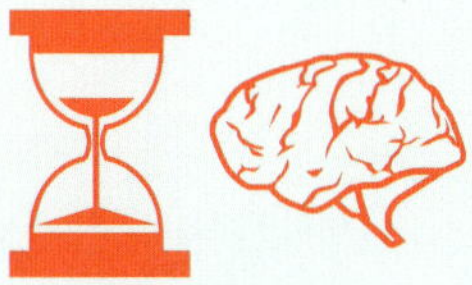
fast learner

numeracy

customer service

interpersonal skills

leadership

research

fluent in languages

attention to detail

negotiating

public speaking

written communication

initiative

telephone manner

work well under pressure

able to drive

project management

time management

businesslike attitude

Aa 43.3 MARK THE CORRECT WORD FOR EACH PICTURE

accurate ☐
creative ☑
ambitious ☐

1 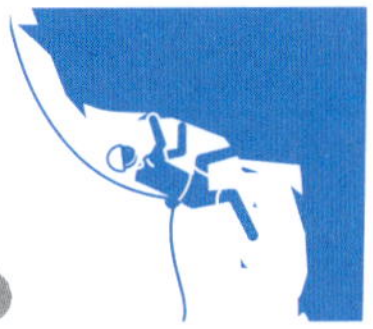

research ☐
administration ☐
determined ☐

2 

organization ☐
calm ☐
reliable ☐

3 

public speaking ☐
energetic ☐
customer service ☐

4 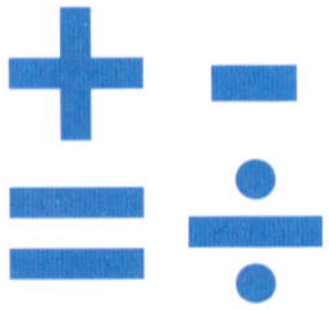

able to drive ☐
numeracy ☐
punctual ☐

5 

honest ☐
calm ☐
flexible ☐

6 

responsible ☐
competitive ☐
motivated ☐

7 

ambitious ☐
accurate ☐
practical ☐

8 

responsible ☐
professional ☐
patient ☐

9 

teamwork ☐
data analysis ☐
honest ☐

10 

organized ☐
research ☐
leadership ☐

11 

adaptable ☐
punctual ☐
IT / computing ☐

12 

initiative ☐
able to drive ☐
hardworking ☐

13 

team player ☐
innovative ☐
fast learner ☐

14 

negotiating ☐
efficient ☐
energetic ☐

Aa 43.4 MARK THE BEGINNING AND ENDING OF EACH WORD IN THE CHAIN OF LETTERS

professional|reliablehardworkingresponsibleadministrationmotivatedresearchorganizedcalm

Aa 43.5 MATCH THE PICTURES TO THE CORRECT WORDS

1 

2 

3 

4 

5 

leadership

problem-solving

customer-focused

time management

fluent in languages

attention to detail

43.6 LISTEN TO THE AUDIO AND CIRCLE THE WORDS YOU HEAR

	teamwork	energetic	team player
1	confident	calm	creative
2	punctual	practical	patient
3	organized	honest	accurate
4	research	reliable	responsible
5	administration	innovative	motivated
6	independent	adaptable	ambitious
7	leadership	efficient	initiative
8	data analysis	professional	fast learner
9	organization	ambitious	flexible
10	negotiating	competitive	confident
11	decision-making	determined	teamwork

Aa 43.7 REWRITE THE WORDS, CORRECTING THE SPELLINGS

inovative

innovative

1 ambicious

2 teem pleyer

3 ennergetic

4 interpersonnel skils

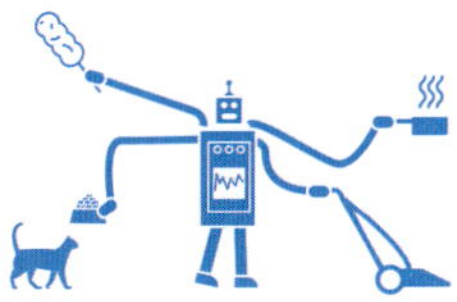

5 eficient

44 Transportation and travel

44.1 FORMS OF TRANSPORTATION

airplane (US)
aeroplane (UK)

car

taxi

bus

coach

train

tram

motorcycle (US)
motorbike (UK)

bicycle / bike

boat

ferry

yacht

ship

helicopter

moped

hot air balloon

truck (US)
lorry (UK)

van

camel

horse

44.2 TRAVEL

passengers

pedestrian

commuters

train station

platform

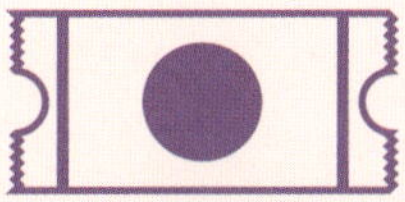
ticket

bus stop

airport

taxi stand (US)
taxi rank (UK)

port

44.3 VERBS

to ride a bike

to ride a horse

to take a flight

to drive a car

to take the bus

to take the train

to walk

to hitchhike

to get on a bus

to get off a bus

to get in a taxi

to get out of a taxi

to catch a train

to miss a train

to give someone a ride (US) / lift (UK)

Aa 44.4 MATCH THE VERBS TO THE CORRECT PICTURES

to hitchhike

1. to give someone a lift
2. to miss a train
3. to get on a bus
4. to catch a train
5. to ride a bike
6. to take a flight
7. to ride a horse
8. to get off a bus
9. to get out of a taxi

A 

B 

C 

D 

E 

F 

G 

H 

I 

Aa 44.5 REWRITE THE WORDS, CORRECTING THE SPELLINGS

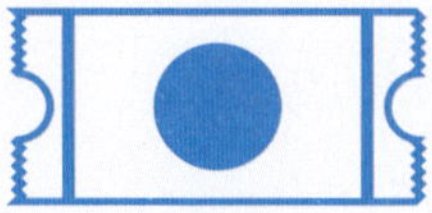

tiket

ticket

1. passagers

2. platforma

3. bycicle

4. pedesstrien

5. comutters

6. couch

7. jacht

8. mopped

9. ven

Aa 44.6 FIND NINE MORE WORDS IN THE GRID THAT MATCH THE PICTURES

A	I	R	P	O	R	T	A	C	T	H
T	A	V	P	Q	H	O	Q	V	R	E
A	E	D	E	M	J	J	M	D	A	L
T	A	X	I	T	E	K	T	I	I	I
L	T	B	C	X	W	N	X	B	N	C
E	E	O	I	C	A	M	E	L	X	O
R	M	A	L	O	L	A	O	Z	B	P
A	B	O	A	T	C	R	Y	C	H	T
V	A	N	P	S	V	V	A	V	O	E
A	E	D	E	R	D	D	C	D	R	R
P	R	I	N	G	I	I	H	I	S	A
F	E	R	R	Y	B	B	T	B	E	O

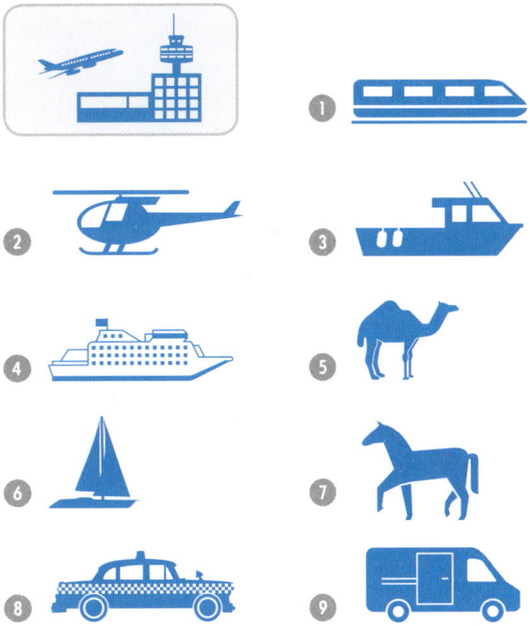

44.7 LISTEN TO THE AUDIO, THEN NUMBER THE PICTURES IN THE ORDER YOU HEAR THEM

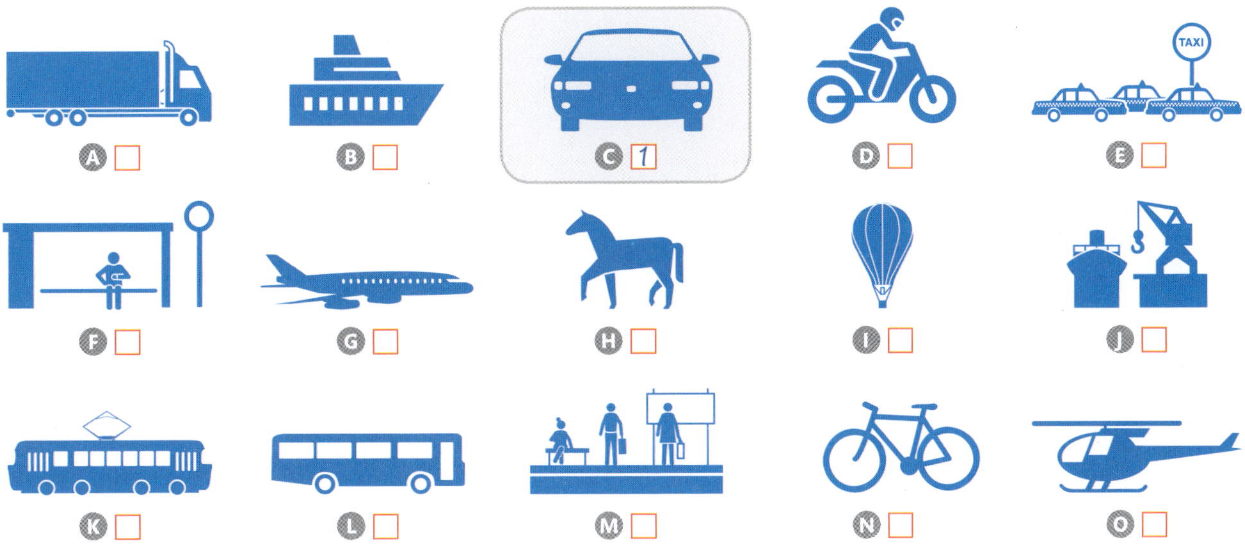

45 Driving a car

45.1 DRIVING VOCABULARY

driver's license (US) / licence (UK)

insurance

seatbelt

gas station (US) petrol station (UK)

engine

turn signal (US) indicator (UK)

steering wheel

fuel

gasoline (US) petrol (UK)

diesel

oil

auto repair shop (US) / garage (UK)

mechanic

flat tire (US) flat tyre (UK)

wipers

pedestrian crossing

traffic lights

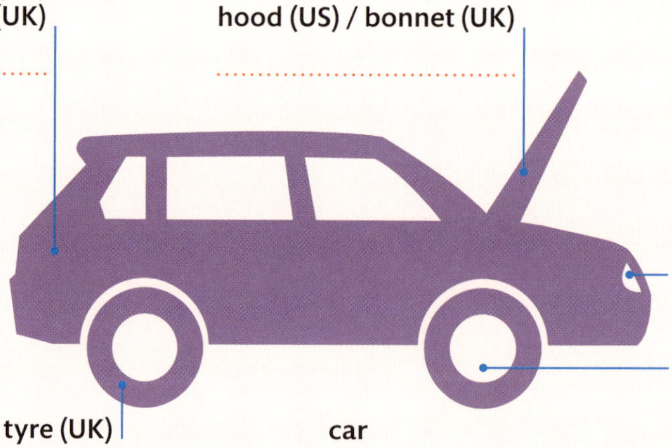

car

parking attendant

speed camera

parking meter

wheel clamp

parking ticket

car wash

speed limit

road sign

traffic jam

parking lot (US)
car park (UK)

45.2 VERBS

to park

to set off

to check the oil

to fill up

to check the tires (US) / tyres (UK)

to service the car

to signal (US)
to indicate (UK)

to brake

to slow down

to speed up

to pick someone up

to drop someone off

to have a car accident

to break down

to pass (US)
to overtake (UK)

Aa 45.3 WRITE THE CORRECT EXPRESSION UNDER EACH PICTURE

mechanic

1 ______

2 ______

3 ______

4 ______

5 ______

6 ______

7 ______

8 ______

9 ______

10 ______

11 ______

12 ______

13 ______

14 ______

Aa 45.4 MARK THE BEGINNING AND ENDING OF EACH WORD OR EXPRESSION IN THE CHAIN OF LETTERS, THEN WRITE THE WORDS YOU FIND

insurance/trunkdieselmechanicgasolinetrafficjamheadlightssteeringwheelparkingattendant

insurance

1 ______

2 ______

3 ______

4 ______

5 ______

6 ______

7 ______

8 ______

Aa 45.5 LOOK AT THE PICTURE AND WRITE THE CORRECT WORD FOR EACH LABEL

45.6 LISTEN TO THE AUDIO AND CIRCLE THE WORDS YOU HEAR

	steering wheel	(headlight)	fuel
1	parking meter	parking lot	gas station
2	flat tire	turn signal	traffic lights
3	driver's license	gas station	car wash
4	wheel	wipers	tire
5	to set off	to speed up	to slow down
6	trunk	insurance	road sign
7	seatbelt	speed limit	speed camera
8	oil	engine	diesel

Aa 45.7 MARK THE CORRECT EXPRESSION FOR EACH PICTURE

- to fill up ☑
- to pass ☐
- to brake ☐

1
- driver's license ☐
- traffic lights ☐
- parking ticket ☐

2
- parking lot ☐
- headlight ☐
- pedestrian crossing ☐

3
- to pick someone up ☐
- to check the oil ☐
- to pass ☐

4
- flat tire ☐
- parking attendant ☐
- wheel clamp ☐

5
- road sign ☐
- parking attendant ☐
- mechanic ☐

6
- to park ☐
- to set off ☐
- to brake ☐

7
- speed limit ☐
- car wash ☐
- insurance ☐

46 Maps and directions

46.1 MAPS AND DIRECTIONS

northwest

north

west

northeast

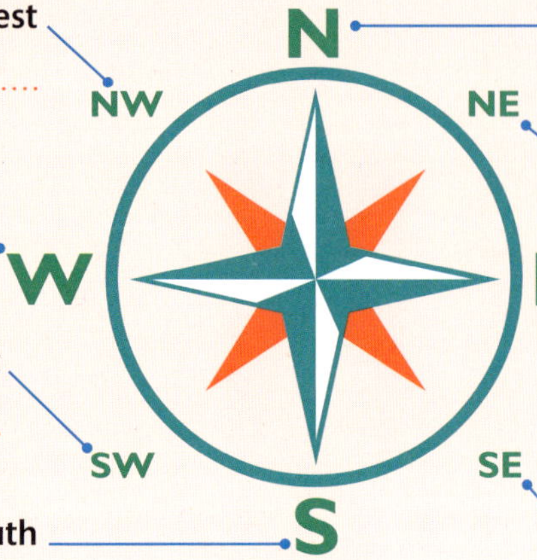

southwest

east

south

southeast

compass

direction

scale

key

roadmap (US)
streetmap (UK)

distance

meter (US)
metre (UK)

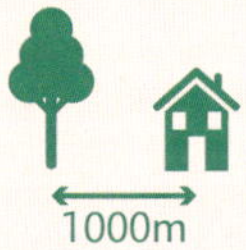

kilometer (US)
kilometre (UK)

mile

yard

intersection (US)
crossroads (UK)

signpost

avenue

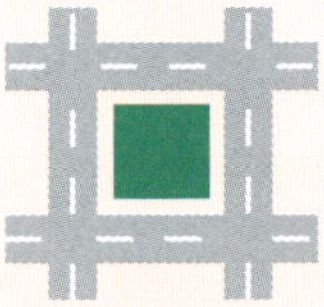

block

street

bend in the road

junction

turn (US)
turning (UK)

main road

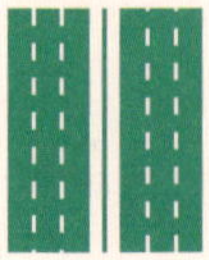

freeway (US)
motorway (UK)

one-way street

sidewalk (US)
pavement (UK)

shoulder (US)
hard shoulder (UK)

footpath

pedestrianized street

46.2 PREPOSITIONS OF PLACE

here

there

next to

across from (US)
opposite (UK)

between

on the corner

behind

in front of

on the right

on the left

46.3 VERBS

to go / turn left

to go / turn right

to go straight ahead (US) / on (UK)

to stop at (the hotel)

to go past (the restaurant)

to take the first left

to take the second right

to read a map

to plan your route

to ask directions

Aa 46.4 LOOK AT THE PICTURE AND WRITE THE CORRECT WORD FOR EACH LABEL

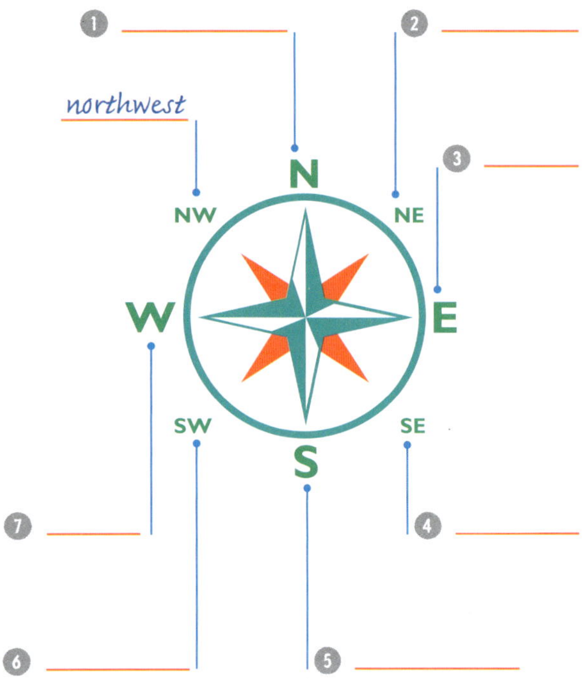

Aa 46.5 REWRITE THE WORDS, CORRECTING THE SPELLINGS

sinepost

signpost

1 tourn

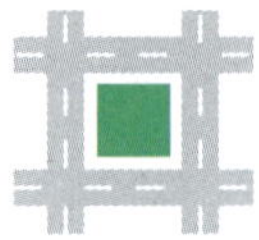

2 bloc

3 meil

4 distence

5 footpeth

Aa 46.6 WRITE THE CORRECT WORD UNDER EACH PICTURE

in front of

1 ________

2 ________

3 ________

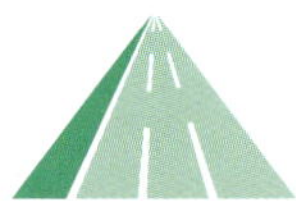

4 ________

5 ________

6 ________

7 ________

8 ________

9 ________

Aa 46.7 MATCH THE PICTURES TO THE CORRECT VERBS

to go / turn right

to read a map

1 

to go / turn left

2 

to go straight ahead (US) / on (UK)

3 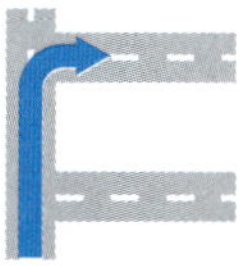

to take the second right

4 

to take the first left

5 

to ask directions

6 

to stop at (the hotel)

7 

46.8 LISTEN TO THE AUDIO AND MARK THE CORRECT PICTURE FOR EACH WORD YOU HEAR

A ☐ B ☑ C ☐

1 

A ☐ B ☐ C ☐

2 

A ☐ B ☐ C ☐

3 

A ☐ B ☐ C ☐

4 

A ☐ B ☐ C ☐

5 

A ☐ B ☐ C ☐

47 Travel and accommodation

47.1 GOING ON VACATION (US) / HOLIDAY (UK)

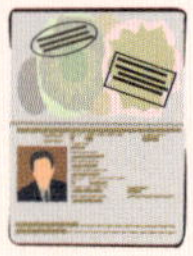
passport

suitcase

luggage

guidebook

phrasebook

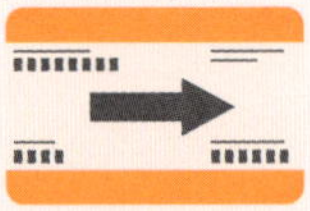
one-way ticket

round-trip (US) / return (UK) ticket

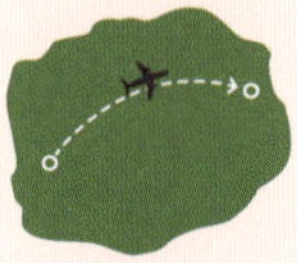
direct flight

window seat

boarding pass

departure gate

passport control

walking vacation (US) / holiday (UK)

all-inclusive

guided tour

47.2 VERBS

to go on a vacation (US) / holiday (UK)

to book a vacation (US) / holiday (UK)

to pack your bags

to board a plane

to land at the airport

to be delayed

to go sightseeing

to go abroad

to go on a cruise

to go on an excursion

47.3 WHERE TO STAY

hotel

apartment

hostel

guesthouse

villa

chalet

cabin

front desk (US)
reception (UK)

single room

double room

twin beds

dorm

en-suite
bathroom (UK)

safe

room service

laundry service

room with a view

no vacancies

vacancies

bed and breakfast

47.4 VERBS

to make a reservation

to rent a cottage

to stay in a hotel

to check in

to check out

Aa 47.5 MATCH THE PICTURES TO THE CORRECT VERBS

1 

2 

3 

4 

to rent a cottage

to make a reservation

to check in

to check out

to stay in a hotel

Aa 47.6 WRITE THE CORRECT WORD OR EXPRESSION UNDER EACH PICTURE

front desk

1 ____________

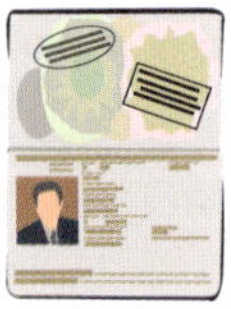

2 ____________

3 ____________

4 ____________

5 ____________

6 ____________

7 ____________

8 ____________

9 ____________

10 ____________

11 ____________

12 ____________

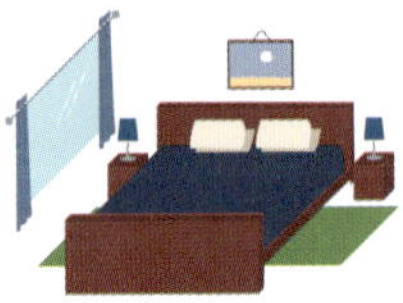

13 ____________

14 ____________

47.7 LISTEN TO THE AUDIO, THEN NUMBER THE PICTURES IN THE ORDER YOU HEAR THEM

A ☐

B 1

C ☐

D ☐

E ☐

F ☐

G ☐

H ☐

I ☐

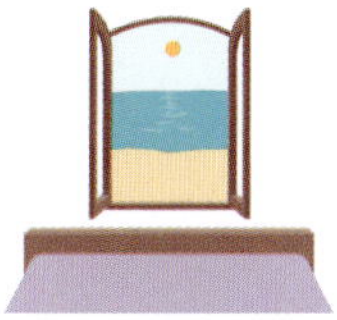
J ☐

K ☐

L ☐

47.8 MARK THE CORRECT WORD OR EXPRESSION FOR EACH PICTURE

- to go on a cruise ☑
- to pack your bags ☐
- to rent a cottage ☐

1
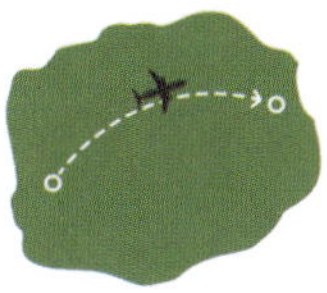

- to go on an excursion ☐
- direct flight ☐
- to make a reservation ☐

2

- to book a vacation ☐
- bed and breakfast ☐
- guided tour ☐

3
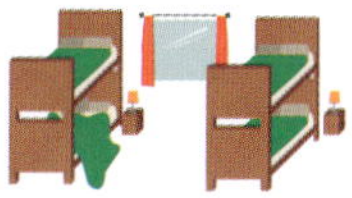

- villa ☐
- dorm ☐
- phrasebook ☐

4

- luggage ☐
- all-inclusive ☐
- walking vacation ☐

5

- room service ☐
- vacancies ☐
- safe ☐

6
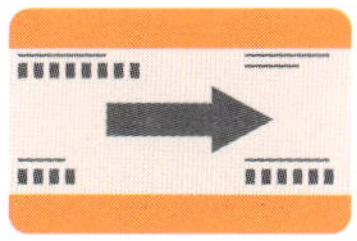

- one-way ticket ☐
- boarding pass ☐
- window seat ☐

7

- hostel ☐
- single room ☐
- safe ☐

48 Travel and tourism

48.1 USEFUL EXPRESSIONS

I love to **get away from it all** when I'm on vacation.

to get away from it all
[to go somewhere relaxing for a break]

The palace is such a **tourist trap** in the summer.

a tourist trap
[a place that attracts too many tourists]

I've won a **once-in-a-lifetime** trip around the world.

once-in-a-lifetime
[unique and unrepeatable]

I don't like going abroad because I **feel homesick**.

to feel homesick
[to be sad because you miss your home and family]

This place is so different from home. It's such a **culture shock**.

a culture shock
[a feeling of confusion or distress when visiting a different place or culture]

We like to stay in places that are **off the beaten path**.

off the beaten path (US) / track (UK)
[a long way from other people, buildings, and roads]

This hotel looks very **run-down**. Let's stay somewhere else.

run-down
[in a bad condition through lack of care or repair]

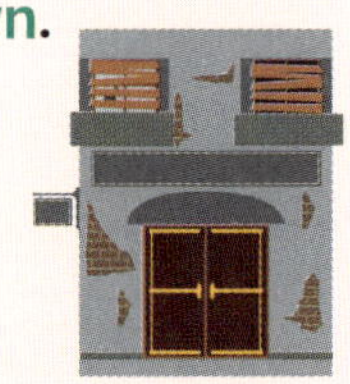

I love going birdwatching in this **unspoiled** countryside.

unspoiled
[not changed, damaged, or built on by people]

Tim has gone abroad again. He's always getting **itchy feet**.

itchy feet
[a desire to travel or move]

Brendan loves sports and has a real **thirst for adventure**.

a thirst for adventure
[a desire for exciting experiences]

I'm taking Clara to look around the park today.

to look around
[to explore an area or place]

We got hopelessly lost when we tried to drive into Tokyo.

hopelessly lost
[totally unable to find your way]

Let's stop off at the gallery before we check into our hotel.

to stop off
[to pause a trip in one place before continuing]

I save lots of money on train tickets by booking in advance.

to book in advance
[to book something several days or weeks before you need it]

I like to travel out of season, when it's nice and quiet.

out of season
[at a time of year when a tourist destination is less popular]

We're checking out the zoo that you recommended.

to check out something / to check something out
[to find out how interesting something is]

The first leg of the trip to Australia is a flight to Bangkok.

a leg of a trip (US) / journey (UK)
[a stage in a trip from one place to another]

We don't need another suitcase. It's just a weekend getaway.

a getaway
[a vacation, particularly a short one]

Zoe is really looking forward to visiting the pyramids.

to look forward to something
[to feel excited about something that is going to happen]

Dan's parents came to the airport to see him off.

to see off somebody / see somebody off
[to go to the station or airport to say goodbye to someone]

Aa 48.2 MATCH THE BEGINNINGS OF THE SENTENCES TO THE CORRECT ENDINGS

	I've won a once-in-a-lifetime	to visiting the pyramids.
1	We like to stay in places that are off	trap in the summer.
2	Zoe is really looking forward	trip around the world.
3	We got hopelessly	the beaten path.
4	The palace is such a tourist	from it all when I'm on vacation.
5	We're checking out	around the park today.
6	I love to get away	lost when we tried to drive into Tokyo.
7	I'm taking Clara to look	by booking in advance.
8	I save lots of money on train tickets	the zoo that you recommended.

Aa 48.3 REWRITE THE SENTENCES, CORRECTING THE ERRORS

Tim has gone abroad again. He's always getting **itchy legs**.
Tim has gone abroad again. He's always getting itchy feet.

1. I don't like going abroad because I **feel housesick**.

2. I save lots of money on train tickets by **booking on advance**.

3. We got **uselessly lost** when we tried to drive into Tokyo.

4. We like to stay in places that are **off a beaten path**.

Aa 48.4 MARK THE SENTENCES THAT ARE CORRECT

The first leg of the trip to Australia is a flight to Bangkok. ☑
The first arm of the trip to Australia is a flight to Bangkok. ☐

1 

Brendan loves sports and has a real hunger for adventure. ☐
Brendan loves sports and has a real thirst for adventure. ☐

2 

I like to travel away from season, when it's nice and quiet. ☐
I like to travel out of season, when it's nice and quiet. ☐

3 

This place is so different from home. It's such a culture shock. ☐
This place is so different from home. It's such a culture clash. ☐

4 

Let's stop off at the gallery before we check into our hotel. ☐
Let's stop in at the gallery before we check into our hotel. ☐

5 

Dan's parents came to the airport to see him out. ☐
Dan's parents came to the airport to see him off. ☐

48.5 LISTEN TO THE AUDIO AND COMPLETE THE SENTENCES THAT DESCRIBE EACH PICTURE

I love going birdwatching in this *unspoiled* countryside.

1 This hotel looks very ____________. Let's stay somewhere else.

2 I don't like going abroad because I feel ____________.

3 I save lots of money on train tickets by ____________.

4 I love to ____________ from it all when I'm on vacation.

5 We don't need another suitcase. It's just a weekend ____________.

49 Camping and cycling

49.1 CAMPING

backpack / rucksack (UK)

campsite

tent peg

tent pole

guyline (US) guy rope (UK)

groundsheet

tent

sleeping bag

to pitch a tent

to build a fire

campfire

camping stove

air bed / air mattress

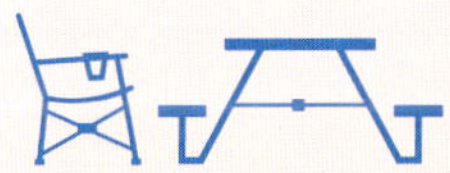
folding chair / table

toilet block

shower block

flashlight (US) torch (UK)

waterproofs

barbecue

hot drink container (US) / flask (UK)

walking boots

insect repellent

caravan

motor home (US) camper van (UK)

49.2 CYCLING

gear

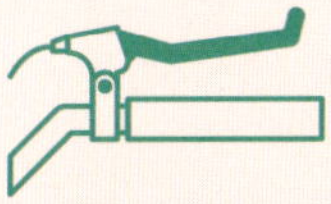

brakes

bicycle / bike

cycling helmet

mountain bike

racing bike

cycling trails

unicycle

cycle pump

tandem

lock

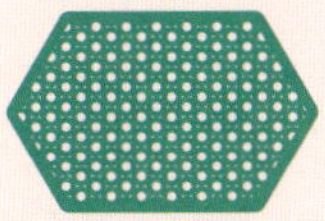

reflector

tire (US)
tyre (UK)

bike rack

basket

bicycle lane

to get on a bike

to get off a bike

to fix a puncture

pothole

Aa 49.3 LOOK AT THE PICTURE AND WRITE THE CORRECT WORD FOR EACH LABEL

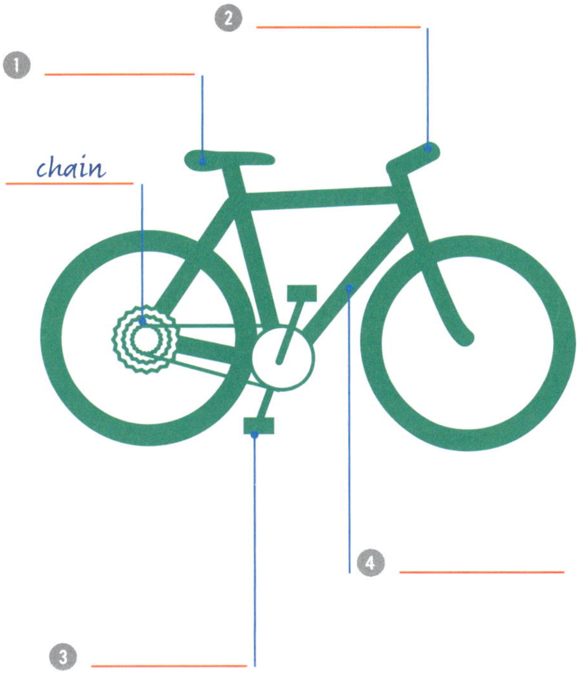

Aa 49.4 MATCH THE PICTURES TO THE CORRECT WORDS

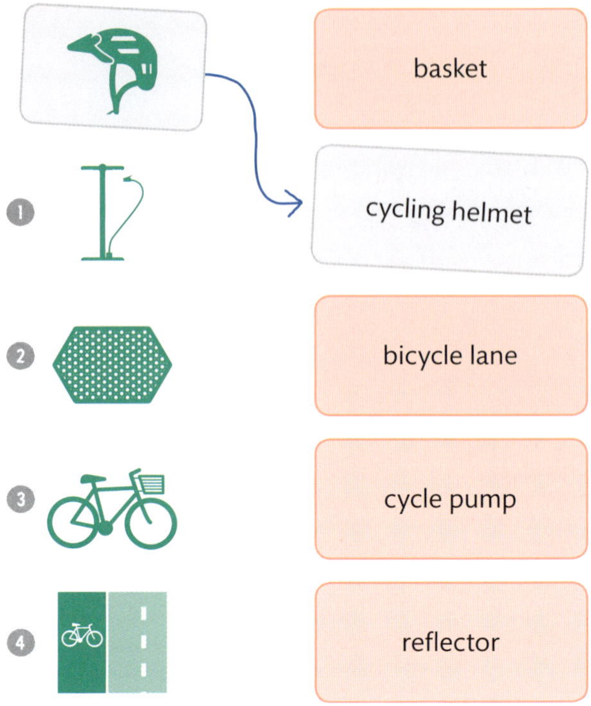

Aa 49.5 WRITE THE CORRECT WORD UNDER EACH PICTURE

Aa 49.6 COMPLETE THE WORDS FOR EACH PICTURE, FILLING IN THE MISSING LETTERS

b a c k p a c k

1  s h _ _ e _ b l _ _ k

2  r _ c i _ g b _ _ e

3  _ n _ c _ c l _

4  w _ t _ r _ r _ o f _

5  b _ _ e r _ c _

6  t _ n _ _ m

7  c _ m p _ _ r _

8  c _ r _ v _ n

9  t _ _ t

10  b _ c _ c l _ l _ n _

11  b _ r b _ c _ _

12 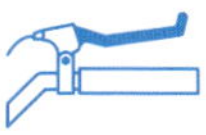 _ r _ _ e s

49.7 LISTEN TO THE AUDIO, THEN NUMBER THE PICTURES IN THE ORDER YOU HEAR THEM

A ☐

B ☐

C 1

D ☐

E ☐

F ☐

G ☐

H ☐

I ☐

J ☐

K ☐

L ☐

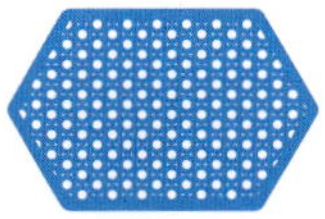
M ☐

N ☐

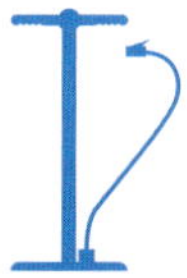
O ☐

P ☐

Q ☐

R ☐

50 Beach

50.1 AT THE BEACH

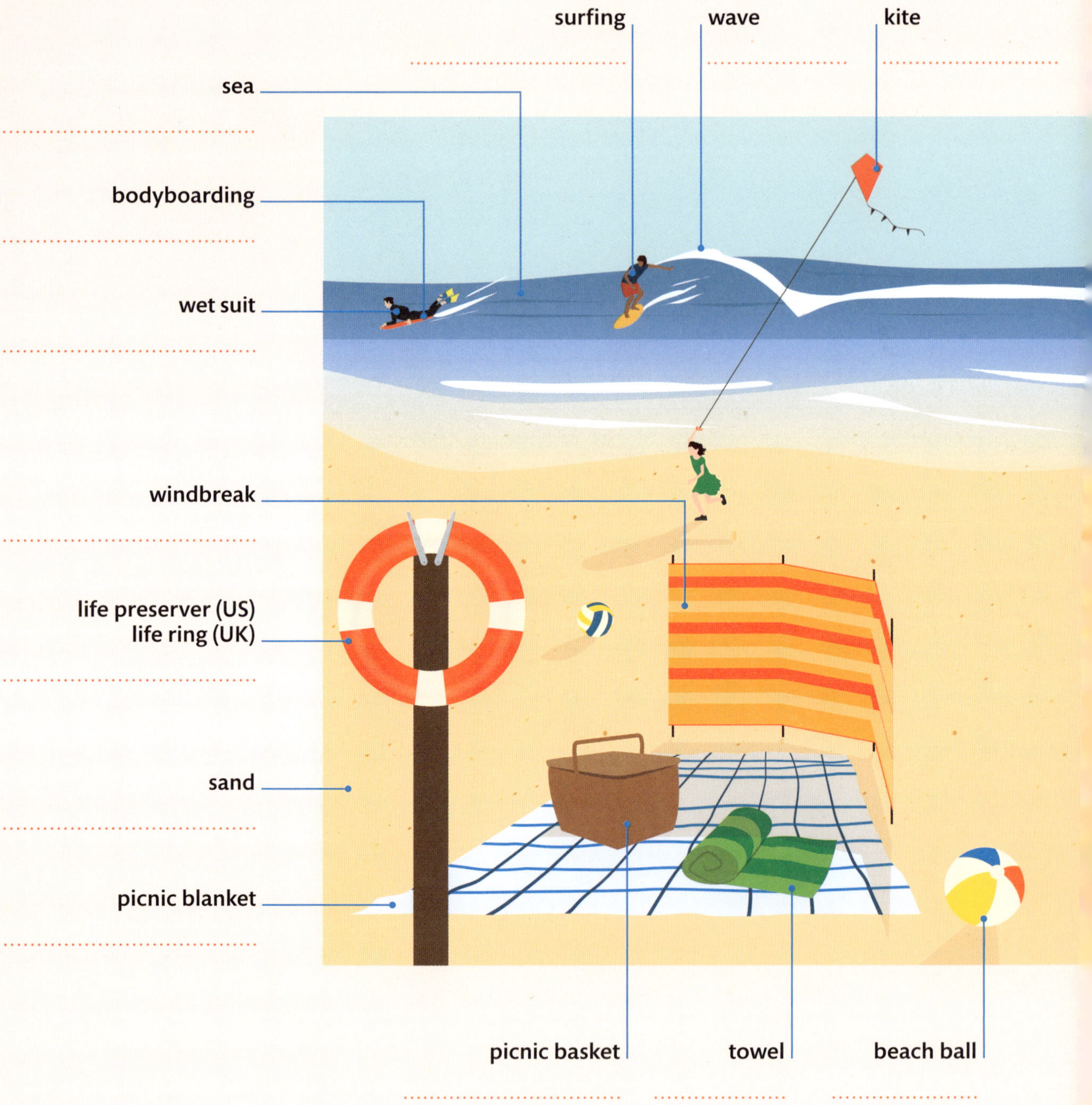

snorkel and mask
jet ski
lifeguard
windsurfing
pail and shovel (US)
bucket and spade (UK)
crab
sandcastle
deck chair
shell
flip-flops
swimsuit
flippers
sunscreen (US)
sun cream (UK)
swimming trunks
sunbathing

Aa 50.2 WRITE THE CORRECT WORD UNDER EACH PICTURE

crab

1 ______

2 ______

3 ______

4 ______

5 ______

6 ______

7 ______

8 ______

9 ______

10 ______

11 ______

12 ______

13 ______

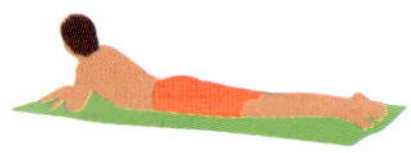

14 ______

Aa 50.3 MARK THE BEGINNING AND ENDING OF EACH WORD OR EXPRESSION IN THE CHAIN OF LETTERS, THEN WRITE THE WORDS YOU FIND

windbreak/wetsuitswimsuitswimmingtrunkssandcastlekitebodyboardinglifepreserverjetski

windbreak

1 ______

2 ______

3 ______

4 ______

5 ______

6 ______

7 ______

8 ______

Aa

50.4 REWRITE THE WORDS, CORRECTING THE SPELLINGS

lifegaurd

lifeguard

1 bodybording

2 windbrake

3 windserfing

4 see

5 krab

6 dek chair

7 flipers

8 picknick blanket

9 sandcassel

50.5 LISTEN TO THE AUDIO AND MARK THE CORRECT PICTURE FOR EACH WORD YOU HEAR

 A ☐  B ☑  C ☐

1  A ☐  B ☐  C ☐

2  A ☐  B ☐  C ☐

3  A ☐ 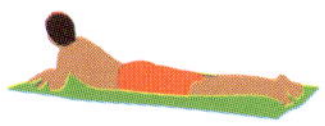 B ☐  C ☐

4  A ☐  B ☐  C ☐

5  A ☐  B ☐  C ☐

6  A ☐  B ☐  C ☐

51 Weather and climate

51.1 WEATHER

humidity

heatwave

tornado

downpour

light shower

overcast

smog

snowdrift

snowstorm

sandstorm

gale

storm

thunder

lightning

wet

dry

rainbow

raindrop

puddle

snowflake

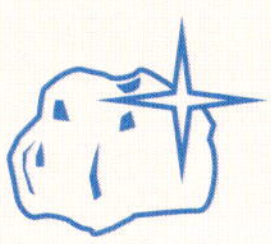
hailstone

blizzard

hurricane

flood

drought

51.2 TEMPERATURE

freezing

cold

chilly

warm

hot

stifling

freezing point

boiling point

minus 10

cool

mild

boiling

25 degrees

Celsius

Fahrenheit

51.3 ADJECTIVES

sun → sunny

cloud → cloudy

fog → foggy

rain → rainy

snow → snowy

ice → icy

frost → frosty

wind → windy

storm → stormy

thunder → thundery

Aa 51.4 COMPLETE THE WORD FOR EACH PICTURE, FILLING IN THE MISSING LETTERS

b o i l i n g

1  c _ _ l

2  s t _ f l _ n g

3  f r _ _ z _ n g

4  d _ _ n p _ _ r

5  F _ h r _ n h _ _ t

6  _ v _ r c _ s t

7  c h _ l _ y

8  t h _ _ d _ r

9  r _ _ n _ r _ p

10  h _ m _ d _ t y

11  f l _ _ d

Aa 51.5 MATCH THE PICTURES TO THE CORRECT WORDS

1 

2 

3 

4 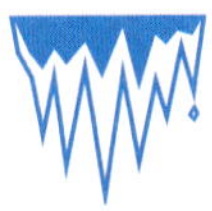

5 

frosty

windy

icy

cloudy

thundery

rainy

Aa 51.6 FIND EIGHT MORE WORDS IN THE GRID THAT MATCH THE PICTURES

R	A	I	N	B	O	W	A	C	S	A
H	A	V	P	L	H	K	Q	V	N	Q
E	E	G	E	I	J	S	E	L	O	L
A	R	A	N	Z	E	R	T	I	W	I
T	T	L	C	Z	W	D	X	B	S	G
W	E	E	I	A	R	Y	A	P	T	H
A	M	Z	L	R	L	A	O	U	O	T
V	E	T	E	D	A	H	V	D	R	N
E	N	X	W	T	P	P	D	D	M	I
D	R	O	U	G	H	T	I	L	L	N
S	N	O	W	F	L	A	K	E	T	G

51.7 LISTEN TO THE AUDIO, THEN NUMBER THE PICTURES IN THE ORDER YOU HEAR THEM

52.1 GEOGRAPHICAL FEATURES

ocean

wave

high tide

low tide

pond

lake

island

cliff

rocks

cave

wood

rain forest (US)
rainforest (UK)

swamp

waterfall

rapids

countryside

field

hill

hedge

farmland

meadow

grassland

plain

desert

oasis

volcano

geyser

mountain range

plateau

valley

canyon

sand dune

polar region

glacier

iceberg

Aa 52.2 WRITE THE CORRECT WORD UNDER EACH PICTURE

island

1 ______

2 ______

3 ______

4 ______

5 ______

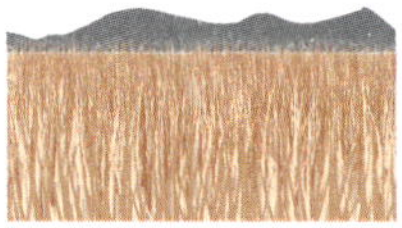

6 ______

7 ______

8 ______

9 ______

10 ______

11 ______

12 ______

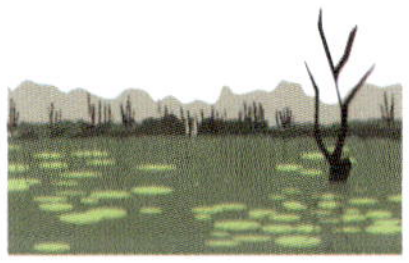

13 ______

14 ______

Aa 52.3 MARK THE BEGINNING AND ENDING OF EACH GEOGRAPHICAL FEATURE IN THE CHAIN OF LETTERS, THEN WRITE THE WORDS YOU FIND

hightide/countrysidecanyonplateauvolcanomeadowrainforestmountainrangepolarregion

high tide

1 ______

2 ______

3 ______

4 ______

5 ______

6 ______

7 ______

8 ______

Aa 52.4 LOOK AT THE PICTURE AND WRITE THE CORRECT WORD FOR EACH LABEL

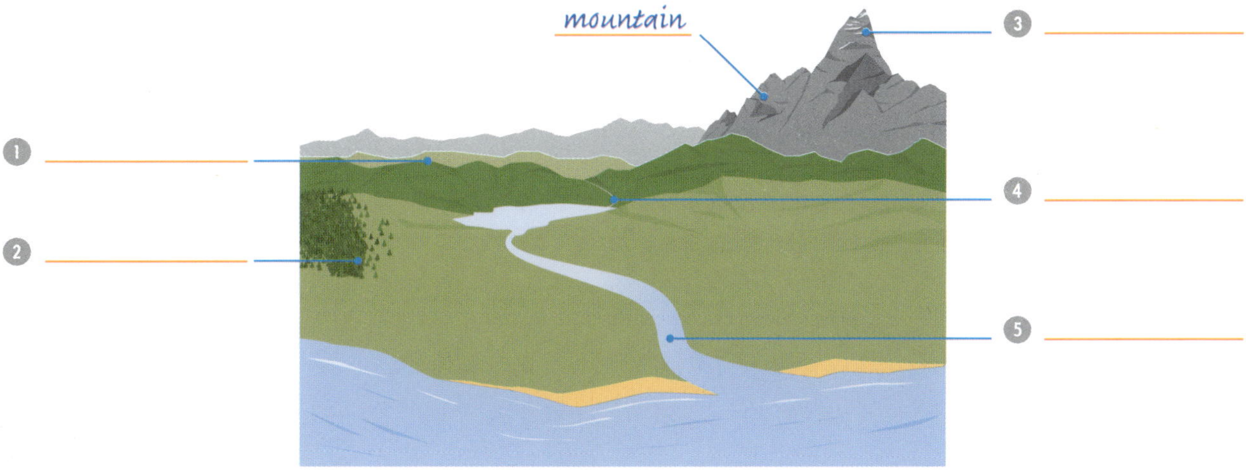

52.5 LISTEN TO THE AUDIO AND MARK THE CORRECT PICTURE FOR EACH WORD YOU HEAR

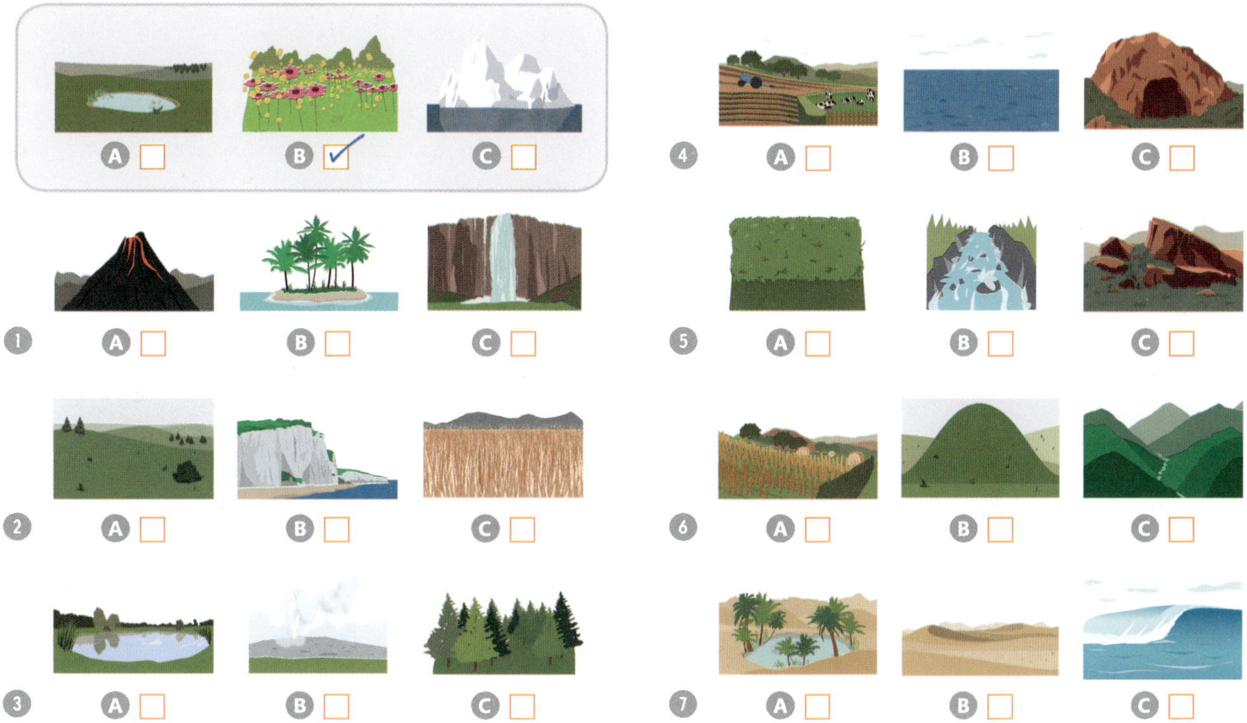

53 Environmental concerns

53.1 USEFUL EXPRESSIONS

Factory emissions are a cause of global warming.

global warming
[the increase in the Earth's temperature]

Climate change is a huge threat to many animals.

climate change
[changes in the Earth's weather patterns]

Carbon dioxide is one of the best-known greenhouse gases.

greenhouse gases
[gases that cause the greenhouse effect, heating up the Earth]

Fossil fuels such as coal and oil produce carbon dioxide.

fossil fuels
[fuels based on oil, coal, and gas]

This space rocket consumes a lot of fuel.

to consume
[to use a supply of something, such as fuel or energy]

You can reduce your carbon footprint by flying less.

to reduce your carbon footprint
[to lower the level of carbon dioxide produced by your actions]

We need to tackle pollution in our rivers.

to tackle pollution
[to deal with the problem of pollution]

We can reduce pollution by using more types of alternative energy.

alternative energy
[energy that does not use fossil fuels]

We must use more green energy sources, like wind and solar.

green energy sources
[types of energy that do not damage the environment]

It can be much cheaper to use renewable energy.

renewable energy
[energy from sources that do not run out]

The traffic in our cities is **harmful to the environment**.

harmful to the environment
[causing damage to the environment]

You can use **solar power** to heat your water.

solar power
[energy created using sunlight]

Some areas use turbines to turn **wind power** into electricity.

wind power
[energy created using the wind]

Years of poaching have made the white rhino **endangered**.

endangered
[at risk of extinction]

We must work together to stop the **destruction** of our forests.

destruction
[the act of damaging something so badly that it cannot survive or be repaired]

Water pollution has **dire consequences** for local wildlife.

dire consequences
[very bad results]

Solar panels on your house can help you save electricity.

a solar panel
[a panel that turns sunlight into electricity]

This **wind farm** has been running for several years.

a wind farm
[a place with many turbines for generating wind power]

Dinosaurs became **extinct** millions of years ago.

extinct
[no longer existing]

If we don't reduce pollution, Earth will undergo **irreversible change**.

irreversible change
[permanent change that cannot be undone]

Aa 53.2 MATCH THE PICTURES TO THE CORRECT SENTENCES

1 

2 

3 

4 

5 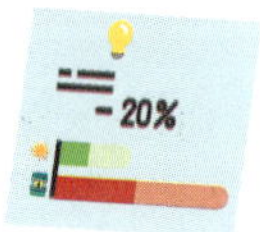

- Fossil fuels such as coal and oil produce carbon dioxide.
- Some areas use turbines to turn wind power into electricity.
- Solar panels on your house can help you save electricity.
- It can be much cheaper to use renewable energy.
- Carbon dioxide is one of the best-known greenhouse gases.
- Factory emissions are a cause of global warming.

Aa 53.3 WRITE THE CORRECT PHRASE NEXT TO ITS DEFINITION, FILLING IN THE MISSING LETTERS

very bad results = d i r e c o n s e q u e n c e s

1 at risk of extinction = e _ d a _ _ e r _ _

2 the increase in the Earth's temperature = _ l _ _ a l w _ r _ i n _

3 energy created using the wind = w _ n _ _ o _ e _

4 energy created using sunlight = _ o _ _ r p _ _ e _

5 energy that does not use fossil fuels = a _ t e _ _ a _ _ _ e _ n _ _ g y

53.4 LISTEN TO THE AUDIO AND COMPLETE THE SENTENCES THAT DESCRIBE EACH PICTURE

This space rocket *consumes* a lot of fuel.

1 We need to ____________ in our rivers.

2 Dinosaurs became ____________ millions of years ago.

3 The traffic in our cities is ____________ ____________.

4 We can reduce pollution by using more types of ____________.

5 ____________ is a huge threat to many animals.

53.5 REWRITE THE SENTENCES, CORRECTING THE ERRORS

You can **reduce your carbon fingerprint** by flying less.

You can reduce your carbon footprint by flying less.

1 This **wind firm** has been running for several years.

____

2 We must work together to stop the **destructing** of our forests.

____

3 **Weather change** is a huge threat to many animals.

____

4 If we don't reduce pollution, Earth will undergo **unreversible change**.

____

54 Pets and farm animals

54.1 PETS AND FARM ANIMALS

54.2 ANIMAL VERBS

to bark

to meow

to gallop

to purr

to molt (US)
to moult (UK)

to hiss

to scratch

to sniff

to crow

to squeak

to snort

to hop

to bleat

to quack

to croak

54.3 ANIMAL EQUIPMENT

fish tank / aquarium

leash (US)
lead (UK)

basket

doghouse (US)
kennel (UK)

cage

rabbit hutch

collar

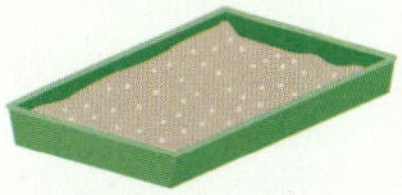
litter box (US)
litter tray (UK)

terrarium

bird seed

Aa 54.4 MATCH THE PICTURES TO THE CORRECT WORDS

1 

2 

3 

4 

5 

6 

7 

8 

- to quack
- bull
- doghouse (US) kennel (UK)
- fish
- hamster
- basket
- parrot
- to squeak
- rabbit hutch

Aa 54.5 REWRITE THE WORDS, CORRECTING THE SPELLINGS

to galop

to gallop

1 hurse

2 terkey

3 shipe

4 to pur

5 to miow

6 mowse

7 to croke

8 donkiy

9 colar

Aa 54.6 LOOK AT THE PICTURE AND WRITE THE CORRECT WORD FOR EACH LABEL

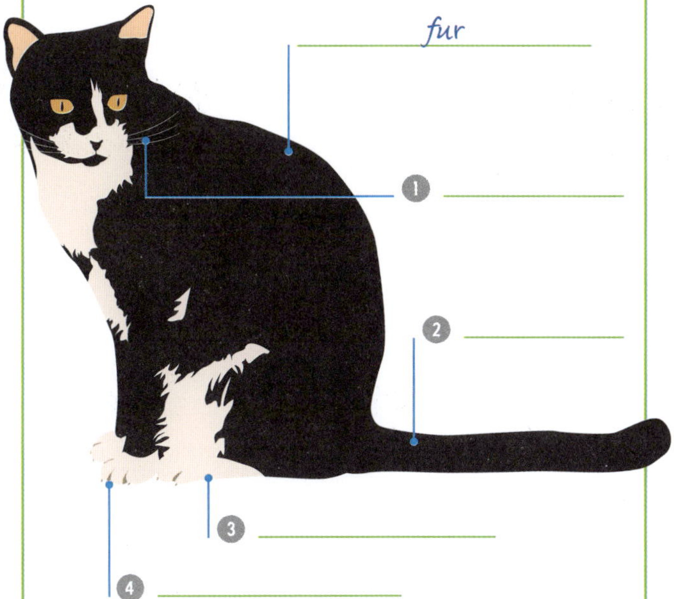

Aa 54.7 COMPLETE THE WORD FOR EACH PICTURE, FILLING IN THE MISSING LETTERS

 c h *i* c k *e* n

1.  t _   s _ r _ t _ h
2.  g _ _ s e
3.  t _ r t _ _ s _
4.  _ q u _ r _ _ m
5.  b _ _ d   s _ _ d

54.8 LISTEN TO THE AUDIO, THEN NUMBER THE PICTURES IN THE ORDER YOU HEAR THEM

A ☐

B ☐

C ☐

D *1*

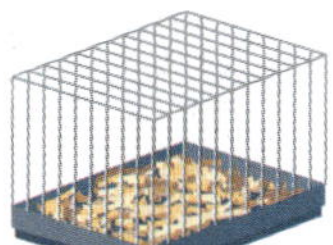
E ☐

F ☐

G ☐

H ☐

I ☐

J ☐

55 Wild animals

55.1 WILD ANIMALS

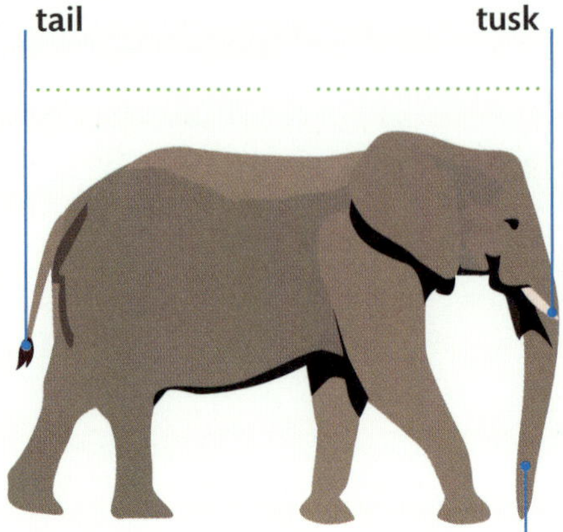

elephant

hippopotamus

rhinoceros

crocodile

snake

lizard

frog

lion

tiger

cheetah

leopard

jaguar

bear

polar bear

panda

koala

kangaroo

monkey

gorilla

boar

fox

wolf

camel

zebra

giraffe

bat

buffalo

bison

yak

moose

deer

gazelle

antelope

mole

beaver

chipmunk

mongoose

meerkat

raccoon

armadillo

sloth

tapir

55.2 VERBS

to roar

to burrow

to hunt

to swing

to prowl

Aa 55.3 MARK THE CORRECT PICTURE FOR EACH WORD

crocodile

A ☑ B ☐ C ☐

1 deer

A ☐ B ☐ C ☐

2 leopard

A ☐ B ☐ C ☐

3 boar

A ☐ B ☐ C ☐

4 fox

A ☐ B ☐ C ☐

5 antelope

A ☐ B ☐ C ☐

55.4 LISTEN TO THE AUDIO AND WRITE THE WORD THAT IS SHOWN IN EACH PICTURE

 *monkey*

1  ______________

2  ______________

3  ______________

4  ______________

5  ______________

6  ______________

7  ______________

Aa 55.5 FIND EIGHT MORE WORDS IN THE GRID THAT MATCH THE PICTURES

C	A	M	E	L	I	R	A	C	S	A	H
T	A	V	L	Q	H	K	Q	V	W	Q	P
A	E	D	E	M	J	S	M	D	H	B	O
H	I	P	P	O	P	O	T	A	M	U	S
Z	T	B	H	X	W	B	X	B	F	F	A
P	E	J	A	G	U	A	R	D	W	F	Y
Q	M	Z	N	O	L	T	O	Z	O	A	M
L	E	D	T	I	G	E	R	D	L	L	J
M	O	N	G	O	O	S	E	Z	F	O	S

1 

2 

3 

4 

5 

6 

7 

8 

Aa 55.6 WRITE THE CORRECT WORD UNDER EACH PICTURE

lizard

1 ____________

2 ____________

3 ____________

4 ____________

5 ____________

6 ____________

7 ____________

8 ____________

9 ____________

10 ____________

11 ____________

12 ____________

13 ____________

14 ____________

56 Birds and bugs

56.1 BIRDS

eagle

hawk

penguin

flamingo

pelican

vulture

stork

kiwi

chicken

swan

dove

woodpecker

crow

toucan

ostrich

parrot

pigeon

hummingbird

duck

goose

seagull

owl

56.2 INSECTS AND BUGS

butterfly

moth

mosquito

bee

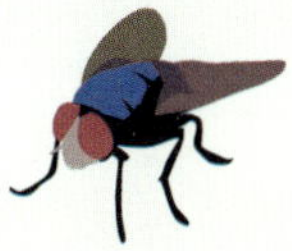
fly

wasp

caterpillar

cockroach

locust

ant

ladybug (US)
ladybird (UK)

beetle

spider

worm

snail

56.3 VERBS FOR BIRDS AND BUGS

to fly

to hoot

to swoop

to flap

to glide

to hatch

to peck

to buzz

to sting

to sing

Aa 56.4 FILL IN THE GAPS, PUTTING THE WORDS FROM THE PANEL INTO THE CORRECT CATEGORIES

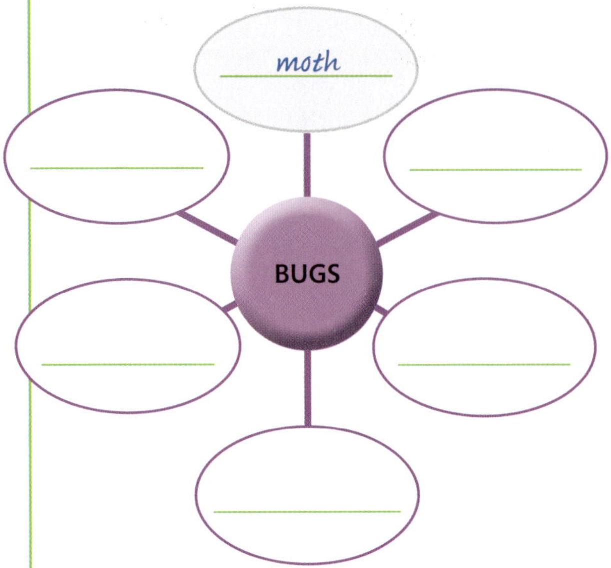

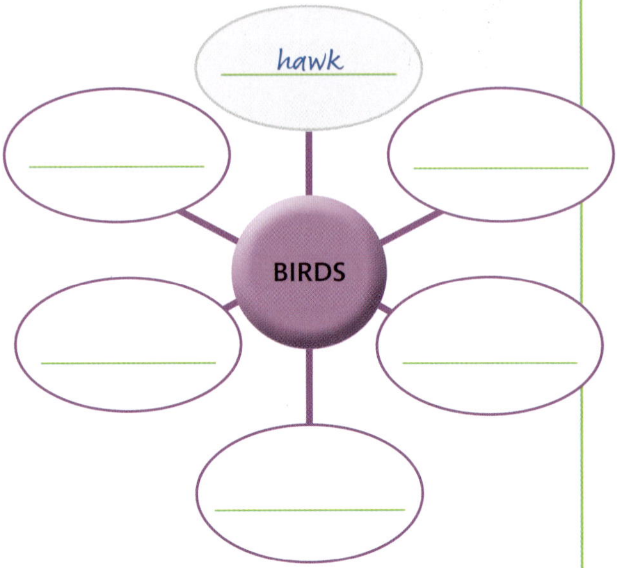

~~moth~~	vulture	spider	penguin	wasp	duck
caterpillar	ant	snail	swan	dove	~~hawk~~

Aa 56.5 MATCH THE PICTURES TO THE CORRECT VERBS

1 

2 

3 

4 

5 

to buzz

to swoop

to peck

to hoot

to hatch

to sing

Aa 56.6 LOOK AT THE PICTURE AND WRITE THE CORRECT WORD FOR EACH LABEL

56.7 LISTEN TO THE AUDIO AND MARK THE WORDS YOU HEAR

owl ☐ beetle ☑ bee ☐

1. crow ☐ kiwi ☐ claw ☐
2. to fly ☐ to flap ☐ to glide ☐
3. toucan ☐ locust ☐ ostrich ☐
4. stork ☐ wing ☐ dove ☐
5. pigeon ☐ pelican ☐ goose ☐
6. seagull ☐ fly ☐ swan ☐
7. bee ☐ beak ☐ eagle ☐
8. feather ☐ mosquito ☐ caterpillar ☐

Aa 56.8 COMPLETE THE WORD FOR EACH PICTURE, FILLING IN THE MISSING LETTERS

h *u* m m *i* n g b *i* r d

1.  w _ _ d p _ c k _ r
2.  w _ r _
3.  _ _ g l _
4.  b _ t _ _ r f l _
5.  b _ _ t l _
6.  c h _ c _ _ n
7.  p _ r _ _ t
8.  c _ _ k r _ _ c _
9.  p _ l _ c _ n

57 Fish, whales, and sea creatures

57.1 FISH AND SEA CREATURES

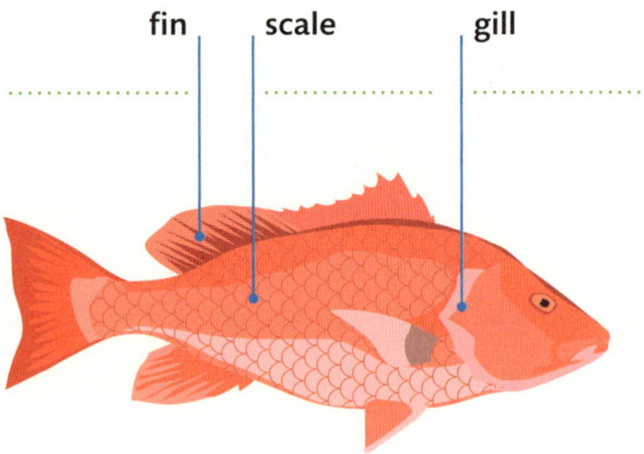

fish

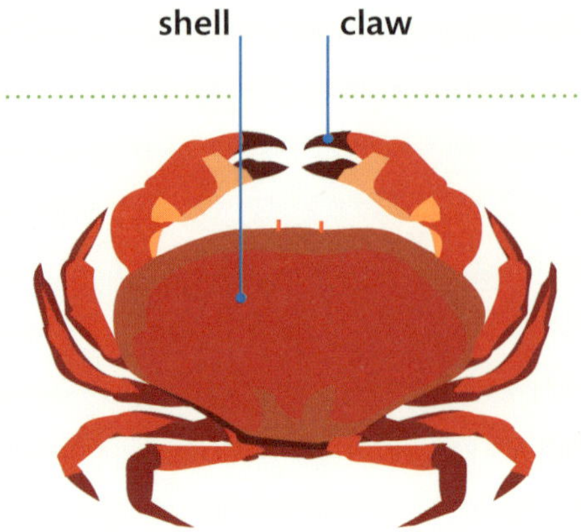

crab

starfish

eel

tuna

trout

salmon

shrimp

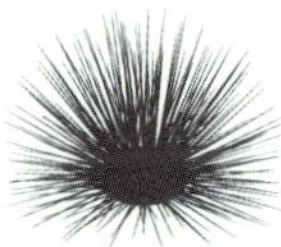

sea urchin

a school of fish

squid

turtle

porpoise

anemone

dolphin

seal

sea lion

walrus

otter

octopus

mussel

clam

oyster

shark

lobster

jellyfish

seahorse

swordfish

ray

57.2 WHALES

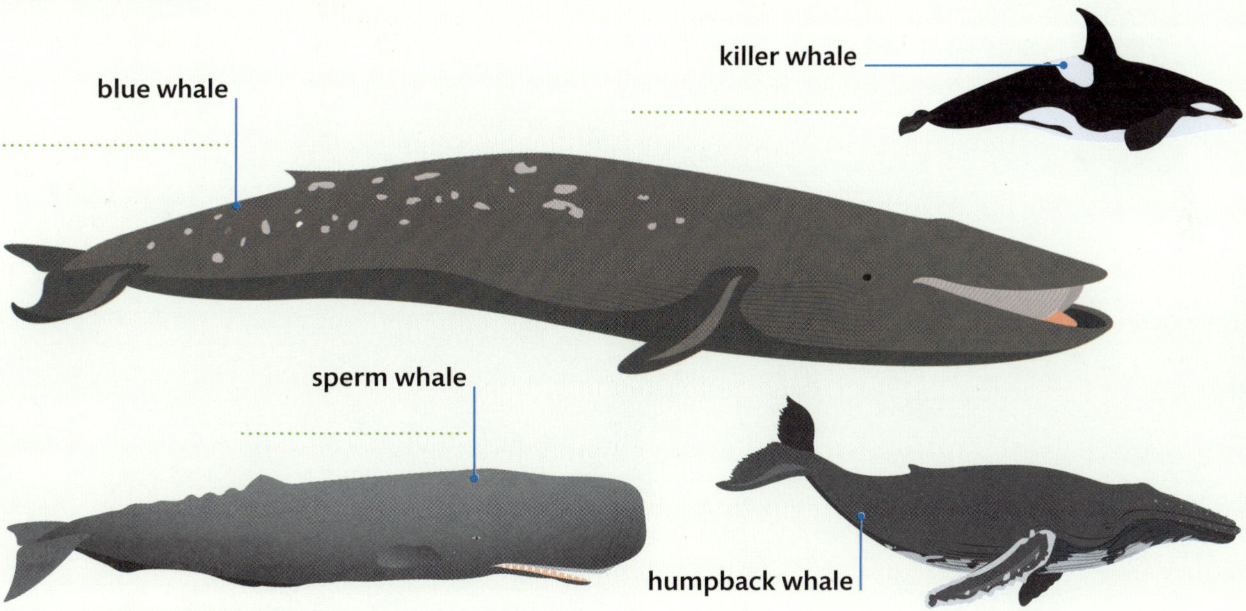

Aa 57.3 MATCH THE WORDS TO THE CORRECT PICTURES

lobster

1. shark
2. sea urchin
3. seahorse
4. octopus
5. salmon

A B C D E

Aa 57.4 LOOK AT THE PICTURE CLUES AND WRITE THE ANSWERS IN THE CORRECT PLACES ON THE GRID

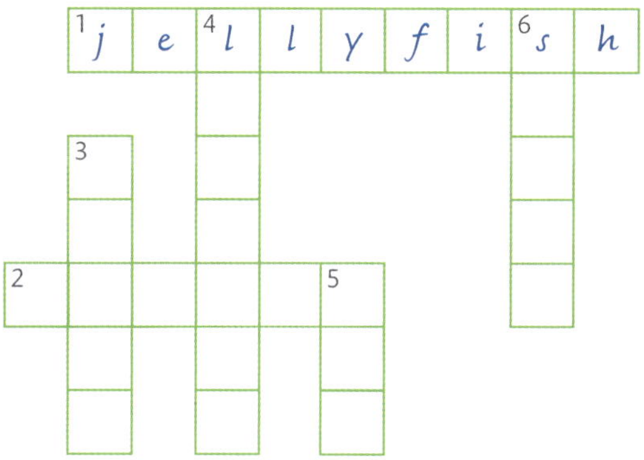

Aa 57.5 MARK THE BEGINNING AND ENDING OF EACH WORD IN THE CHAIN OF LETTERS

seahorse/dolphinottermussellobstercraywalrusclamswordfishoysterjellyfishoctopuscrabseal

57.6 LISTEN TO THE AUDIO AND MARK THE CORRECT PICTURE FOR EACH WORD YOU HEAR

A ☐ B ☑ C ☐

1 A ☐ B ☐ C ☐

2 A ☐ B ☐ C ☐

3 A ☐ B ☐ C ☐

4 A ☐ B ☐ C ☐

5 A ☐ B ☐ C ☐

6 A ☐ B ☐ C ☐

57.7 WRITE THE CORRECT WORD UNDER EACH PICTURE

swordfish

1 ______

2 ______

3 ______

4 ______

5 ______

6 ______

7 ______

8 ______

9 ______

58 Free time activities

58.1 FREE TIME ACTIVITIES

to do puzzles

to play cards

to play chess

to play board games

to go to a book club

to play video games

to read

to draw

to write

to paint

to take photos

to play a musical instrument

to walk / to hike

to cook

to bake

to sew

to knit

to go to a party

to do karaoke

to watch television

to watch a movie

to see a play

to do exercise

to go to the gym

to do yoga

to listen to music

to go camping

to go birdwatching

to go out for a meal

to do the gardening

to visit a museum / gallery

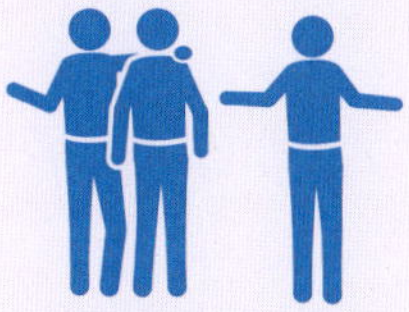
to meet friends

to go on vacation (US)
to go on holiday (UK)

to go shopping

to go to a concert

to stay (at) home

to have a picnic

to collect stamps

to do pottery

to make models

to surf / browse the internet

to call friends

to go to an evening class

to go to the beach

to fly a kite

to ride a horse

to go jogging

to sing in a choir

to arrange flowers

to go foraging

Aa 58.2 MARK THE CORRECT VERB FOR THE ACTIVITY IN EACH PICTURE

to draw ☐
to play cards ☑
to collect stamps ☐

1

to meet friends ☐
to make models ☐
to sew ☐

2

to take photos ☐
to go shopping ☐
to do karaoke ☐

3

to collect stamps ☐
to cook ☐
to do puzzles ☐

4

to call friends ☐
to take photos ☐
to paint ☐

5

to read ☐
to go to a party ☐
to go camping ☐

6

to walk / hike ☐
to fly a kite ☐
to ride a horse ☐

7

to see a play ☐
to bake ☐
to go foraging ☐

8

to have a picnic ☐
to listen to music ☐
to knit ☐

9

to write ☐
to paint ☐
to go jogging ☐

10

to fly a kite ☐
to knit ☐
to play chess ☐

11

to watch television ☐
to sing in a choir ☐
to do puzzles ☐

Aa 58.3 MATCH THE ACTIVITIES TO THE CORRECT PICTURES

to go birdwatching

1 to go to an evening class

2 to watch a movie

3 to go out for a meal

4 to sing in a choir

A

B

C

D

58.4 LISTEN TO THE AUDIO AND WRITE THE ACTIVITY THAT IS SHOWN IN EACH PICTURE

to do pottery

1  ______________________

2  ______________________

3  ______________________

4  ______________________

5  ______________________

6  ______________________

7  ______________________

8  ______________________

9  ______________________

58.5 WRITE THE CORRECT ACTIVITY UNDER EACH PICTURE

to go shopping

1 ______________________

2 ______________________

3 ______________________

4 ______________________

5 ______________________

6 ______________________

7 ______________________

8 ______________________

9 ______________________

10 ______________________

11 ______________________

12 ______________________

13 ______________________

14 ______________________

59 Abilities and actions

59.1 ABILITIES AND ACTIONS

to see

to lick

to taste

to smell

to listen

to work

to play

to kick

to throw

to hit

to whisper

to dance

to run

to crawl

to jump

to repair

to shake

to make (a snowman)

to do (homework)

to think

to understand

to spell

to move

to dig

to fall

to carry

to climb

to stand up

to sit down

to lift

to add

to subtract

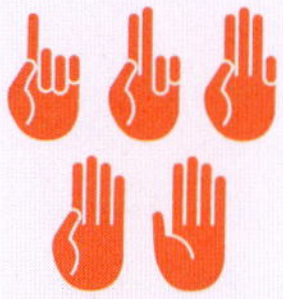
to count

to sing

to catch

to talk

to speak

to shout

to push

to pull

to act

to blow

to copy

to decide

to remember

to hold

to point

to pack

to fly

to ride

59.2 WRITE THE CORRECT ACTION UNDER EACH PICTURE

to catch

1 ______
2 ______
3 ______
4 ______
5 ______
6 ______
7 ______
8 ______
9 ______
10 ______
11 ______
12 ______
13 ______
14 ______

59.3 LISTEN TO THE AUDIO, THEN NUMBER THE ACTIONS IN THE ORDER YOU HEAR THEM

A ☐
B ☐
C 1
D ☐
E ☐
F ☐
G ☐
H ☐
I ☐
J ☐
K ☐
L ☐
M ☐
N ☐

Aa 59.4 MATCH THE ACTIONS TO THE CORRECT PICTURES

to dance

1. to crawl
2. to act
3. to push
4. to dig
5. to play

A B C D E

Aa 59.5 MARK THE CORRECT PICTURE FOR EACH ACTION

to jump

A ☐ B ☐ C ☑

3. to hit

A ☐ B ☐ C ☐

1. to shake

A ☐ B ☐ C ☐

4. to climb

A ☐ B ☐ C ☐

2. to add

A ☐ B ☐ C ☐

5. to throw

A ☐ B ☐ C ☐

60 Sports

60.1 SPORTS

judo

boxing

archery

gymnastics

discus

high jump

long jump

baseball

cricket

field hockey (US)
hockey (UK)

badminton

soccer (US)
football (UK)

rugby

volleyball

basketball

golf

cycling

fishing

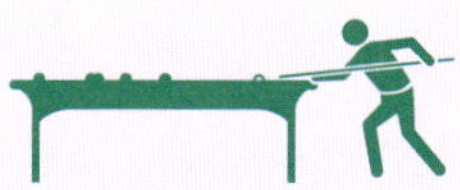
pool

roller-skating

canoeing / kayaking

surfing

swimming

sailing

rowing

javelin

running

running a marathon

hockey (US)
ice hockey (UK)

tennis

squash

football (US)
American football (UK)

horse riding

motor racing

skating

skiing

diving

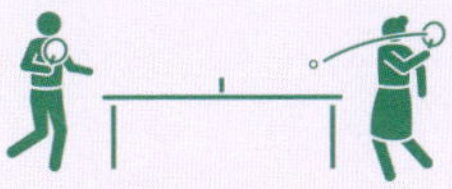
table tennis

bowling

skateboarding

60.2 ADVENTURE SPORTS

abseiling

bungee jumping

hang gliding

paragliding

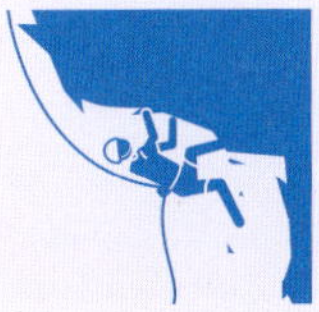
rock climbing

scuba diving

skydiving

snorkeling (US)
snorkelling (UK)

snowboarding

windsurfing

Aa 60.3 LOOK AT THE PICTURE CLUES AND WRITE THE ANSWERS IN THE CORRECT PLACES ON THE GRID

Aa 60.4 MARK THE BEGINNING AND ENDING OF EACH SPORT IN THE CHAIN OF LETTERS, THEN WRITE THE WORDS YOU FIND

hockey/rockclimbingsurfingjudomotorracingvolleyballparaglidingskydivingskateboarding

hockey

1 ______

2 ______

3 ______

4 ______

5 ______

6 ______

7 ______

8 ______

60.5 LISTEN TO THE AUDIO AND MARK THE CORRECT PICTURE FOR EACH SPORT YOU HEAR

A ☑ B ☐ C ☐

1 A ☐ B ☐ C ☐

2 A ☐ B ☐ C ☐

3 A ☐ B ☐ C ☐

4 A ☐ B ☐ C ☐

5 A ☐ B ☐ C ☐

6 A ☐ B ☐ C ☐

60.6 COMPLETE THE WORDS FOR EACH PICTURE, FILLING IN THE MISSING LETTERS

h o r s e r i d i n g

1  b _ d m _ n t _ n

2  b _ s _ b _ l l

3  g _ m n _ s t _ c s

4  c _ c l _ n g

5  s q _ _ s h

6  s k _ t _ b _ _ r d _ n g

7  s c _ b _ d _ v _ n g

8  t _ b l _ t _ n n _ s

9  s k _ d _ v _ n g

10  v _ l l _ y b _ l l

11  _ b s _ _ l _ n g

12  _ w _ m _ i _ g

61 Soccer

61.1 SOCCER GAME

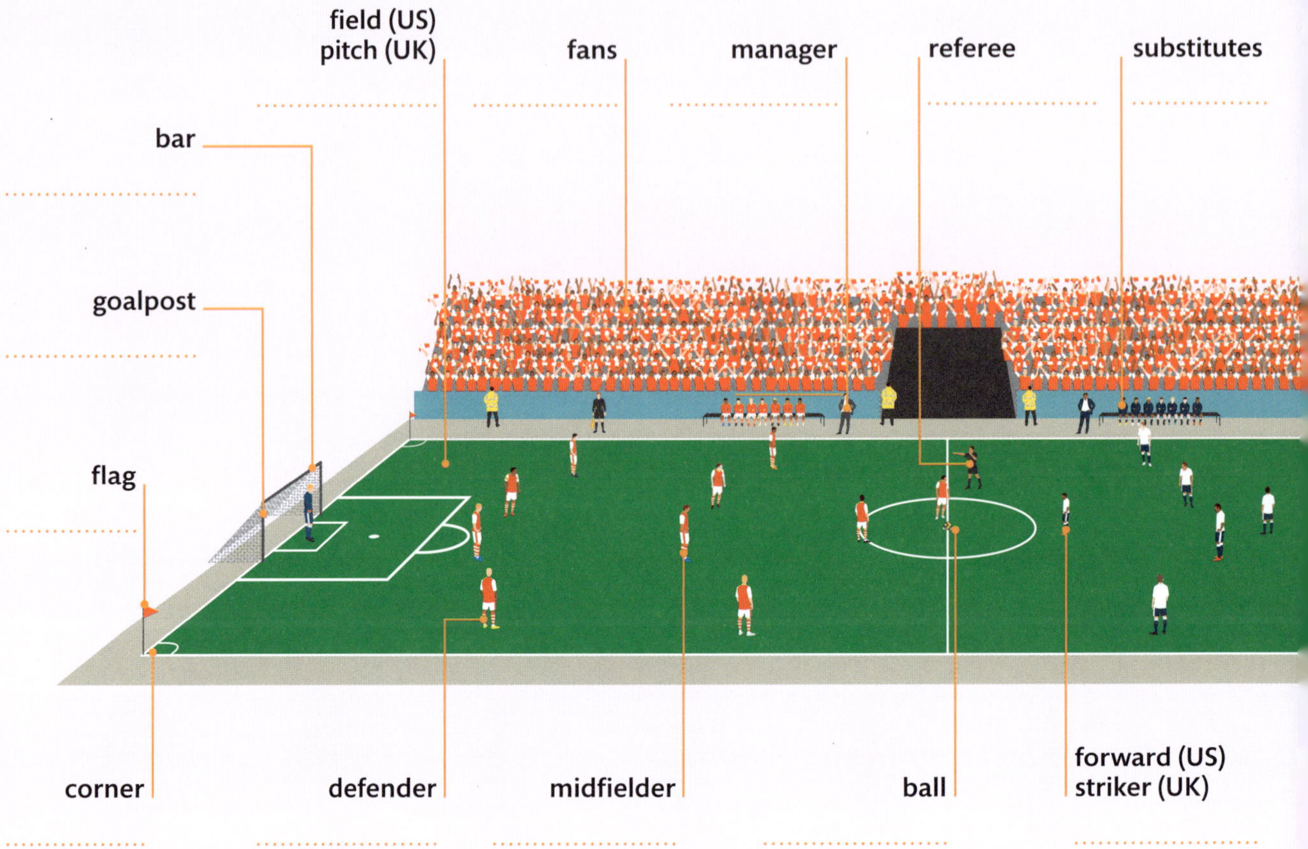

61.3 TIMINGS AND RULES

kickoff

half time

full time

stoppage time (US)
injury time (UK)

final whistle

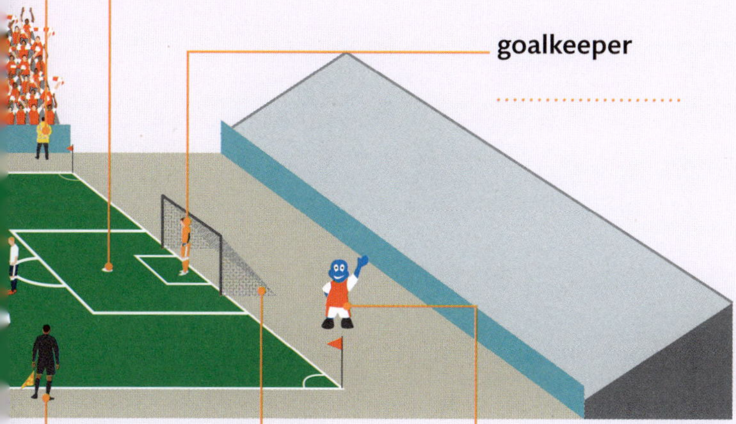

61.2 VERBS

to tackle

to kick

to score a goal

to be booked

to be sent off

to win

to lose

to tie (US)
to draw (UK)

corner kick

throw-in

penalty

yellow card

red card

Aa 61.4 WRITE THE CORRECT WORD OR EXPRESSION UNDER EACH PICTURE

kickoff

1 ______

2 ______

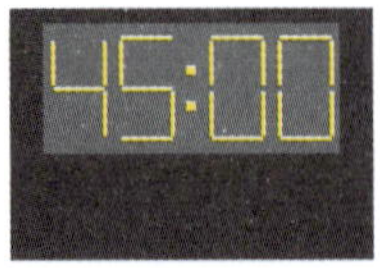

3 ______

4 ______

5 ______

6 ______

7 ______

8 ______

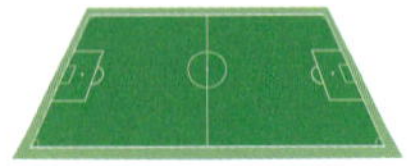
9 ______

10 ______

11 ______

12 ______

13 ______

14 ______

Aa 61.5 MARK THE CORRECT WORD OR EXPRESSION FOR EACH PICTURE

- to tackle ☐
- to win ☐
- throw-in ☑

1

- to be booked ☐
- to lose ☐
- to score a goal ☐

2

- to kick ☐
- to tie ☐
- goalkeeper ☐

3

- to lose ☐
- to be sent off ☐
- to win ☐

4

- final whistle ☐
- kickoff ☐
- bar ☐

5

- substitutes ☐
- security ☐
- fans ☐

6

- manager ☐
- mascot ☐
- security ☐

7

- stoppage time ☐
- kickoff ☐
- to tackle ☐

8

- full time ☐
- stoppage time ☐
- red card ☐

9

- to lose ☐
- to tie ☐
- to be booked ☐

61.6 LISTEN TO THE AUDIO, THEN NUMBER THE PICTURES IN THE ORDER YOU HEAR THEM

A ☐

B 1

C ☐

D ☐

E ☐

F ☐

G ☐

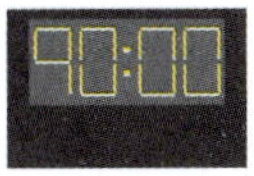
H ☐

I ☐

J ☐

K ☐

L ☐

Aa 61.7 CIRCLE THE WORD THAT DOES NOT BELONG IN EACH LIST

	goalkeeper	manager	(stoppage time)
1	to be booked	to tackle	to kick
2	kickoff	penalty spot	half time
3	to lose	to kick	to win
4	mascot	goalpost	net
5	to be booked	to be sent off	to tie
6	goalpost	bar	throw-in
7	referee	forward	linesman
8	red card	stoppage time	full time
9	midfielder	defender	linesman
10	corner kick	bar	penalty
11	net	fans	flag
12	kickoff	full time	midfielder

Aa 61.8 MATCH THE WORDS TO THE CORRECT PICTURES

yellow card

1 fans

2 to tackle

3 net

4 corner

5 linesman

A 

B 

C 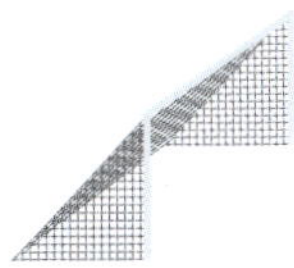

D 

E 

62 Sports equipment and venues

62.1 EQUIPMENT

baseball bat

golf club

hockey stick

tennis racket

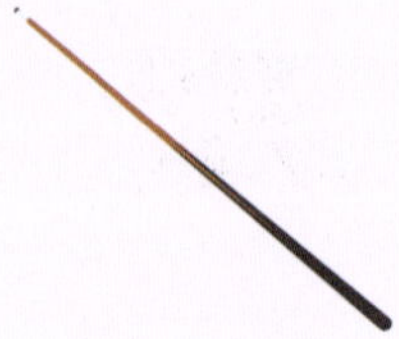
pool cue

soccer cleats (US)
football boots (UK)

ice skates

roller skates

skis

boxing gloves

swimming cap

goggles

armband

swimsuit

float

swimming trunks

swimming gear

flipper

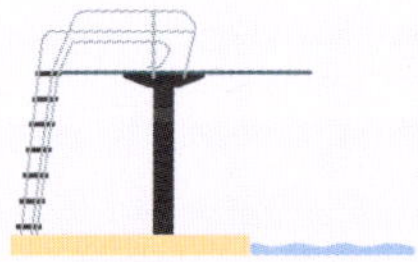
diving board

lifejacket

oars

helmet

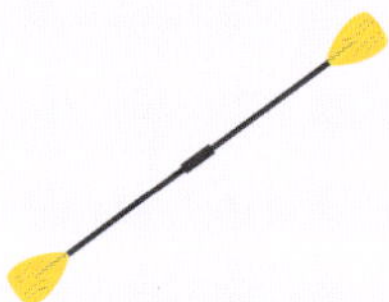
paddle

harness

ball

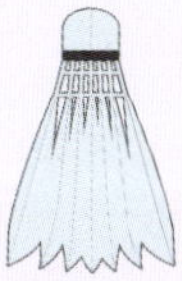
shuttlecock

bowling pins

skateboard

surfboard

snowboard

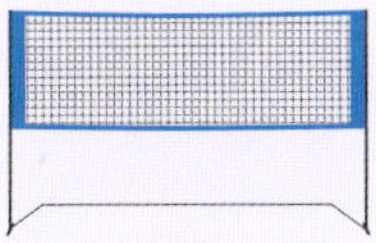
net

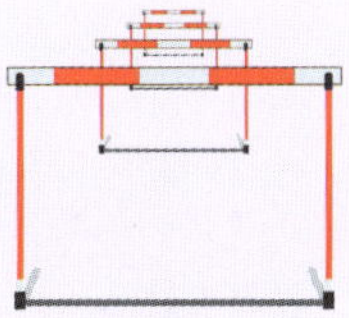
hurdles

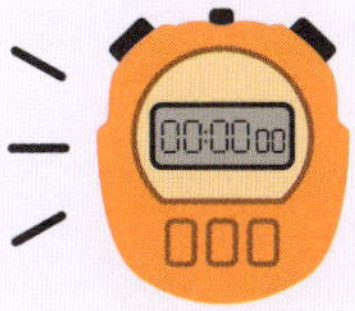
stopwatch

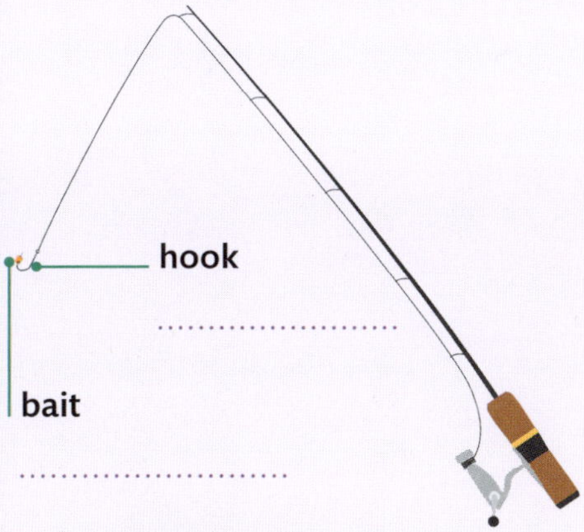
hook

bait

fishing rod

bow

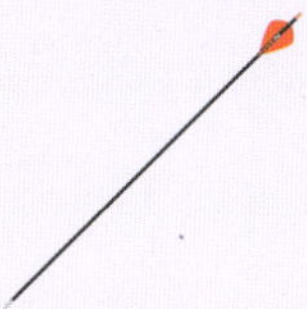
arrow

62.2 VENUES

field (US) / pitch (UK)

stadium

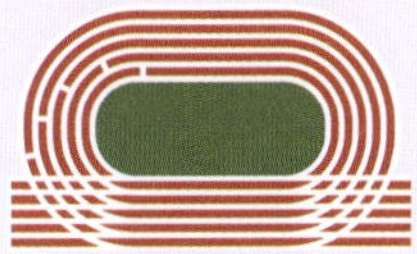
running track

golf course

tennis court

gym

boxing ring

swimming pool

ice rink

ski slope

Aa 62.3 MATCH THE WORDS TO THE CORRECT PICTURES

golf course

1 swimming pool

2 stadium

3 boxing ring

4 ice rink

5 field (US) / pitch (UK)

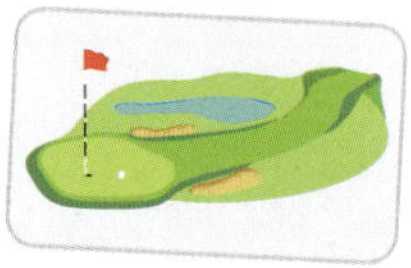

A 

B 

C 

D 

E 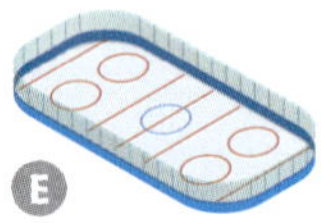

Aa 62.4 LOOK AT THE PICTURE AND WRITE THE CORRECT WORD FOR EACH LABEL

goggles

1 ______

2 ______

3 ______

4 ______

5 ______

6 ______

62.5 LISTEN TO THE AUDIO AND CIRCLE THE WORDS YOU HEAR

ice skates   roller skates   skateboard

1	gym	diving board	boxing ring
2	oars	arrow	ball
3	float	flipper	field
4	stopwatch	snowboard	surfboard
5	harness	net	hurdles
6	bow	bait	hook
7	golf club	gym	armbands
8	stadium	skis	ski slope
9	lifejacket	tennis racket	ball
10	paddle	pitch	pool cue

Aa 62.6 FILL IN THE GAPS, PUTTING THE WORDS FROM THE PANEL INTO THE CORRECT CATEGORIES

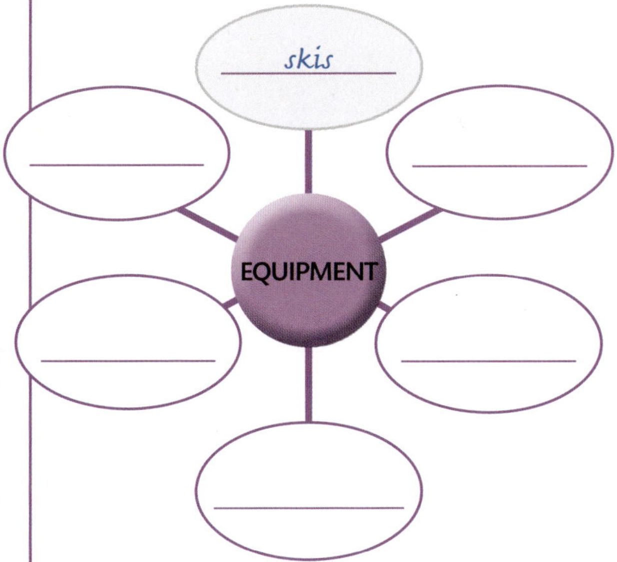

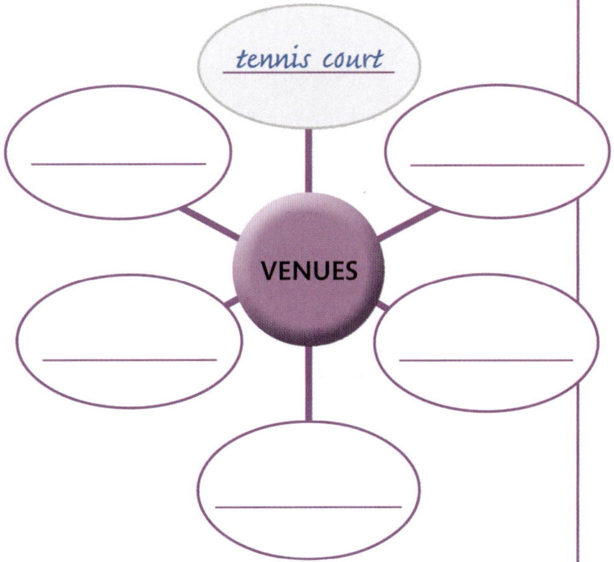

~~tennis court~~	ice rink	pool cue	stadium	fishing rod	helmet
ski slope	roller skates	golf course	running track	baseball bat	~~skis~~

Aa 62.7 REWRITE THE WORDS, CORRECTING THE SPELLINGS

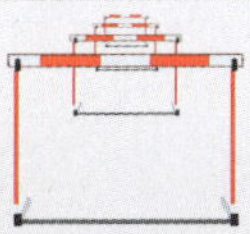
herdles
hurdles

1 paddel

2 arow

3 shutelcock

4 snowbored

5 helmut

6 bolling pines

7 harnes

63 Books and reading

63.1 BOOKS

illustration

page

cover

book

spine

author

novel

chapter

hardback

paperback

e-reader

63.2 USEFUL EXPRESSIONS

His new novel has received **glowing reviews** from all the critics.

glowing reviews

[highly positive reviews]

I **flipped through** the guidebook and decided to buy it.

to flip (US) / flick (UK) through

[to take a quick look inside a book]

I find the **plot** difficult to understand in most fantasy novels.

a plot

[a series of events that make up a story]

Her latest novel is a **bestseller** around the world.

a bestseller

[a book that sells a large number of copies]

I'm reading a crime novel. It's a real **page-turner**.

a page-turner

[a novel that makes you want to read more]

The novel was too **highbrow** for me. I prefer popular fiction.

highbrow

[containing difficult or intellectual ideas]

63.3 READING AND GENRES

fiction

romance

crime fiction

science-fiction

fantasy

non-fiction

biography

autobiography

humor (US)
humour (UK)

self-help

nature writing

travel writing

guidebook

cookbook

textbook / course book

dictionary

encyclopedia

comic

gossip magazine

TV guide

newspaper

puzzles

horoscope

coloring book (US)
colouring book (UK)

Aa 63.4 WRITE THE CORRECT WORD UNDER EACH PICTURE

fantasy

1 ______

2 ______

3 ______

4 ______

5 ______

6 ______

7 ______

8 ______

9 ______

10 ______

11 ______

12 ______

13 ______

14 ______

Aa 63.5 LOOK AT THE PICTURE CLUES AND WRITE THE ANSWERS IN THE CORRECT PLACES ON THE GRID

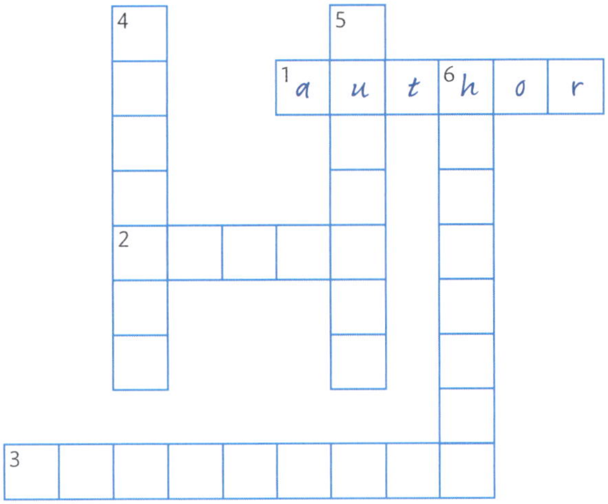

1

2

3

4

5

6

Aa 63.6 MATCH THE BEGINNINGS OF THE SENTENCES TO THE CORRECT ENDINGS

The novel was too highbrow for me. → I prefer popular fiction.

1. I flipped through the guidebook
2. His new novel has received
3. I'm reading a crime novel.
4. I find the plot difficult to
5. Her latest novel is a

- It's a real page-turner.
- understand in most fantasy novels.
- I prefer popular fiction.
- bestseller around the world.
- and decided to buy it.
- glowing reviews from all the critics.

63.7 LISTEN TO THE AUDIO, THEN NUMBER THE PICTURES IN THE ORDER YOU HEAR THEM

A ☐

B ☐

C ☐

D 1

E ☐

F ☐

G ☐

H ☐

I ☐

J ☐

64 Music

64.1 MUSICAL INSTRUMENTS

64.2 VERBS

to practice (US)
to practise (UK)

to rehearse

to play the trumpet

to sing

to conduct

to listen

to perform

to busk

to compose

to record

64.3 MUSICAL GENRES

hip-hop

classical

jazz

country

opera

soul

rap

rock

pop

latin

64.4 PERFORMANCE

orchestra

band

group

choir

lyrics

solo

composer

guitar player

concert

festival

singer

album

dance

microphone

conductor

Aa 64.5 LOOK AT THE PICTURE AND WRITE THE CORRECT WORD FOR EACH LABEL

1. ______
2. ______
3. ______
4. ______
5. ______
6. ______
7. ______
8. ______
9. ______

drum

Aa 64.6 MARK THE CORRECT WORD OR EXPRESSION FOR EACH PICTURE

- to listen ☐
- to record ☐
- to sing ☑

1

- to rehearse ☐
- to perform ☐
- to record ☐

2

- soul ☐
- latin ☐
- opera ☐

3

- to play the trumpet ☐
- to compose ☐
- to conduct ☐

4

- classical ☐
- rock ☐
- latin ☐

5

- to conduct ☐
- to listen ☐
- to busk ☐

6

- to record ☐
- to rehearse ☐
- to compose ☐

7

- country ☐
- hip-hop ☐
- classical ☐

8

- to compose ☐
- to listen ☐
- to perform ☐

9

- country ☐
- rap ☐
- jazz ☐

Aa 64.7 MATCH THE PICTURES TO THE CORRECT WORDS

1 

2 

3 

4 

5 

6 

7 

8 

- choir
- singer
- solo
- lyrics
- group
- guitar player
- festival
- microphone
- conductor

64.8 LISTEN TO THE AUDIO AND MARK THE CORRECT PICTURE FOR EACH WORD YOU HEAR

A ☐ B ☐ C ☑

1 A ☐ B ☐ C ☐

2 A ☐ B ☐ C ☐

3 A ☐ B ☐ C ☐

4 A ☐ B ☐ C ☐

5 A ☐ B ☐ C ☐

6 A ☐ B ☐ C ☐

65 Movies and plays

65.1 MOVIES

movie theater (US)
cinema (UK)

movie (US)
film (UK)

movie star (US)
film star (UK)

main character

hero

villain

director

drama

musical

science fiction

thriller

comedy

action movie

horror

cartoon

romantic comedy

crime drama

western

special effects

stunt

audience

screen

box office

multiplex

popcorn

65.2 PLAYS AND SHOWS

opera

opera house

ballet

tragedy

sets

props

costumes

cast

performance

script

program (US)
programme (UK)

applause

dialog (US)
dialogue (UK)

encore

standing ovation

usher

Aa 65.3 MATCH THE PICTURES TO THE CORRECT WORDS

1 

2 

3 

4 

5 

director | horror | thriller

romantic comedy | opera | ballet

Aa 65.4 CIRCLE THE WORD THAT DOES NOT BELONG IN EACH LIST

	hero	villain	stage
1	western	costumes	science fiction
2	multiplex	sets	props
3	comedy	tragedy	script
4	applause	popcorn	encore
5	multiplex	screen	villain
6	usher	opera	ballet
7	cartoon	curtain	balcony
8	audience	cast	stunt
9	thriller	director	drama

65.5 LISTEN TO THE AUDIO AND CIRCLE THE WORDS YOU HEAR

	stunt	screen	science fiction
1	cast	sets	script
2	hero	horror	western
3	villain	movie	musical
4	dialog	director	drama
5	applause	multiplex	encore
6	usher	popcorn	audience
7	tragedy	ballet	box office
8	cartoon	crime drama	curtain
9	script	props	performance
10	villain	thriller	ballet

Aa 65.6 LOOK AT THE PICTURE AND WRITE THE CORRECT WORD FOR EACH LABEL

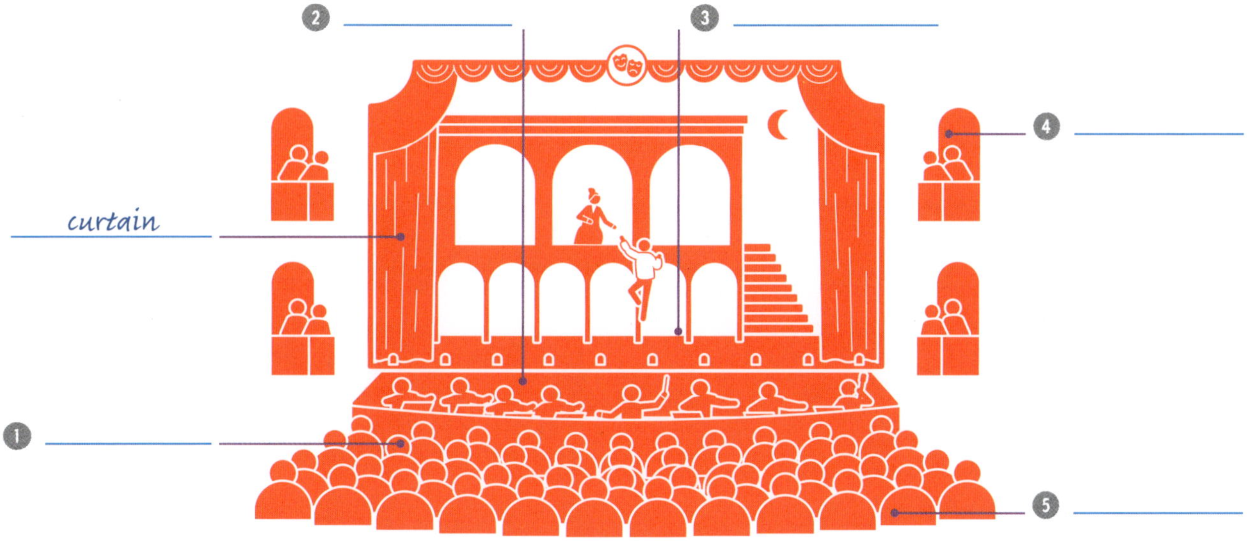

Aa 65.7 REWRITE THE WORDS, CORRECTING THE SPELLINGS

opara

opera

1 screne

2 custumes

3 acton movie

4 movee star

5 audeince

6 carton

7 encor

66 TV

66.1 WATCHING TELEVISION

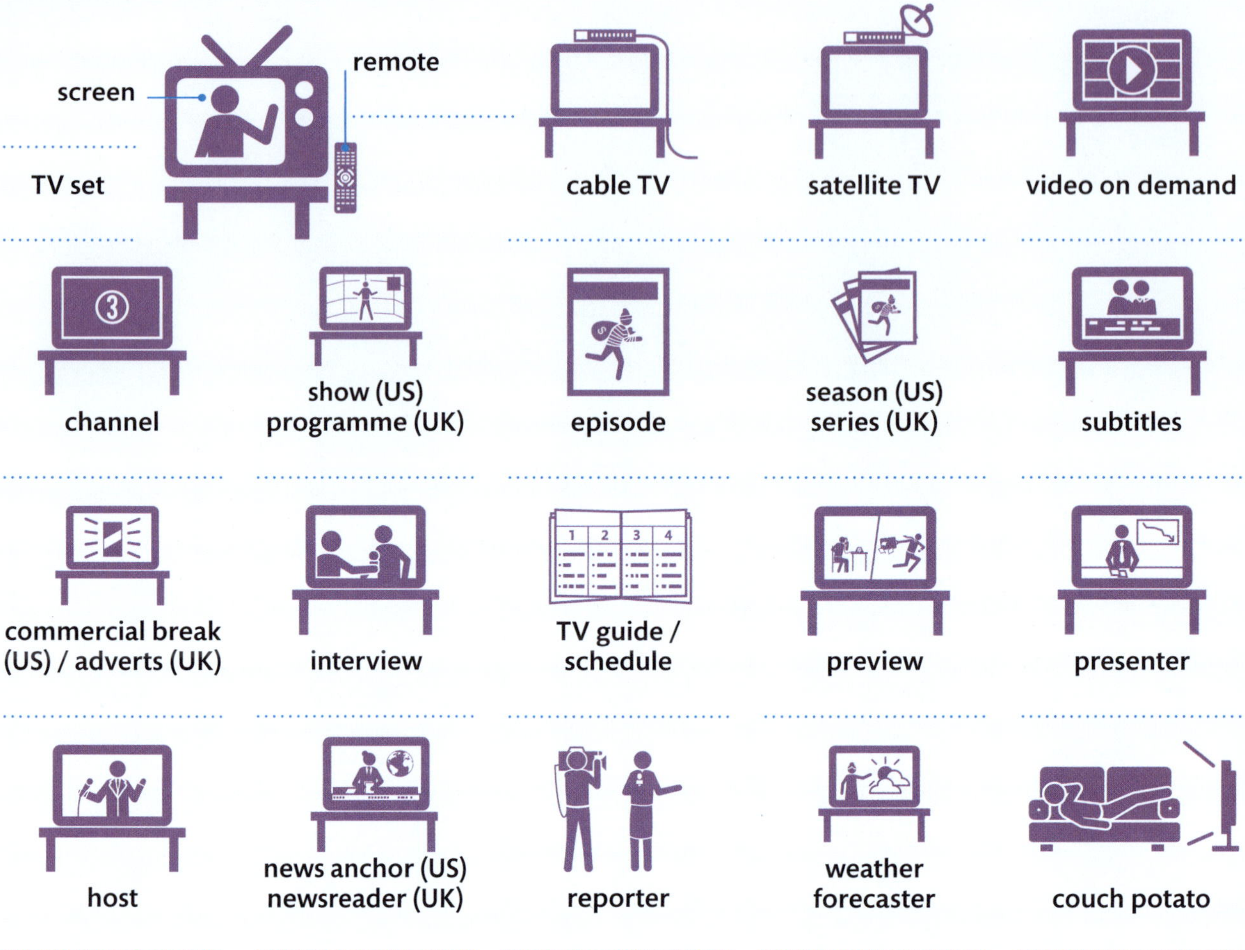

66.2 VERBS

66.3 TV SHOWS AND CHANNELS

cooking show

talk show (US) / chat show (UK)

sports show (US) / programme (UK)

documentary

nature documentary

period / costume drama

sitcom

quiz show

current affairs

news

weather

soap opera

game show

comedy

drama

cartoon

crime

thriller

satire

children's show (US) / TV (UK)

breakfast TV

reality TV

catch-up TV

shopping channel

music channel

Aa 66.4 MATCH THE PICTURES TO THE CORRECT WORDS

1 

2 

3 

4 

5 

6 

- comedy
- cartoon
- talk show (US) / chat show (UK)
- children's show (US) / children's TV (UK)
- period / costume drama
- cooking show
- news

66.5 LISTEN TO THE AUDIO, THEN NUMBER THE PICTURES IN THE ORDER YOU HEAR THEM

A ☐

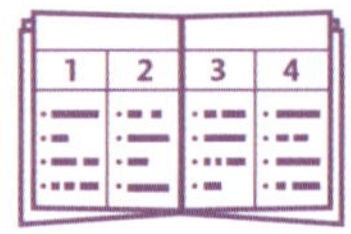

B ☐

C ☐

D ☐

E 1

F ☐

G ☐

H ☐

I ☐

J ☐

K ☐

L ☐

Aa 66.6 MARK THE BEGINNING AND ENDING OF EACH WORD IN THE CHAIN OF LETTERS

episode/documentarychannelremotesatirereporterweatherdramascreenpreviewsitcom

Aa 66.7 WRITE THE CORRECT WORD UNDER EACH PICTURE

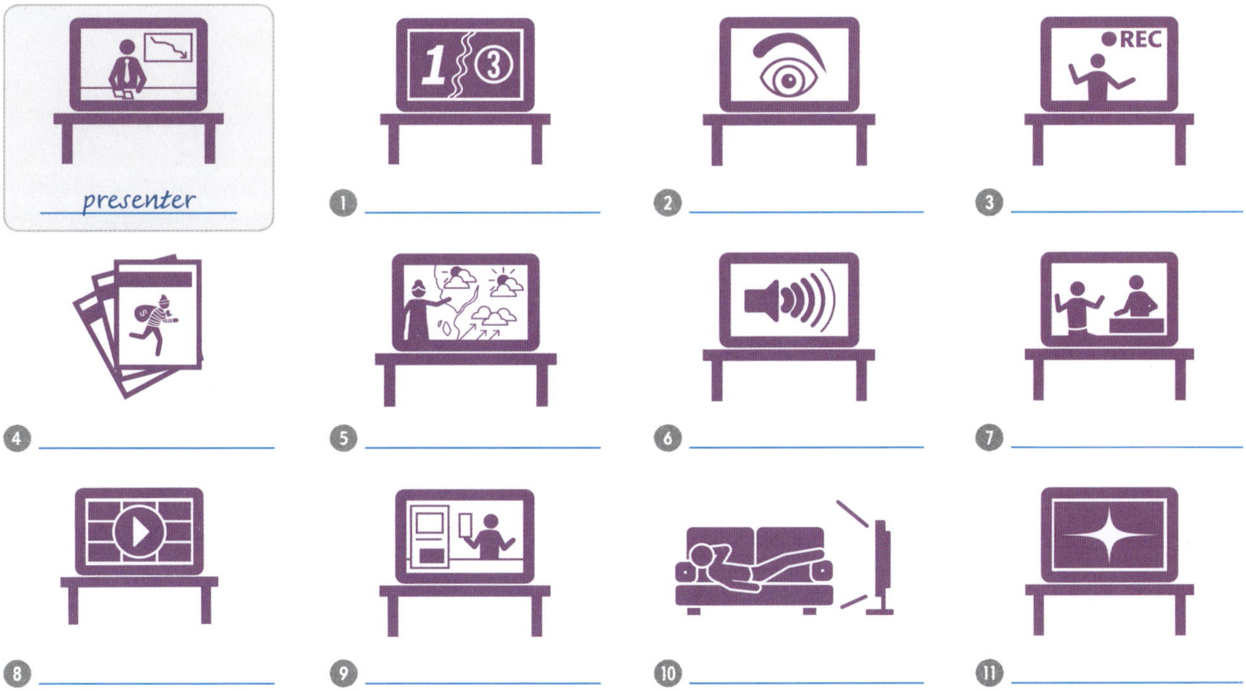

Aa 66.8 FIND EIGHT MORE WORDS IN THE GRID THAT MATCH THE PICTURES

T	H	R	I	L	L	E	R	C	S	L	H
R	A	J	Q	X	W	E	A	T	H	E	R
E	E	D	E	M	J	D	M	D	A	N	E
P	C	I	N	C	A	R	T	O	O	N	N
O	T	S	C	X	W	A	X	B	L	A	C
R	E	H	C	R	I	M	E	D	E	H	I
T	M	O	L	O	L	A	O	Z	R	C	L
E	A	W	E	I	C	H	A	N	N	E	L
R	E	I	N	T	E	R	V	I	E	W	L

67 Media and celebrity

67.1 USEFUL EXPRESSIONS

I think the newspaper has sensationalized this story.

to sensationalize
[to make something more dramatic or exciting than it is]

The politician's lies were exposed in the interview.

to expose
[to reveal something hidden]

Politicians can easily be exploited by the media.

to exploit
[to use something or someone for your own gain]

You don't always need to be talented to become a celebrity.

to become a celebrity
[to become a famous person]

This chef has been a household name for years.

a household name
[someone who is known by most people]

John would really love to have his name in lights.

to have your name in lights
[to be very famous]

The success of her latest movie has gone to her head.

to go to somebody's head
[to make somebody feel more important than they are]

Lucinda is used to being in the public eye.

in the public eye
[seen and well known by the public]

This morning's newspaper headline is shocking!

a newspaper headline
[the large text at the top of a newspaper page]

This singer's wedding was headline news last week.

headline news
[news that is widely reported]

Social media has supported the rise of celebrity culture.

celebrity culture
[the popular culture that surrounds famous people]

Some people go on talent shows to become famous.

a talent show
[a competition with performances by entertainers showcasing their skills]

It's not fair when the paparazzi invade people's privacy.

the paparazzi
[photographers who take pictures of famous people without their consent]

My favorite actors were on the red carpet this evening.

the red carpet
[a carpet for important guests to walk or stand on at an event]

Read our exclusive interview with the stars of the movie tomorrow!

an exclusive interview
[an interview that no other source has obtained]

Lee's claim to fame was that he could eat five burgers in five minutes.

a claim to fame
[the thing that somebody or something is known for, often said jokingly]

I enjoy reality shows because I'm nosy about people's lives.

a reality show
[a show based on or around real-life events]

The opening night of the show was a great success.

the opening night
[the first night of a show or movie]

Kelly has had a truly meteoric rise in the music industry.

a meteoric rise
[a very rapid rise, often in a career]

Everyone was talking about her attention-grabbing dress.

attention-grabbing
[designed or intended to get your attention quickly]

67.2 REWRITE THE SENTENCES, CORRECTING THE ERRORS

This chef has been a **homehold name** for years.
This chef has been a household name for years.

1. Lee's **call to fame** was that he could eat five burgers in five minutes.

2. **The beginning night** of the show was a great success.

3. Lucinda is used to being **in the people's eye**.

4. The success of her latest movie has **gone to her heart**.

67.3 MATCH THE PICTURES TO THE CORRECT SENTENCES

1. 

2. 

3. 

4. 

- My favorite actors were on the red carpet this evening.
- I enjoy reality shows because I'm nosy about people's lives.
- This singer's wedding was headline news last week.
- Everyone was talking about her attention-grabbing dress.
- Social media has supported the rise of celebrity culture.

67.4 MATCH THE BEGINNINGS OF THE SENTENCES TO THE CORRECT ENDINGS

I think the newspaper has → sensationalized this story.

1. John would really love to have
2. This morning's newspaper
3. Kelly has had a truly meteoric
4. Some people go on talent
5. Politicians can easily
6. The politician's lies were

- headline is shocking!
- shows to become famous.
- sensationalized this story.
- his name in lights.
- be exploited by the media.
- exposed in the interview.
- rise in the music industry.

67.5 LISTEN TO THE AUDIO, THEN NUMBER THE SENTENCES IN THE ORDER YOU HEAR THEM

A  You don't always need to be talented to become a celebrity. ☐

B  The opening night of the show was a great success. [1]

C  It's not fair when the paparazzi invade people's privacy. ☐

D  This singer's wedding was headline news last week. ☐

E  The politician's lies were exposed in the interview. ☐

F 

John would really love to have his name in lights. ☐

68 Sickness

68.1 SICKNESS AND CONDITIONS

flu

cold

hay fever / allergies

virus

infection

tonsillitis

appendicitis

food poisoning

indigestion

migraine

nosebleed

eczema

measles

mumps

chickenpox

asthma

diabetes

high blood pressure

stress

insomnia

68.2 ADJECTIVES FOR SICKNESS

sick (US) / ill (UK)

sore

itchy

swollen

painful

68.3 SYMPTOMS

symptoms

fever (US)
temperature (UK)

cough

runny nose

sore throat

headache

backache

stomachache (US)
stomach ache (UK)

pain

diarrhea (US)
diarrhoea (UK)

68.4 VERBS FOR SYMPTOMS

to vomit

to cough

to sneeze

to hurt / to ache

to bleed

68.5 ACCIDENTS AND INJURIES

accident

broken bone

sprain

wound

bruise

burn

bite

sting

splinter

cut

Aa 68.6 MARK THE CORRECT PICTURE FOR EACH WORD

to vomit

A ☐ B ☑ C ☐

❶ insomnia

A ☐ B ☐ C ☐

❷ hay fever / allergies

A ☐ B ☐ C ☐

❸ sting

A ☐ B ☐ C ☐

❹ headache

A ☐ B ☐ C ☐

❺ cut

A ☐ B ☐ C ☐

68.7 LISTEN TO THE AUDIO AND WRITE THE WORD THAT IS SHOWN IN EACH PICTURE

 cough

❶  ______________

❷  ______________

❸  ______________

❹  ______________

❺  ______________

❻  ______________

❼  ______________

Aa 68.8 FILL IN THE GAPS, PUTTING THE WORDS FROM THE PANEL INTO THE CORRECT CATEGORIES

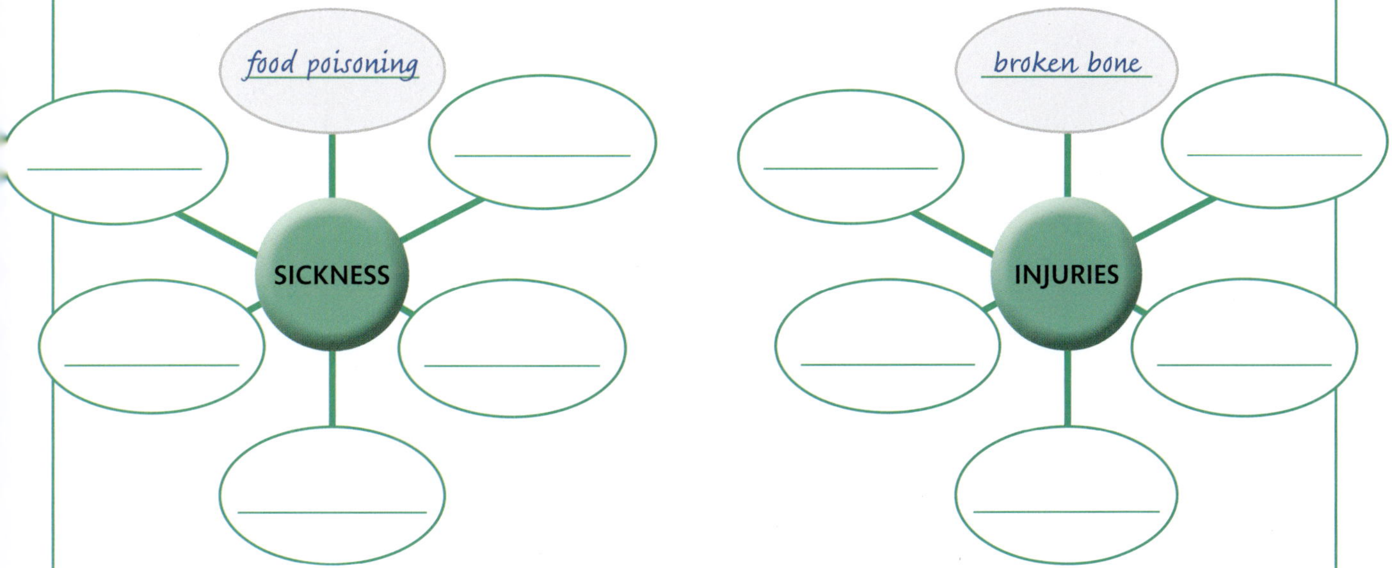

~~food poisoning~~	wound	diabetes	appendicitis	bruise	burn
chickenpox	mumps	sting	cut	cold	~~broken bone~~

Aa 68.9 LOOK AT THE PICTURE CLUES AND WRITE THE ANSWERS IN THE CORRECT PLACES ON THE GRID

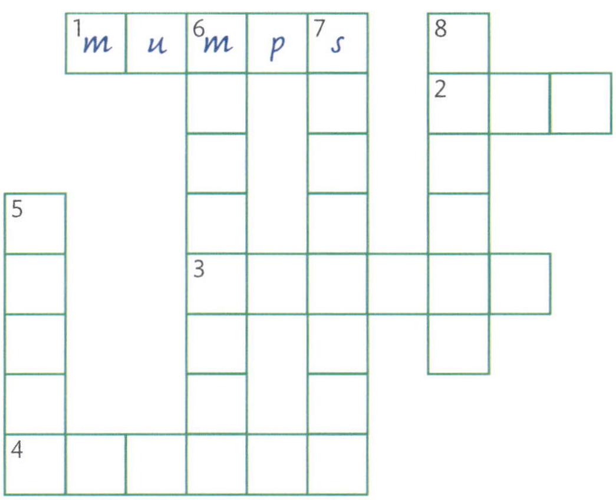

69 Medicine and treatment

69.1 MEDICINE AND TREATMENT

doctor

nurse

patient

clinic (US) / doctor's surgery (UK)

hospital

waiting room

appointment

prescription

ambulance

paramedic

medicine / medication

pills / tablets

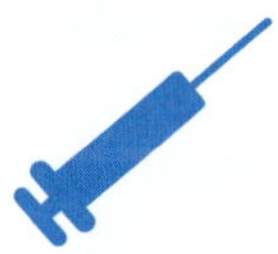

injection

blood test

test results

treatment

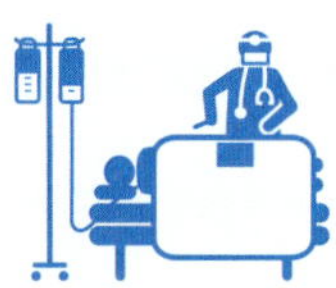

operation

physical therapy (US) physiotherapy (UK)

stitches

X-ray

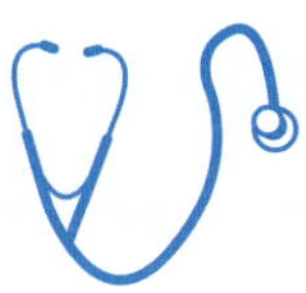

stethoscope

inhaler

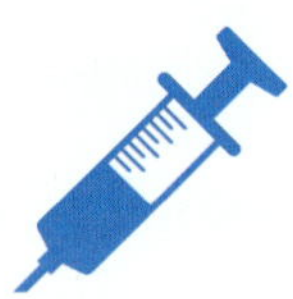

syringe

scales

thermometer

69.2 FIRST AID

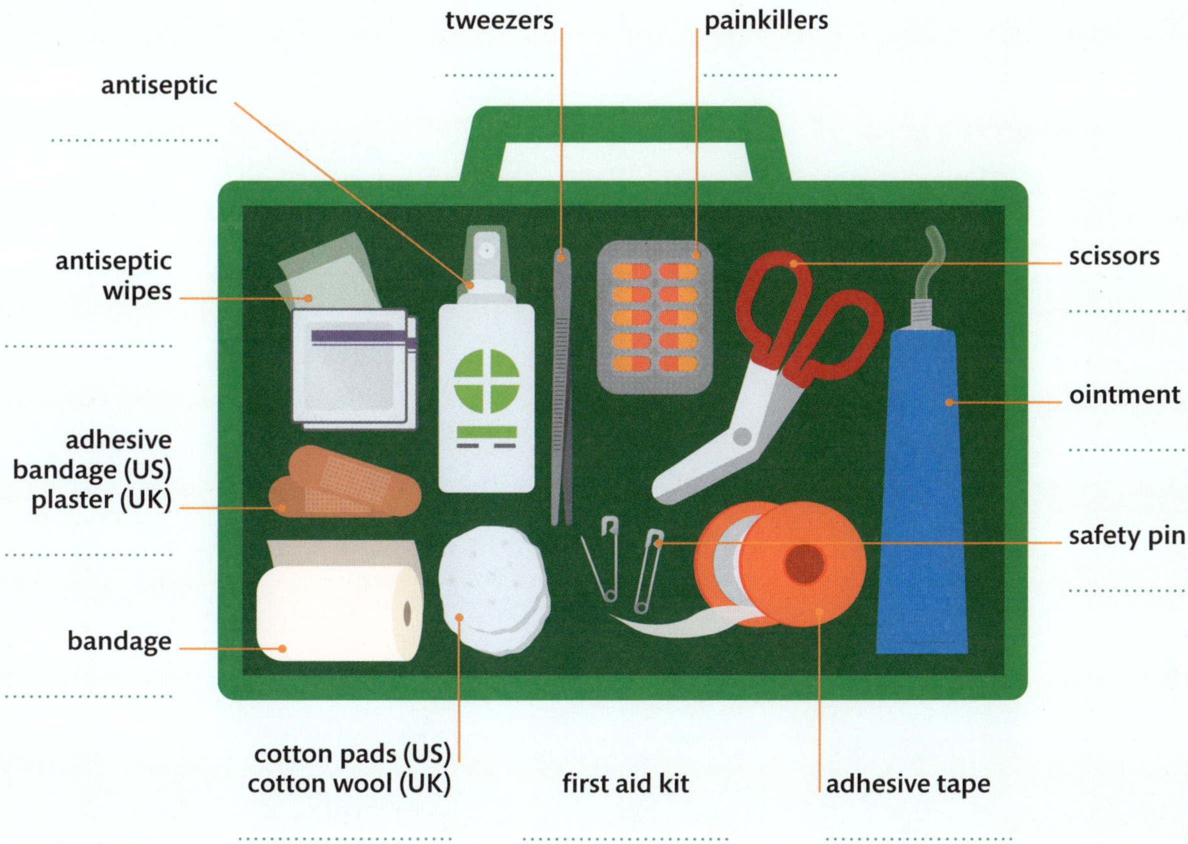

69.3 VERBS

69.4 MATCH THE WORDS TO THE CORRECT PICTURES

X-ray

1. thermometer
2. waiting room
3. pills / tablets
4. scales
5. doctor
6. to recover
7. nurse
8. blood test
9. to gain weight

A 

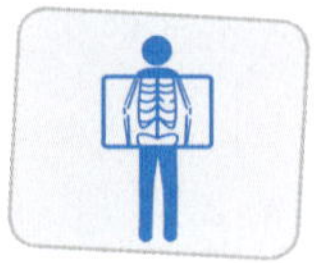

B 

C 

D 

E 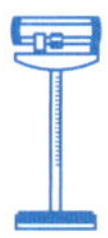

F 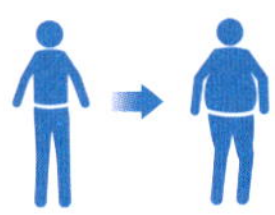

G 

H 

I 

69.5 REWRITE THE WORDS, CORRECTING THE SPELLINGS

stiches
stitches

1.  proscription ______
2.  ambulence ______
3.  apointment ______
4. 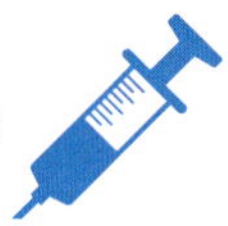 siringe ______
5.  to heel ______
6.  to excercise ______
7. 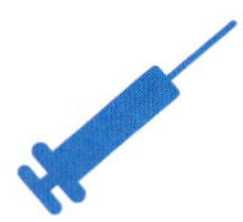 injecsion ______
8.  tretment ______
9.  to resussitate ______

Aa 69.6 LOOK AT THE PICTURE AND WRITE THE CORRECT WORD FOR EACH LABEL

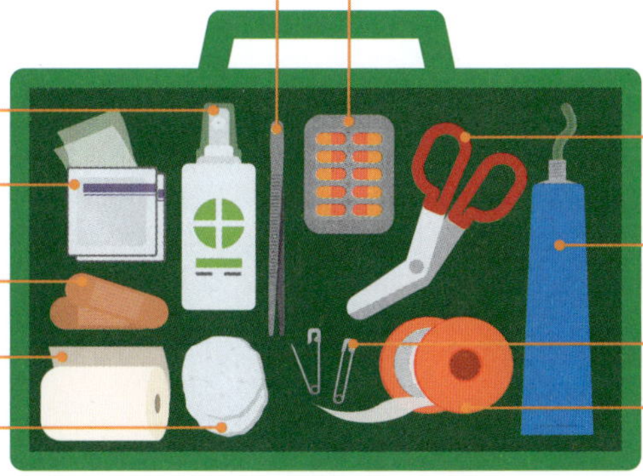

antiseptic

1 ______

2 ______

3 ______

4 ______

5 ______

6 ______

7 ______

8 ______

9 ______

10 ______

Aa 69.7 MARK THE BEGINNING AND ENDING OF EACH WORD IN THE CHAIN OF LETTERS

stethoscope|physicaltherapyoperationpatientbloodtestinhalerparamedicbandageointment

69.8 LISTEN TO THE AUDIO, THEN NUMBER THE PICTURES IN THE ORDER YOU HEAR THEM

A ☐

B ☐

C ☐

D 1

E ☐

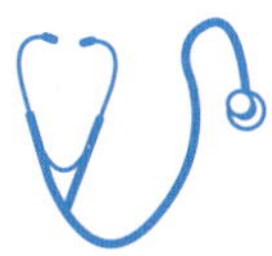
F ☐

G ☐

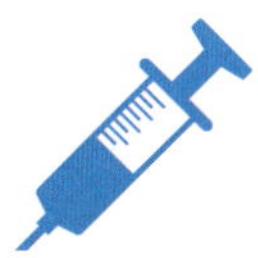
H ☐

I ☐

J ☐

K ☐

L ☐

M ☐

N ☐

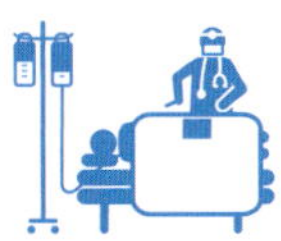
O ☐

P ☐

70 Healthy eating

70.1 NUTRITION AND DIETS

protein

carbohydrates

fiber (US)
fibre (UK)

dairy

legumes (US)
pulses (UK)

sugar

salt

saturated fat

unsaturated fat

calories / energy

vitamins

minerals

calcium

iron

cholesterol

superfoods

processed food

a balanced diet

a calorie-controlled diet

a detox

vegetarian

vegan

pescatarian

gluten-free

dairy-free

70.2 USEFUL EXPRESSIONS

You should eat smaller portions if you want to lose weight.

a portion
[the amount of food you eat in one meal]

Fish is very good for you because it's high in protein.

high in something
[containing a large amount of something]

I'm trying to cut down on sugary drinks because I know they're bad for me.

to cut down on something
[to eat or drink less of something]

I'm trying to eat more vegetables because they're low in fat.

low in something
[containing a small amount of something]

Pedro has given up chocolate this month.

to give up something / to give something up
[to stop eating or drinking something]

Brown bread is a good source of fiber.

a good source of something
[containing a lot of something healthy]

No dessert for me, thank you. I'm watching my weight.

to watch your weight
[to try to avoid gaining weight]

It's okay to eat treats like cake in moderation.

to eat something in moderation
[to avoid eating too much of something]

Mia must not eat nuts because she's allergic to them.

allergic to something
[unable to eat or drink something without having a bad reaction]

Convenience food saves people time, but isn't always good for them.

convenience food
[food that is quick and easy to make]

Aa 70.3 MATCH THE WORDS TO THE CORRECT PICTURES

vegan → 

A 

1 cholesterol

2 carbohydrates

3 legumes (US) pulses (UK)

4 dairy-free

5 pescatarian

6 vitamins

7 calcium

8 dairy

9 a balanced diet

B 

C 

D 

E 

F 

G 

H 

I 

70.4 LISTEN TO THE AUDIO AND MARK THE CORRECT PICTURE FOR EACH WORD YOU HEAR

A ☑ B ☐ C ☐

1 A ☐ B ☐ C ☐

2 A ☐ B ☐ C ☐

3 A ☐ B ☐ C ☐

4 A ☐ B ☐ C ☐

5 A ☐ B ☐ C ☐

6 A ☐ B ☐ C ☐

7 A ☐ B ☐ C ☐

Aa 70.5 MARK THE SENTENCES THAT ARE CORRECT

No dessert for me, thank you. I'm watching my weight. ☑
No dessert for me, thank you. I'm seeing my weight. ☐

1. Pedro has given up chocolate this month. ☐
Pedro has given for chocolate this month. ☐

2. I'm trying to eat more vegetables because they're low of fat. ☐
I'm trying to eat more vegetables because they're low in fat. ☐

3. Brown bread is a good source of fiber. ☐
Brown bread is a good cause of fiber. ☐

4. You should eat smaller portions if you want to lose weight. ☐
You should eat smaller partions if you want to lose weight. ☐

5. Convenient food saves people time, but isn't always good for them. ☐
Convenience food saves people time, but isn't always good for them. ☐

Aa 70.6 REWRITE THE SENTENCES, CORRECTING THE ERRORS

Fish is very good for you because it's **high of** protein.
Fish is very good for you because it's high in protein.

1. I'm trying to **reduce down on** sugary drinks because I know they're bad for me.
____

2. Mia must not eat nuts because she's **allergic for** them.
____

3. I'm trying to eat more vegetables because they're **down in** fat.
____

4. It's okay to **eat** treats like cake **on moderation**.
____

71 Fitness and well-being

71.1 AT THE GYM

71.2 VERBS FOR FITNESS

71.3 FITNESS

locker room (US)
changing room (UK)

lockers

jump rope (US)
skipping rope (UK)

push-up (US)
press-up (UK)

sit-up

heart rate

circuit training

boot camp

exercise class

aerobics

71.4 WELL-BEING

to relax /
to chill out

to meditate

to sleep well

deep breathing

massage

spa

sauna

steam room

hot tub

Pilates

yoga

acupuncture

reflexology

aromatherapy

counseling (US)
counselling (UK)

Aa 71.5 MARK THE CORRECT WORD FOR EACH PICTURE

to run ☑
to stretch ☐
sit-up ☐

1

aerobics ☐
circuit training ☐
to squat ☐

2

to skip ☐
lockers ☐
to stretch ☐

3

to cool down ☐
sit-up ☐
heart rate ☐

4

push-up ☐
sauna ☐
locker room ☐

5

Pilates ☐
steam room ☐
spa ☐

6

to warm up ☐
to meditate ☐
exercise class ☐

7

to jog ☐
to squat ☐
boot-camp ☐

8

acupuncture ☐
reflexology ☐
aromatherapy ☐

9

massage ☐
yoga ☐
hot tub ☐

Aa 71.6 LOOK AT THE PICTURE AND WRITE THE CORRECT WORD FOR EACH LABEL

rowing machine

1 ______

2 ______

3 ______

4 ______

5 ______

6 ______

71.7 LISTEN TO THE AUDIO AND WRITE THE WORD THAT IS SHOWN IN EACH PICTURE

aerobics

1.  ______________
2.  ______________
3.  ______________
4.  ______________
5.  ______________
6.  ______________
7.  ______________
8.  ______________
9.  ______________
10.  ______________
11.  ______________
12.  ______________
13.  ______________

71.8 CIRCLE THE WORD THAT DOES NOT BELONG IN EACH LIST

	circuit training	exercise class	hot tub
1	to stretch	to warm up	personal trainer
2	treadmill	massage	acupuncture
3	to chill out	to jog	to run
4	yoga	boot camp	to meditate
5	treadmill	spa	weights
6	lockers	Pilates	reflexology
7	sit-up	steam room	push-up

71.9 COMPLETE THE WORD FOR EACH PICTURE, FILLING IN THE MISSING LETTERS

d e e p b r e a t h i n g

1.  r _ f l _ _ _ l _ g _
2.  _ x _ r c _ s _ c l _ _ s
3.  s _ _ n _
4.  s _ _ _ m r _ _ m
5.  t _ s l _ _ p w _ _ l
6.  t _ w _ r _ _ p

72 Around town

72.1 AROUND TOWN

street map

village

town

city

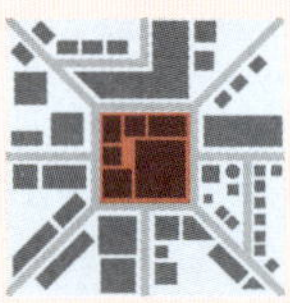

downtown (US)
city centre (UK)

commercial district

historic quarter

police station

bus station

train station

fire station

airport

factory

post office

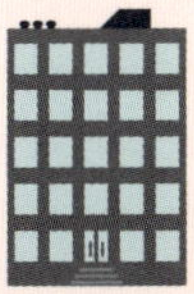
office building

park

bridge

swimming pool

café

bar

theater (US)
theatre (UK)

movie theater (US)
cinema (UK)

hotel

church

mosque

synagogue

temple

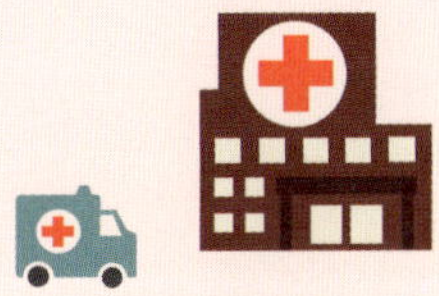
hospital

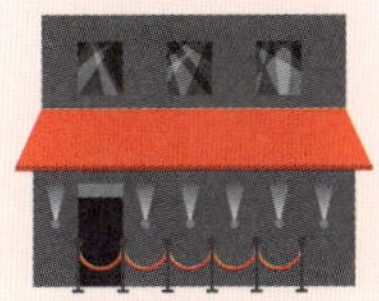
nightclub

gas station (US)
petrol station (UK)

government building

law court

skyscraper

shopping mall

tourist office (US) /
information (UK)

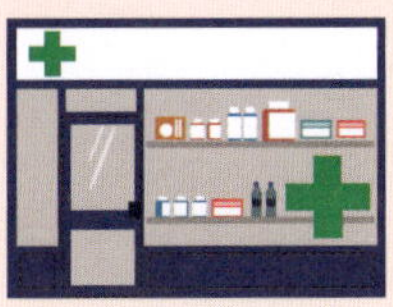
pharmacy

cemetery

sports / leisure
center (centre)

concert hall

Aa 72.2 LOOK AT THE PICTURE AND WRITE THE CORRECT WORD FOR EACH LABEL

1 ______

2 ______

3 ______

4 ______

5 ______

6 ______

7 ______

museum

Aa 72.3 FIND FIVE MORE WORDS IN THE GRID THAT MATCH THE PICTURES

H O T E L I R A C S A F
T E M P L E K Q H T Q A
A E D E M J S M E A M C
P H A R M A C Y D P T T
L T B C X W D X I L X O
E E N I G H T C L U B R
H O S P I T A L T R O Y

1 

2 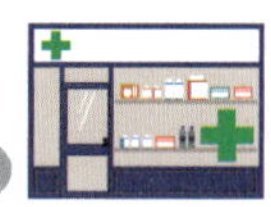

3 

4 

5 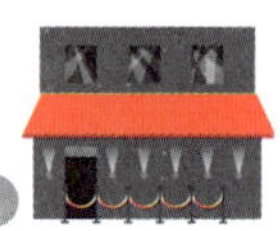

72.4 LISTEN TO THE AUDIO AND MARK THE CORRECT PICTURE FOR EACH WORD YOU HEAR

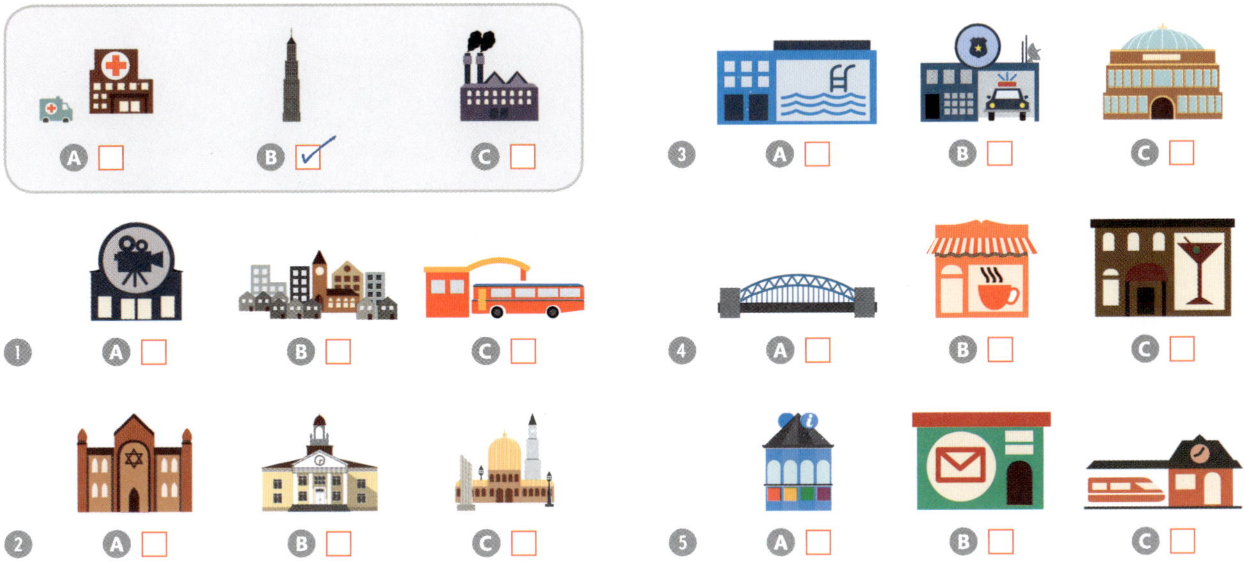

72.5 WRITE THE CORRECT WORD UNDER EACH PICTURE

73 Shopping

73.1 STORES (US) / SHOPS (UK)

butcher

baker

bookstore (US)
bookshop (UK)

fish dealer (US)
fishmonger (UK)

greengrocer

boutique

shoe store (US)
shoe shop (UK)

street market

delicatessen

jewelers (US)
jewellers (UK)

dry cleaners

florist

hardware store

bank

toy store (US)
toy shop (UK)

73.2 VERBS

to choose

to sell

to want

to fit

to buy

to pay

to try on

to haggle

to exchange

to refund

73.3 USEFUL EXPRESSIONS

I love going bargain-hunting at my local market.

bargain-hunting

[searching for goods that are cheaper than normal]

It's always worth shopping around when buying a new car.

to shop around

[to compare prices at various stores]

You can buy almost anything you want at the flea market in town.

a flea market

[an open-air market that sells old or used items]

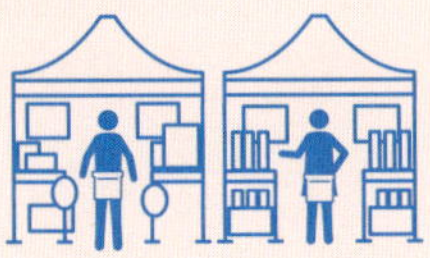

My new phone was a real rip-off. It broke after only a couple of weeks.

a rip-off

[a low-quality product that costs more than it should]

I spent Saturday morning window shopping with my friends.

window shopping

[looking at goods in store windows without buying them]

There's 50 percent off all winter coats at this department store.

50 percent off

[a 50 percent reduction]

I'm on a tight budget. I can't afford to buy many Christmas presents.

on a tight budget

[having only a small amount of money to spend]

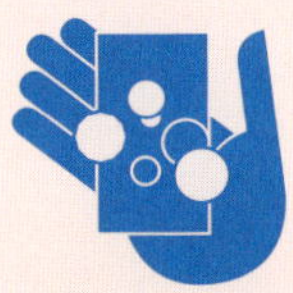

I got a good deal on my new pair of shoes. They were reduced by $20.

a good deal

[a good price]

The local hardware store has slashed its prices. You can find some real bargains.

to slash prices

[to reduce prices dramatically]

I thought the restaurant was overpriced. The food was very disappointing.

overpriced

[costing too much]

Aa 73.4 WRITE THE CORRECT WORD UNDER EACH PICTURE

dry cleaners

1 ____________

2 ____________

3 ____________

4 ____________

5 ____________

6 ____________

7 ____________

8 ____________

9 ____________

Aa 73.5 MARK THE CORRECT WORD FOR EACH PICTURE

to pay ☑
to fit ☐
to try on ☐

1
to buy ☐
to try on ☐
to haggle ☐

2
bank ☐
bookstore ☐
butcher ☐

3
to refund ☐
to sell ☐
to choose ☐

4
dry cleaners ☐
boutique ☐
jewelers ☐

5
to haggle ☐
to exchange ☐
to buy ☐

6
hardware store ☐
toy store ☐
fishmonger ☐

7
to refund ☐
to fit ☐
to want ☐

8
to choose ☐
to pay ☐
to haggle ☐

9
hardware store ☐
dry cleaners ☐
delicatessen ☐

73.6 LISTEN TO THE AUDIO AND COMPLETE THE SENTENCES THAT DESCRIBE EACH PICTURE

I spent Saturday morning *window shopping* with my friends.

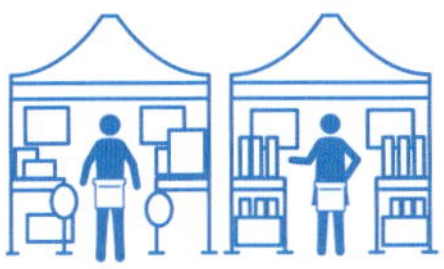

1. You can buy almost anything you want at the __________ in town.

2. It's always worth __________ when buying a new car.

3. I love going __________ at my local market.

4. I thought the restaurant was __________. The food was very disappointing.

5. The local electrical store has __________. You can find some real bargains.

73.7 MATCH THE DEFINITIONS TO THE CORRECT PHRASES

costing too much → overpriced

1. a good price
2. to reduce prices dramatically
3. having only a small amount of money to spend
4. an open-air market that sells old or used items
5. to compare prices at various stores
6. a low-quality product that costs more than it should
7. searching for goods that are cheaper than normal

- to slash prices
- a flea market
- bargain-hunting
- overpriced
- a rip-off
- a good deal
- on a tight budget
- to shop around

74 At the supermarket

74.1 SUPERMARKET

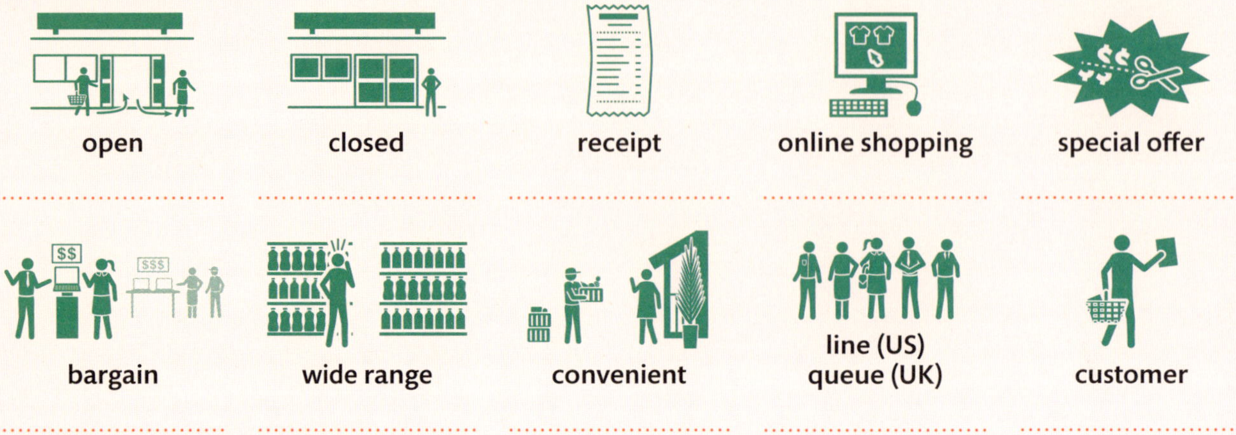

74.2 AT THE CHECKOUT

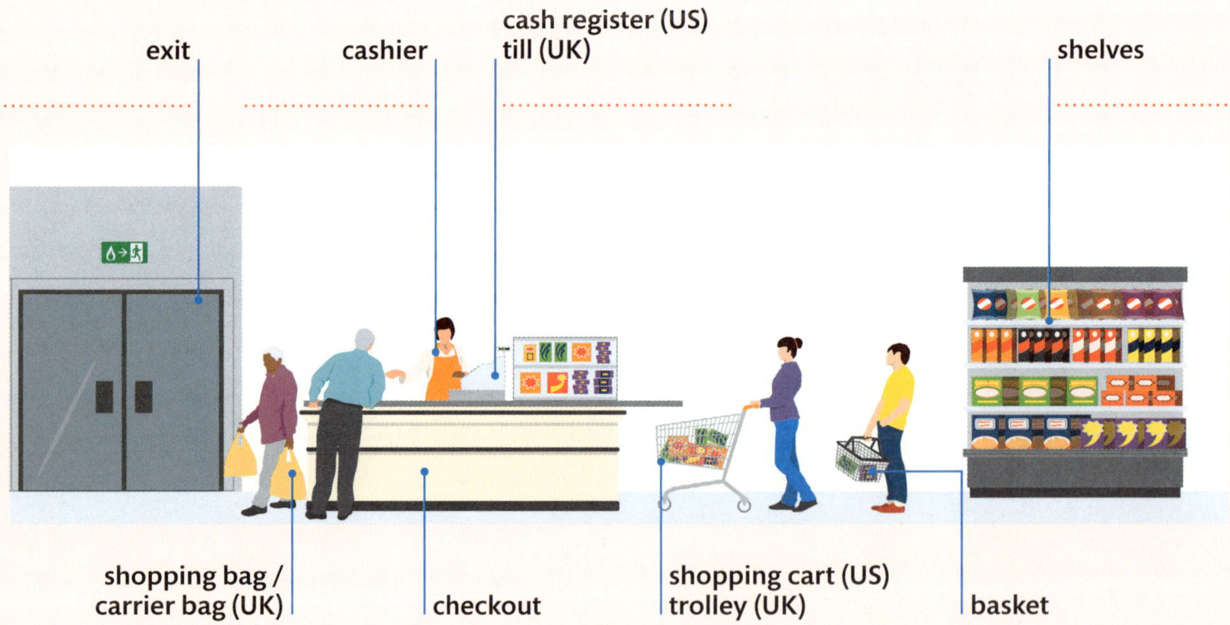

74.3 DEPARTMENT STORE

escalator

elevator (US)
lift (UK)

guarantee

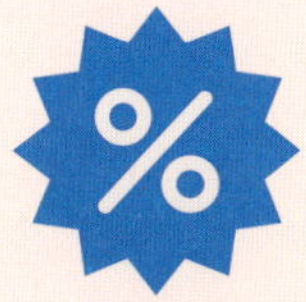
sale

price tag

first floor (US)
ground floor (UK)

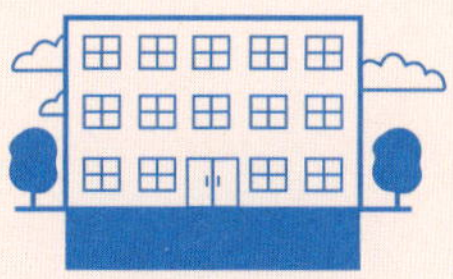
basement

loyalty card

upmarket

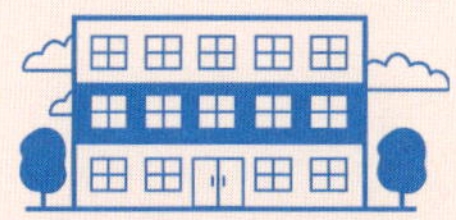
second floor (US)
first floor (UK)

designer labels

men's wear

women's wear

children's
department

customer service

kitchenware

home furnishings

changing rooms

baby changing
facilities

food court

lingerie

cosmetics (US)
perfumery (UK)

beauty

electrical
appliances

lighting

Aa 74.4 LOOK AT THE PICTURE AND WRITE THE CORRECT WORD FOR EACH LABEL

Aa 74.5 REWRITE THE WORDS, CORRECTING THE SPELLINGS

bargin

bargain

1 conveniente

______

2 reciept

______

3 speciel ofer

______

4 basment

______

5 custommer

______

6 garantee

______

7 escallator

______

Aa 74.6 MATCH THE WORDS TO THE CORRECT PICTURES

customer service → 

1. elevator (US) / lift (UK)
2. children's department
3. home furnishings
4. line (US) / queue (UK)

A 

B 

C 

D 

Aa 74.7 COMPLETE THE WORD FOR EACH PICTURE, FILLING IN THE MISSING LETTERS

 k *i* t c h *e* n w *a* r *e*

1.  f _ _ d c _ u _ t
2.  _ p _ a _ k e _
3.  c _ o _ e _
4.  p _ i c _ t _ g

74.8 LISTEN TO THE AUDIO, THEN NUMBER THE PICTURES IN THE ORDER YOU HEAR THEM

A ☐

B 1

C ☐

D ☐

E ☐

F ☐

G ☐

H ☐

I ☐

J ☐

K ☐

L ☐

75 Urban life

75.1 USEFUL EXPRESSIONS

It's sometimes impossible to get on the bus during rush hour.

rush hour
[the period of the day when most people travel to or from work]

The vandalism in my area makes the buildings look very ugly.

vandalism
[illegal damage to or destruction of property]

There's a greater choice of cafés and restaurants in large cities.

a greater choice
[a larger number of shops, restaurants, and services]

There are lots of green spaces in the city for people to relax in the summer.

green spaces
[outdoor areas with grass or vegetation]

The crime rate in most cities has been dropping in recent years.

the crime rate
[the frequency of crimes in an area]

I offer guided tours of the city's historic buildings.

historic buildings
[buildings that have been important in history]

A good way to avoid traffic jams is to travel by train.

a traffic jam
[a line of traffic that is unable to move]

I live in a poor part of town with many derelict buildings.

derelict buildings
[buildings that have not been repaired for many years]

I live in a suburb, but I can walk downtown.

a suburb
[an urban area that is outside the center of a town or city]

New York is one of the world's most cosmopolitan cities.

cosmopolitan
[containing people or cultures from around the world]

Dan found life in the city too **fast-paced**, so he moved to the countryside.

fast-paced
[active and full of energy]

Good **infrastructure**, such as roads and telecommunications, is essential for a modern city.

infrastructure [the basic services that a city needs to run well]

There is a huge **carnival** in Rio de Janeiro in the spring.

a carnival
[a festival that often involves people dancing in the street]

Greater **work opportunities** are one reason why people move to the city.

work opportunities
[the chances you have of finding a job]

Overcrowding on London's trains means it's often hard to find a seat.

overcrowding
[when there are too many people in one place]

The **road work** meant that it took me two hours to arrive at the office today.

road work (US) / roadworks (UK)
[repairs that are made to roads]

Moscow has a **lively nightlife**, with bars and nightclubs that stay open until dawn.

a lively nightlife
[nighttime entertainment such as bars, cafés, and nightclubs]

The **pollution** in my city can be terrible in the summer months.

pollution
[harmful substances in air or water]

The Eiffel Tower is the best-known **tourist attraction** in Paris.

a tourist attraction
[a place that attracts large numbers of tourists]

The pace of life is much faster in the city than in the countryside.

the pace of life
[how quickly people lead their lives]

Aa 75.2 FILL IN THE GAPS USING THE WORDS IN THE PANEL

The crime ___rate___ in most cities has been dropping in recent years.

1. There are lots of green ______________ in the city for people to relax in the summer.
2. There's a greater ______________ of cafés and restaurants in large cities.
3. Moscow has a ______________ nightlife, with bars and nightclubs that stay open until dawn.
4. The ______________ work meant that it took me two hours to arrive at the office today.
5. It's sometimes impossible to get on the bus during ______________ hour.
6. The ______________ in my city can be terrible in the summer months.

rush | pollution | choice | spaces | lively | road | ~~rate~~

Aa 75.3 MATCH THE PICTURES TO THE CORRECT SENTENCES

1 

2 

3 

Overcrowding on London's trains means it's often hard to find a seat.

Dan found life in the city too fast-paced, so he moved to the countryside.

Good infrastructure, such as roads and telecommunications, is essential for a modern city.

I offer guided tours of the city's historic buildings.

75.4 LISTEN TO THE AUDIO, THEN NUMBER THE SENTENCES IN THE ORDER YOU HEAR THEM

A  Moscow has a lively nightlife, with bars and nightclubs that stay open until dawn. ☐

B  I live in a suburb, but I can walk downtown. ☐

C  There is a huge carnival in Rio de Janeiro in the spring. ☐

D  The Eiffel Tower is the best-known tourist attraction in Paris. ☐

E  New York is one of the world's most cosmopolitan cities. [1]

75.5 FILL IN THE GAPS, PUTTING THE WORDS IN THE CORRECT ORDER

a | poor | in | town | of | many | with | part

I live *in a poor part of town with many* derelict buildings.

much | city | faster | of | is | in | the | pace | life

1. The ___ ___ ___ ___ ___ ___ ___ ___ ___ than in the countryside.

in | area | my | makes | vandalism

2. The ___ ___ ___ ___ ___ the buildings look very ugly.

avoid | to | way | to | jams | traffic | is

3. A good ___ ___ ___ ___ ___ ___ ___ travel by train.

took | work | it | me | that | meant | road

4. The ___ ___ ___ ___ ___ ___ ___ two hours to arrive at the office today.

76 Technology and gadgets

76.1 DIGITAL TECHNOLOGY

hands-free headset

keypad

charger

smartphone

plug

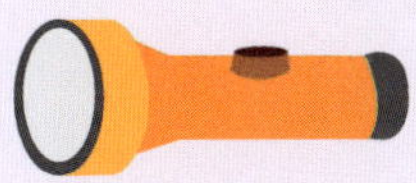

flashlight (US)
torch (UK)

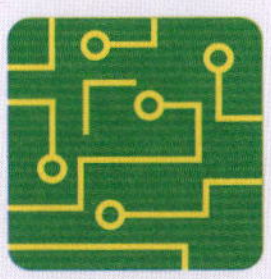

circuit

remote control

camcorder

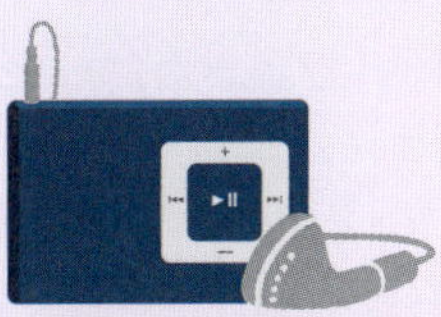

MP3 player

webcam

artificial intelligence

password

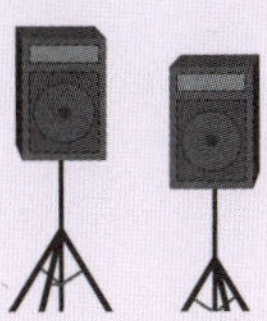

speakers

voice recorder

76.2 VERBS

to turn on

to turn off

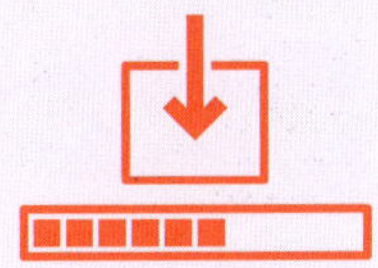

to download

to upload

to click

to log in

to log out

to back up

to plug in

to delete

Aa 76.3 WRITE THE CORRECT WORD UNDER EACH PICTURE

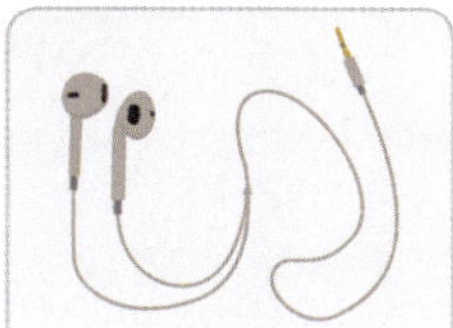

earphones

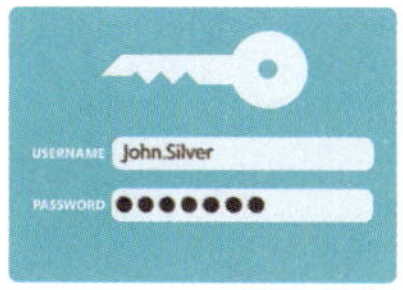

1 ______

2 ______

3 ______

4 ______

5 ______

6 ______

7 ______

8 ______

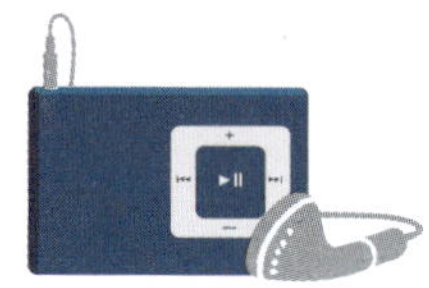

9 ______

10 ______

11 ______

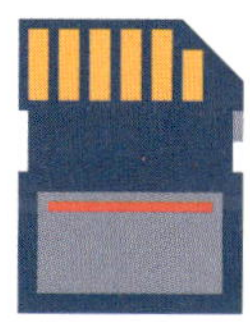

12 ______

13 ______

14 ______

Aa 76.4 MATCH THE VERBS TO THE CORRECT PICTURES

to plug in

1 to turn on

2 to click

3 to delete

4 to turn off

5 to back up

A 

B 

C 

D 

E 

76.5 LISTEN TO THE AUDIO AND WRITE THE WORD THAT IS SHOWN IN EACH PICTURE

camcorder

1  ______

2  ______

3  ______

4  ______

5  ______

6  ______

7  ______

8  ______

9  ______

10  ______

11  ______

12  ______

13  ______

76.6 LOOK AT THE PICTURE AND WRITE THE CORRECT WORD FOR EACH LABEL

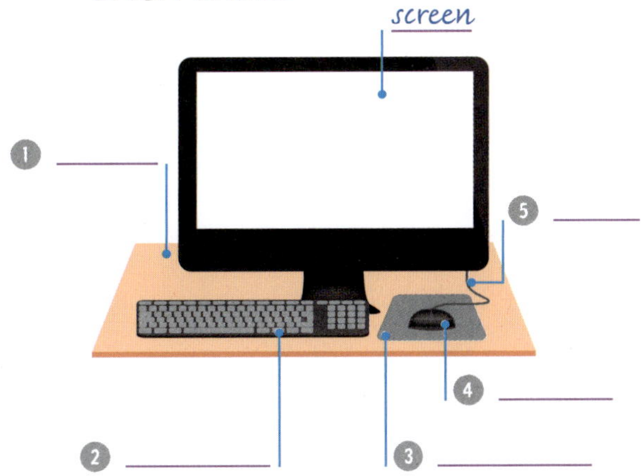

76.7 LOOK AT THE PICTURE CLUES AND WRITE THE ANSWERS IN THE CORRECT PLACES ON THE GRID

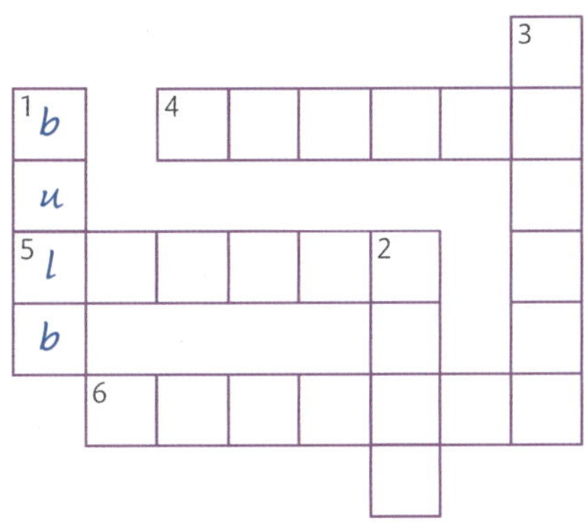

1 

2 

3 

4 

5 

6 

77 Technology and the future

77.1 USEFUL EXPRESSIONS

The internet has had an impact on how we communicate at work.

to have an impact on something
[to affect something powerfully]

Laila is making predictions about what will happen in the new year.

to make predictions
[to say what you think might happen in the future]

None of us can know exactly what the future holds.

what the future holds
[what will happen in the future]

The car was expensive, but it will save us money in the long run.

in the long run
[eventually, after a long time]

In this digital age, many people have a laptop and smartphone.

a digital age
[an era based on digital information, when technology is dominant]

Ruth's new product won an award for technical innovation.

innovation
[inventiveness or creation of new ideas]

The internet has caused a revolution in the way we learn.

a revolution
[a huge change in ideas or methods]

His cutting-edge designs have made millions of dollars.

cutting-edge
[extremely modern and innovative]

Higher prices could be the shape of things to come.

the shape of things to come
[the way things are likely to develop in the future]

I really want to buy the latest model of their smartphone.

the latest model
[the most recent version of a product]

The research scientists made an amazing breakthrough.

a breakthrough
[an important discovery or achievement]

You need to be computer literate to find a good job these days.

computer literate
[able to use computer technology effectively]

Our customers love our state-of-the-art kitchen equipment.

state-of-the-art
[very modern and up-to-date]

Seb's such a technophile. He has to have the latest phone.

a technophile
[a person who enjoys using new technology]

We must future-proof our designs or our sales will start to fall.

to future-proof
[to design something to work in the future, even if technology changes]

My uncle's a technophobe. He still uses a typewriter.

a technophobe
[a person who dislikes or refuses to use new technology]

It's only a matter of time before we sell one of these paintings.

only a matter of time
[sure to happen at some point in the future]

CDs and cassettes have become obsolete because of online streaming.

obsolete / out of date
[no longer needed or useful because of a new invention]

Only time will tell whether we will live on Mars one day.

only time will tell
[the results will only become clear in the future]

My new smartphone is light-years ahead of my old one.

light-years ahead
[much more advanced than its competitors]

Aa 77.2 CROSS OUT THE INCORRECT WORDS IN EACH SENTENCE

None of us can know exactly what the future ~~carries~~ / **holds** / ~~bears~~.

1.  The car was expensive, but it will save us money in the long **walk** / **time** / **run**.

2.  Higher prices could be the **shape** / **size** / **sound** of things to come.

3.  It's only a matter of **age** / **time** / **future** before we sell one of these paintings.

4.  Laila is **making** / **doing** / **taking** predictions about what will happen in the new year.

Aa 77.3 MATCH THE PICTURES TO THE CORRECT SENTENCES

1. 

2. 

3. 

4. 

My uncle's a technophobe. He still uses a typewriter.

The research scientists made an amazing breakthrough.

I really want to buy the latest model of their smartphone.

Seb's such a technophile. He has to have the latest phone.

The internet has caused a revolution in the way we learn.

77.4 FILL IN THE GAPS, PUTTING THE WORDS IN THE CORRECT ORDER

will | Only | tell | time

Only *time* *will* *tell* whether we will live on Mars one day.

be | to | literate | to | computer

1 You need ______ ______ ______ ______ ______ find a good job these days.

of | light-years | ahead | is

2 My new smartphone ______ ______ ______ ______ my old one.

obsolete | of | become | because

3 CDs and cassettes have ______ ______ ______ ______ online streaming.

age, | digital | many | this

4 In ______ ______ ______ ______ people have a laptop and smartphone.

breakthrough | made | amazing | an

5 The research scientists ______ ______ ______ ______ .

77.5 LISTEN TO THE AUDIO, THEN NUMBER THE SENTENCES IN THE ORDER YOU HEAR THEM

A  Ruth's new product won an award for technical innovation. ☐

B  We must future-proof our designs or our sales will start to fall. ☐

C  The internet has had an impact on how we communicate at work. ☐

D  His cutting-edge designs have made millions of dollars. ☐

E  Our customers love our state-of-the-art kitchen equipment. [1]

78 Science

78.1 SCIENCE AND SCIENTIFIC EQUIPMENT

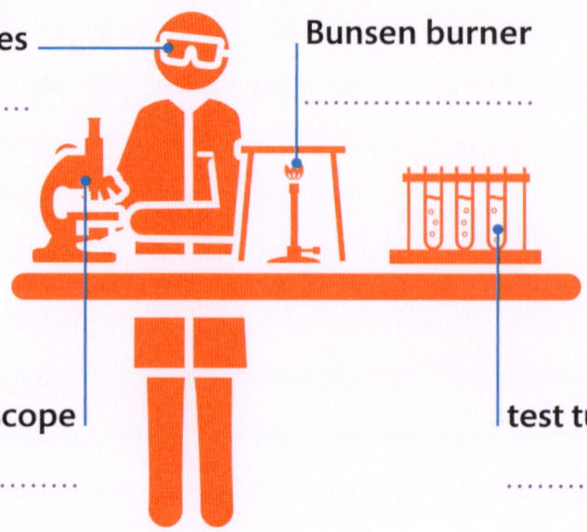

laboratory

biology

physics

chemistry

scientist

biologist

physicist

chemist

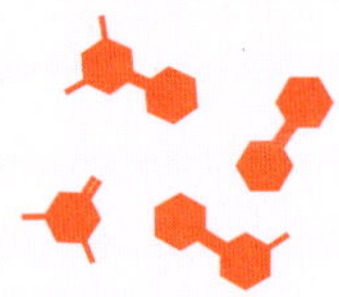

chemicals

magnet

solid

liquid

gas

steam

crystals

DNA

cloning

genetic engineering

cells

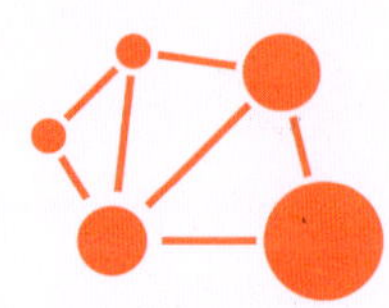

molecules

experiment

hypothesis

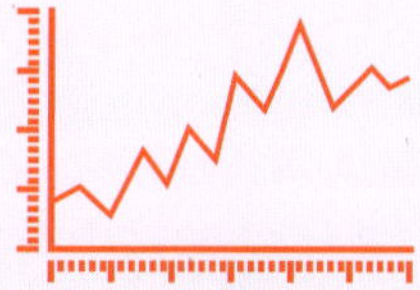
results

reaction

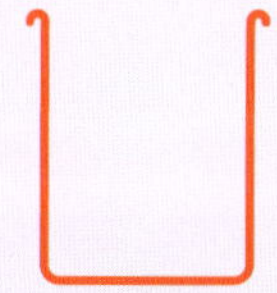
beaker

static electricity

electric shock

battery

pestle

mortar

78.2 VERBS

to record

to observe

to attract

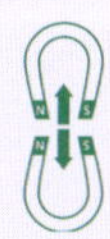
to repel

to pour

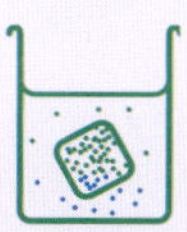
to dissolve

to heat

to burn

to boil

to evaporate

to cool

to freeze

to melt

to float

to sink

Aa 78.3 CIRCLE THE WORD THAT DOES NOT BELONG IN EACH LIST

	biology	(beaker)	physics
1	pestle	steam	mortar
2	to attract	to record	to repel
3	to observe	to freeze	to melt
4	chemist	crystals	physicist
5	liquid	solid	cloning
6	DNA	cells	battery
7	hypothesis	microscope	Bunsen burner

Aa 78.4 LOOK AT THE PICTURE AND WRITE THE CORRECT WORD FOR EACH LABEL

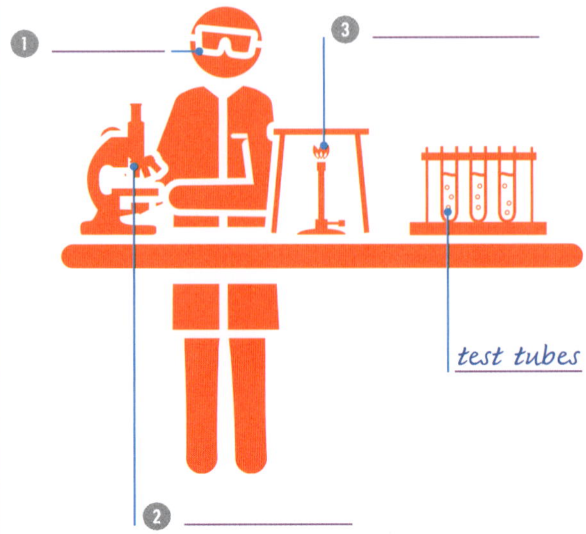

Aa 78.5 REWRITE THE WORDS, CORRECTING THE SPELLINGS

batery
battery

1 cristals ______

2 pessel ______

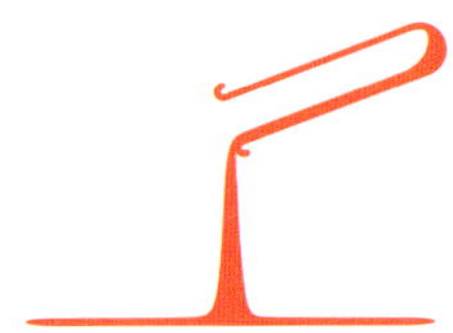
3 to poor ______

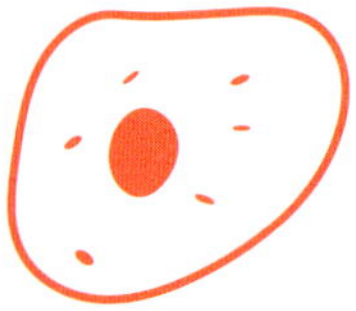
4 sells ______

5 phisycs ______

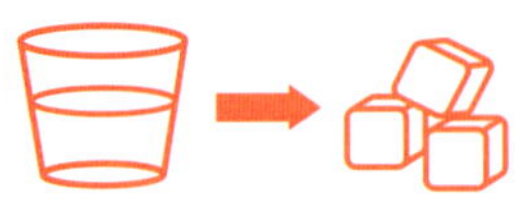
6 to frieze ______

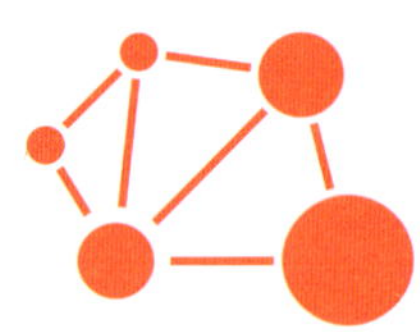
7 mollecules ______

Aa 78.6 MARK THE CORRECT WORD ILLUSTRATED IN EACH PICTURE

- [x] magnet
- [ ] steam
- [ ] cells

1
- [ ] to float
- [ ] to dissolve
- [ ] to boil

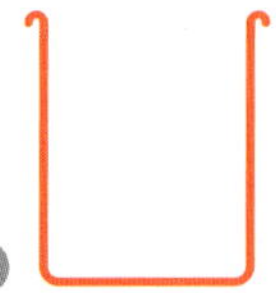

2
- [ ] beaker
- [ ] chemistry
- [ ] DNA

3
- [ ] chemicals
- [ ] cloning
- [ ] gas

4
- [ ] to record
- [ ] to observe
- [ ] to melt

5
- [ ] biology
- [ ] results
- [ ] electric shock

6
- [ ] to sink
- [ ] to burn
- [ ] to evaporate

7
- [ ] steam
- [ ] electric shock
- [ ] magnet

8
- [ ] scientist
- [ ] mortar
- [ ] reaction

9
- [ ] static electricity
- [ ] solid
- [ ] experiment

78.7 LISTEN TO THE AUDIO AND MARK THE CORRECT PICTURE FOR EACH WORD YOU HEAR

A [ ]

B [x]

C [ ]

3

A [ ]

B [ ]
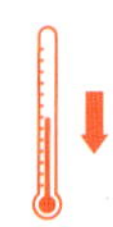
C [ ]

1

A [ ]

B [ ]

C [ ]

4

A [ ]

B [ ]

C [ ]

2

A [ ]

B [ ]

C [ ]

5

A [ ]

B [ ]

C [ ]

Answers

01

1.3
1. India
2. Germany
3. Mongolia
4. Egypt
5. Canada
6. Thailand
7. Slovakia
8. Russia
9. Japan

1.4
1. Indonesia
2. France
3. China
4. Pakistan
5. South Korea
6. Brazil
7. Singapore
8. Argentina

1.5
1. Indian
2. Turkish
3. Greece
4. Netherlands
5. Portuguese
6. German
7. Mongolian
8. China

1.6
COUNTRIES:
Russia, **United Kingdom / UK**, **Poland**, **Pakistan**, **Japan**
NATIONALITIES:
Russian, **British**, **Polish**, **Pakistani**, **Japanese**

1.7
1. Portugal
2. Greece
3. Philippines
4. Turkey
5. Spain
6. United States of America (US)
7. New Zealand
8. Republic of Ireland (ROI)
9. Poland

02

2.5
1. twelve
2. twenty
3. thirty
4. one hundred and ten
5. thirteen
6. one thousand, one hundred
7. seventeen
8. eight

2.6
1. a hundred
2. eighth
3. a thousand
4. forty
5. thirteen
6. twentieth
7. nineteen
8. ninety
9. twelfth
10. fifty

2.7
1 B 2 C 3 B 4 A 5 C 6 A

2.8
1. one thousand, two hundred
2. three hundred and forty-two
3. seven hundred and fifty
4. six point three
5. five hundred and forty-two
6. forty-five percent
7. three point nine five

2.9
1 a third 2 a half
3 a quarter 4 two thirds

03

3.3
1 Tuesday 2 decade
3 November 4 week
5 August 6 year

3.4
1 October 2 hour 3 Friday
4 millennium 5 winter 6 century
7 minute 8 hourly 9 often

3.5
1. spring
2. decade
3. day
4. Friday
5. April
6. never

3.6
1 A 2 A 3 B 4 C 5 A 6 C 7 B

3.7
1. weekly
2. September
3. afternoon
4. hourly
5. sometimes
6. every day
7. usually
8. twice a week

04

4.2
1 B 2 C 3 C 4 A 5 B

4.3
1. to wash the dishes
2. to arrive late
3. to wash your face
4. to put the children to bed
5. to do the housework

4.4
1. to check your emails
2. to iron a shirt
3. to walk the dog
4. to go to bed
5. to brush your teeth
6. to make the bed
7. to take / have a shower
8. to wake up
9. to finish work
10. to catch the train
11. to shave
12. to have / eat dinner
13. to start work
14. to dry your hair

4.5
A 11 B 12 C 2 D 7 E 4 F 9
G 1 H 8 I 6 J 3 K 10 L 5

05

5.4
1. brown
2. cream
3. orange
4. yellow
5. purple

6 blue
7 green

5.5
1 wool
2 silk
3 glass
4 fabric

5.6
1 near
2 clean
3 loose
4 high
5 light
6 short

5.7
1 C 2 A 3 A 4 B 5 B

5.8
A 5 B 1 C 3 D 2 E 8 F 4
G 6 H 7

06

6.4
POSITIVE:
fantastic, **breathtaking**, **incredible**, **fun**, **amazing**, **exciting**
NEGATIVE:
awful, **disastrous**, **annoying**, **nasty**, **disgusting**, **terrible**

6.5
1 magnificent
2 wonderful
3 disappointing
4 outstanding
5 respectable
6 delicious
7 special
8 pretty

6.6
1 irritating
2 thrilling
3 frightening
4 graceful
5 old-fashioned

6.7
1 tiring 2 unpleasant 3 boring
4 important 5 harmless 6 relaxing

6.8
1 ugly
2 stunning
3 useless
4 beautiful
5 respectable

07

7.5
1 title
2 middle name
3 last name
4 street address
5 cell phone number (US) / phone number (UK)
6 email address
7 city

7.6
1 name 2 job title
3 company name 4 business card

7.7
1 to send
2 to print
3 to forward
4 to reply
5 inbox
6 to reply all
7 signature
8 attachment
9 subject

7.8
1 trash
2 spam
3 memo
4 mail
5 state
6 contact
7 outbox
8 website
9 draft
10 phone call
11 title

7.9
1 text message 2 phone call 3 note
4 letter 5 email 6 online chat

08

8.2
1 Tamsin got cold feet about giving a presentation to the sales team.
2 I'm so tired today! I'm really not on the ball.
3 Susan is feeling under the weather today. I think she should go home.
4 I have to face the music and tell Julia that I broke her new vase.

8.3
1 I didn't mean to offend Luisa, but I think her reaction was over the top.
2 Hamid is working against the clock to finish his report this week.
3 Leo has a heart of gold. He always helps his grandma with her shopping.
4 I don't know who to vote for yet. I'm still on the fence.
5 You two really let your hair down at Sunita's party last night.

8.4
1 You're so right about Jim. He's really lazy! **You've hit the nail on the** head.
2 I'm planning a surprise party for Joe. Don't **let the cat out of** the bag.
3 You can't believe all her stories. **Take them with a pinch of** salt.
4 If **you cut corners to** finish a project on time, the quality will suffer.

8.5
A 2 B 1 C 4 D 3 E 5

09

9.2
1 bedroom
2 light
3 table
4 rug
5 shower
6 dresser (US) / chest of drawers (UK)
7 trash can (US) / bin (UK)
8 window

9.3
1 cabinet
2 bed
3 table
4 roof
5 kitchen
6 sink
7 lamp
8 living room

9.4
1 upstairs 2 downstairs
3 basement 4 stairs
5 yard (US) / garden (UK)

9.5
A 6 B 1 C 5 D 7 E 4
F 3 G 9 H 2 I 10 J 8

9.6

KITCHEN:
dishwasher, **refrigerator / fridge**, **stove (US) / cooker (UK)**, **cabinet (US) / cupboard (UK)**

BATHROOM:
bathtub (US) / bath (UK), **toilet**, **sink**, **shower**

LIVING ROOM:
armchair, **cushion**, **couch (US) / sofa (UK)**, **television / TV**

BEDROOM:
bed, **bedside table**, **lamp**, **wardrobe**

10

10.3

KITCHEN:
whisk, **knife**, **frying pan**, **bowl**, **plate**, **cup**

BATHROOM:
mouthwash, **conditioner**, **sponge**, **shampoo**, **soap**, **toothbrush**

10.4

1 shaving foam 2 spatula
3 microwave 4 toothpaste
5 peeler 6 moisturizer
7 dental floss 8 colander

10.5

1 toaster 2 scissors
3 corkscrew 4 blender
5 spatula 6 grater
7 wok 8 mug
9 can opener (US) / tin opener (UK)

10.6

1 C 2 A 3 C 4 A 5 B 6 A 7 C

11

11.3

1 cloth
2 bucket
3 dustpan
4 mop
5 brush
6 duster
7 scouring pad
8 polish

11.4

1 laundry detergent
2 sponge
3 recycling bin
4 to scrub the floor
5 to clear the table
6 bleach
7 to load the dishwasher

11.5

1 C 2 A 3 D 4 B
5 G 6 H 7 F 8 E

11.6

1 washing machine
2 to fold clothes
3 tumble dryer
4 to set the table
5 to mop the floor

11.7

1 clothes line 2 rubber gloves
3 bucket 4 iron

12

12.5

1 to plant bulbs
2 to put up shelves
3 to mow the lawn
4 to water the flowers
5 to paint a room
6 to plaster the walls
7 to trim a hedge

12.6

1 wrench (US) / spanner (UK)
2 shears 3 nail 4 vise (US) / vice (UK)
5 fork 6 tool box 7 saw

12.7

TOOLS:
paintbrush, **hammer**, **hacksaw**, **plane**, **file**, **jigsaw**

GARDENING EQUIPMENT:
hoe, **rake**, **sprinkler**, **hose**, **wheelbarrow**, **trowel**

12.8

1 C 2 B 3 B

13

13.3

1 keys 2 boxes 3 landlord
4 cottage 5 storage 6 rent

13.4

A 12 B 11 C 1 D 9 E 4 F 3
G 6 H 2 I 5 J 8 K 10 L 7

13.5

1 unfurnished
2 landlord
3 tenant
4 apartments
5 storage

13.6

1 real estate (US) / property (UK)
2 a residential area
3 local
4 a deposit
5 including utilities

13.7

1 We had a **house-warming** party to celebrate buying our new apartment.
2 We have a **roomer** who lives in our spare bedroom.
3 My **roommate** never does the dishes.
4 We **gave** notice to our landlord two months before moving out.
5 We live in an attractive **residential** area with lots of parks.

14

14.3

1 head 2 chin 3 chest 4 finger
5 shin 6 toe 7 neck 8 shoulder
9 waist 10 hip 11 thigh 12 knee 13 foot

14.4

eyelashes, teeth, nose, mouth, eyebrow, nostrils, ear, ankle, lips, forehead, thigh, finger, stomach, chin, hip

14.5

1 to wave
2 to shiver
3 to shrug
4 to cry
5 to breathe
6 to lick
7 to yawn
8 to sigh
9 to nod

14.6

1 B 2 C 3 B 4 A 5 A

15

15.4

1 jacket
2 sweater (US) / jumper (UK)
3 blouse

4 pants (US) / trousers (UK)
5 skirt
6 t-shirt
7 boxer shorts
8 dress
9 uniform

15.5
1 cuff 2 sleeve 3 button

15.6
1 bathrobe 2 coat 3 raincoat
4 shorts 5 socks 6 tie
7 denim 8 suit 9 leather
10 bra 11 t-shirt

15.7
A 10 B 8 C 9 D 1 E 5
F 7 G 2 H 4 I 6 J 3

15.8
1 striped 2 plain
3 polka dot 4 leather
5 denim 6 cotton
7 silk 8 woolen

16

16.4
1 handkerchief
2 sandals
3 backpack
4 scarf
5 wallet

16.5
1 shoes
2 belt
3 hair band
4 eyeliner
5 handkerchief
6 scarf
7 umbrella

16.6
A 3 B 6 C 2 D 1 E 4
F 5 G 8 H 10 I 9 J 7

16.7
1 nail polish 2 bow tie
3 high heels 4 lipstick
5 flip-flops 6 ring
7 purse (US) / handbag (UK) 8 hat

16.8
1 brooch 2 earrings
3 umbrella 4 comb
5 perfume 6 sunglasses
7 necklace

17

17.5
1 D 2 A 3 F 4 H 5 B
6 I 7 C 8 G 9 E

17.6
1 brown hair
2 to style your hair
3 middle-aged
4 facial hair
5 to shave
6 curly hair
7 blond hair
8 sideburns
9 to have / get your hair cut

17.7
1 short hair
2 fair skin
3 beard
4 frizzy hair
5 red hair
6 to grow your hair
7 bald
8 to style your hair
9 glamorous
10 straight hair
11 black hair

17.8
1 C 2 B 3 B 4 A 5 B

18

18.2
1 assertive 2 rude
3 impatient 4 unreliable
5 lazy 6 considerate
7 talented 8 approachable
9 insensitive

18.3
1 optimistic 2 brave
3 arrogant 4 laid-back
5 assertive 6 insensitive

18.4
1 caring
2 mean
3 eccentric
4 assertive
5 talented
6 passionate
7 calm
8 unapproachable
9 generous

18.5
1 B 2 A 3 B
4 A 5 B 6 C

18.6
1 secretive
2 passionate
3 calm
4 mean
5 shy
6 critical
7 silly
8 impatient
9 reliable

19

19.2
1 jealous
2 calm
3 disgusted
4 surprised
5 frightened
6 serious
7 delighted
8 exhausted
9 amused
10 irritated
11 cheerful
12 nervous
13 grateful
14 angry / mad (US)
15 unenthusiastic
16 curious
17 proud
18 worried
19 disappointed

19.3
delighted, annoyed, grateful, embarrassed, ecstatic, worried, curious, unenthusiastic, jealous, confused

19.4
1 disgusted 2 grateful
3 amazed 4 scared
5 interested 6 disappointed
7 depressed 8 annoyed
9 bored 10 proud
11 relaxed 12 miserable

19.5
1 happy
2 interested
3 nervous
4 calm
5 miserable
6 proud
7 amused

19.6
A 11 B 1 C 7 D 5 E 14
F 2 G 12 H 16 I 8 J 4
K 15 L 6 M 9 N 3 O 10 P 13

20

20.8
1 grandfather
2 grandparents
3 mother / mom (US) / mum (UK)
4 aunt
5 sister-in-law
6 wife
7 cousin
8 son
9 children
10 granddaughter
11 grandson
12 grandchildren

20.9
1 adults
2 girl
3 triplets
4 baby
5 male

20.10
1 widower 2 grandmother
3 boyfriend and girlfriend
4 twins 5 grandfather

20.11
1 father / dad
2 stepsister
3 stepbrother

20.12
1 female
2 partner
3 nephew
4 daughter
5 husband
6 widow
7 girlfriend

21

21.2
1 I love playing with my grandson. I think the world of him.
2 My siblings are always falling out with each other.
3 We often bump into Mary at the local store.
4 We see eye to eye about most important issues.

21.3
1 Caroline **looks** up to her eldest brother.
2 Sadie takes **after** her mother. They are both very kind.
3 My cousin **gave** birth to a baby boy last year.
4 I stick **up** for my friends if people are mean to them.
5 I **made** friends with Miguel after he moved to my town.

21.4
A 6 B 3 C 2 D 5 E 1 F 4

21.5
1 Jo **gets along with** her boss.
2 We've been **close friends** since we shared an apartment.
3 I love playing with my grandson. I **think the world of** him.
4 We **broke up** because I didn't love him any more.
5 My siblings are always **falling out with** each other.

22

22.3
1 B 2 A 3 D
4 E 5 F 6 C

22.4
A 14 B 7 C 6 D 1 E 8 F 13
G 2 H 5 I 3 J 15 K 4 L 9
M 10 N 16 O 12 P 11

22.5
booties, nursery, toy, sandbox, swings, train set, doll, marbles, bottle, kite, puppet, changing table, rattle

22.6
EQUIPMENT:
baby monitor, **bottle**, **bib**, **potty**, **high chair**, **wet wipe**
TOYS:
spinning top, **puppet**, **building blocks**, **playing cards** **kite**, **slide**

22.7
1 snowsuit
2 rattle
3 doll
4 diaper
5 marbles
6 toy
7 mobile
8 high chair

23

23.4
1 C 2 A 3 A 4 B 5 C

23.5
1 to fail
2 classroom
3 law
4 medicine
5 degree

23.6
1 art
2 business studies
3 professor
4 exercise book
5 physics
6 history
7 school
8 drama
9 biology
10 laboratory
11 to study a subject
12 lecture
13 exam

23.7
1 math (US) / maths (UK)
2 college (US) / university (UK)
3 architecture
4 essay
5 teacher
6 student
7 music
8 psychology
9 geography

24

24.2
1 Rowena is taking a year off before she starts college.
2 Practicing for her class presentation made a world of difference.
3 I expect my students to attend classes every week.
4 Their views on teaching a class are polar opposites.
5 Chris passed his final college exams with flying colors.

24.3
1 When Gavin was a **freshman**, he was very nervous about starting college.
2 There is a **clear distinction** between these two experiments.

3 Emma **took her driving test** last week, and she passed.
4 It's important to give students **regular feedback** on their work.
5 Amira is studying for a **graduate degree** in chemistry.
6 Boris almost **missed the deadline** for his research project.

24.4
1 an undergraduate
2 a first draft
3 a freshman (US) / fresher (UK)
4 continuous assessment
5 to pass with flying colors

24.5
1 I like **continuous assessment** more than just taking final exams.
2 I've finished the **first draft** of my essay, but I'm sure that I'll have to make lots of changes to it.
3 Matt **enrolled in** a computer science course last month.
4 I'd like you to **compare and contrast** these two pictures.
5 Many **undergraduates** live in a dormitory in their first year of college.

25

25.2
1 After only a few weeks living in Italy, I was able to **make** myself understood.
2 I have a good **ear** for languages. I learned Swahili in six months.
3 The language **barrier** stopped me from talking to Wen.
4 My uncle is fluent **in** five different languages.
5 I speak **conversational** German, but my grammar is awful.
6 Juan finds the **pronunciation** of the word "squirrel" impossible.

25.3
1 an accent
2 bilingual
3 a native speaker
4 speaking
5 to speak accurately
6 vocabulary
7 fluent in

25.4
1 I was taught French **by a native speaker from** Marseilles.
2 English **acts as a lingua franca for** the people at the conference.
3 I understand some Hebrew, **but find the writing** impossible.
4 Although Pedro has **a strong accent, he does speak** accurately.

25.5
A 2 B 6 C 3 D 5 E 1 F 4

26

26.2
1 Do you **really believe in ghosts**?
2 I really enjoy **reading fairy tales to my** grandchildren.
3 We **have a sneaking suspicion that** Tim won't come to the party with us.
4 Farah **started a rumor** that Kerry stole a car.

26.3
1 Tara is **dropping** a hint that she would like new shoes for her birthday.
2 Jenna told a **white** lie and said she liked Barry's new suit.
3 I've never played this game, so I'm hoping for **beginner's** luck.
4 He has a very old-fashioned **set** of beliefs.

26.4
1 to make a wish
2 pure luck
3 an urban myth
4 folklore
5 to gossip

26.5
1 I often find out about new products **by word of mouth**.
2 Anyone can win this game. It's a game of **pure luck**.
3 You shouldn't be a **tattletale** at school.
4 To some people, a black cat is a **good omen**; to others, a **bad omen**.
5 Martin loves **to gossip** about other people's relationships.

27

27.4
1 shoplifting
2 hacking
3 burglary
4 fine
5 smuggling

27.5
1 law court 2 judge 3 trial

27.6
1 B 2 C 3 A 4 A 5 B

27.7
1 The recent crime wave in my home town is very worrying.
2 The jury found Colin guilty of car theft.
3 The burglar wouldn't admit he had committed a crime.
4 After discussing all the evidence, the jury reached a verdict.
5 It's a police officer's job to enforce the law.

27.8
1 The police officer **arrested** Tina for shoplifting.
2 It's a police officer's job to **enforce** the law.
3 **Street crime**, such as mugging, can be a problem in our cities.
4 Paul was **sentenced** to 100 hours of community service.
5 André is trained to deal with **white-collar crime**, such as fraud.

28

28.5
MEAT:
sausages, **chicken**,
lamb, **ham**
SEAFOOD:
sardines, **salmon**,
lobster, **sushi**
DAIRY:
milk, **fried egg**,
butter, **cheese**
FAST FOOD:
hot dog, **fries (US) / chips (UK)**,
pizza, **kebab**

28.6
1 cream 2 soup 3 bacon
4 beef 5 mackerel

28.7
1 soup
2 scrambled eggs
3 salad
4 wrap
5 chips (US) / crisps (UK)
6 scallops
7 cottage cheese
8 burger

28.8
A 5 B 8 C 1 D 4
E 9 F 7 G 10
H 2 I 3 J 6

29

29.3
1 apricot
2 kiwi fruit
3 banana
4 cherries
5 grapes
6 coconut
7 papaya
8 lemon
9 pear
10 pomegranate
11 blackberries
12 gooseberries
13 starfruit
14 watermelon

29.4
1 peanut
2 pistachio
3 walnut
4 hazelnut
5 raisin
6 golden raisin (US) / sultana (UK)
7 currant
8 fig
9 date

29.5
1 fries
2 quince
3 salmon
4 pistachio
5 yolk
6 soup
7 lamb
8 pizza

29.6
A 7 B 2 C 3 D 8 E 1
F 5 G 9 H 6 I 4

29.7
1 watermelon
2 mango
3 walnut
4 papaya
5 pear
6 passion fruit

30

30.2
1 butternut squash
2 lettuce
3 cauliflower
4 garlic
5 beans
6 sweetcorn / corn
7 avocados
8 eggplants (US) / aubergines (UK)
9 carrots
10 onions
11 zucchini (US) / courgettes (UK)
12 peppers
13 asparagus
14 broccoli

30.3
1 artichokes
2 spinach
3 mushrooms
4 cauliflower
5 cucumbers
6 eggplants
7 asparagus
8 sweetcorn

30.4
1 B 2 A 3 B 4 C 5 A

30.5
1 cabbage
2 tomatoes
3 leeks
4 cucumbers
5 butternut squash
6 mushrooms
7 spinach
8 artichokes
9 sweet potatoes

31

31.3
1 C 2 C 3 A 4 B 5 B

31.4
1 flour
2 noodles
3 dumplings
4 pancakes
5 chocolate

31.5
1 oil
2 mint
3 soy sauce
4 ketchup
5 pepper
6 jam
7 peanut butter
8 basil
9 spices
10 chutney
11 honey
12 toast
13 pancakes
14 mustard
15 parsley
16 noodles
17 salt

31.6
1 marmalade
2 spaghetti
3 roll
4 mayonnaise
5 cupcake
6 chili flakes (US) / chilli flakes (UK)
7 meringue

32

32.5
1 C 2 E 3 A 4 B 5 G
6 D 7 F 8 I 9 H

32.6
1 strong
2 gone off
3 sour
4 fresh
5 iced
6 sweet
7 tasty
8 delicious
9 savory
10 bitter
11 disgusting
12 spicy

32.7
1 B 2 A 3 C 4 A 5 C
6 A 7 B

32.8
1 to gulp
2 to drink
3 to taste
4 to bite
5 to eat
6 to dine
7 to chew
8 to nibble
9 to swallow

33

33.5
1 to whisk
2 to roast

3. to simmer
4. to mash
5. to grate
6. to bake
7. to fry
8. to peel
9. to cut

33.6
1. tip
2. lunch
3. menu
4. breakfast
5. dinner
6. buffet

33.7
1. napkin
2. dessert / pudding (UK)
3. appetizer (US) / starter (UK)
4. check (US) / bill (UK)
5. restaurant
6. waitress
7. snack
8. café
9. chef
10. to slice
11. entrée (US) / main course (UK)
12. to stir
13. food stall
14. buffet

33.8
A 7 B 12 C 1 D 14 E 6
F 4 G 11 H 8 I 2 J 13
K 10 L 9 M 3 N 15 O 5

34

34.2
1. writer
2. mechanic
3. librarian
4. pilot
5. dentist
6. actor
7. plumber
8. scientist
9. tour guide
10. lawyer
11. sales assistant
12. waitress
13. fashion designer
14. gardener

34.3
psychologist, judge, driver, photographer, paramedic, businessman, journalist, engineer, scientist

34.4
1 B 2 D 3 A 4 E 5 C

34.5
1. lawyer
2. teacher
3. scientist
4. artist
5. train driver
6. butcher
7. librarian
8. mechanic
9. chef
10. psychologist
11. designer
12. architect

34.6
1. judge
2. businessman
3. dentist
4. scientist
5. waiter
6. nurse
7. teacher
8. actor
9. plumber
10. farmer
11. train driver

35

35.4
1. assistant
2. manager
3. employee
4. intern
5. staff
6. client
7. apprentice

35.5
1. to call in sick
2. to work from home
3. to work full-time
4. to earn
5. to have a day off
6. to work shifts
7. to get fired
8. to go on maternity leave
9. to work part-time

35.6
1. The store pays its staff an **hourly rate** of $15.
2. We will pay **overtime** to all staff who are willing to work weekends.
3. I'm looking for a job with a **salary** of at least $25,000.
4. **Benefits** include gym membership and health insurance.
5. My **bonus** this year was $1,000, so I'm going to go on vacation.
6. I had to find a new job last year because I **was laid off**.
7. I got a **promotion** after working for the company for only six months.

35.7
1. benefits
2. wages
3. a pay cut
4. a raise
5. an hourly rate

36

36.3
1 C 2 A 3 B 4 G 5 H 6 E
7 D 8 I 9 F

36.4
1. healthcare
2. agriculture
3. finance
4. shipping
5. energy
6. advertising
7. journalism
8. tourism
9. aerospace

36.5
A 3 B 2 C 9 D 8
E 4 F 1 G 6 H 10
I 7 J 11 K 12 L 5

36.6
1. Human Resources (HR)
2. Accounts / Finance
3. Legal
4. Administration
5. Public Relations (PR)
6. Sales
7. Marketing

37

37.4
1. trays
2. desk
3. bulletin board (US) / notice board (UK)
4. water cooler
5. trash can (US) / bin (UK)
6. filing cabinet
7. chair

37.5
1 laptop
2 envelope
3 stapler
4 paper
5 printer
6 pencil

37.6
1 B 2 A 3 C
4 A 5 B 6 A

37.7
1 calendar
2 scissors
3 photocopier
4 rubber bands
5 clipboard
6 laptop
7 shredder
8 paper clips
9 scanner
10 highlighter
11 envelope
12 hole punch

38

38.3
1 currency
2 cash machine
3 bank loan
4 check
5 stock exchange
6 bank statement
7 interest rate
8 mobile banking
9 PIN
10 credit card
11 wallet
12 mortgage
13 cash register
14 coins

38.4
mortgage
cash machine
invoice
wallet
coins
bank
receipt
check
mobile banking
stock exchange

38.5
1 The store has gone out of business because most people download movies now.
2 The bank charges $10 per month for overdrafts.
3 The exchange rate has made trips to some countries more expensive.
4 If we can't sell more products, we will get into debt.
5 Our income fell after we lost an important client.

38.6
1 B 2 A 3 A
4 B 5 A

39

39.2
1 to get ahead
2 to take off
3 to take someone on
4 give and take
5 to step down

39.3
1 All our employees are fully trained and have **hands-on experience**.
2 Gavin **was fired** because he was caught stealing from the warehouse.
3 Bruno's career **took off** after he won an important new client.
4 People who work in childcare **have their hands full** all day.
5 We've **set our sights on** winning more industry awards.
6 I need to **tackle this problem head-on** or it will get worse.
7 Working well with clients involves a lot of **give and take**.

39.4
1 My boss started working here **at the bottom of the career** ladder.
2 Lucas has been **stuck in a dead-end job** for two years.
3 I don't work **a nine-to-five job** because I have two young children.
4 I'm **stepping down from this job** because I need more training.

39.5
1 Elena's chosen career **path** involves a lot of travel.
2 Can I call you back later? I'm **snowed** under right now.
3 Clive always goes the extra **mile** to deliver our products on time.
4 Some of the factory workers were laid **off** after our profits fell.

40

40.2
1 We easily reached a consensus on the best poster design.
2 Stefan is on vacation and will be absent from this meeting.
3 I'm sorry to interrupt, but your client is waiting in reception.
4 Our poor sales figures will be on the agenda today.

40.3
A 3 B 4 C 1 D 5 E 2

40.4
1 on the agenda
2 to sum up
3 to attend a meeting
4 the main objective
5 to reach a consensus
6 absent
7 to run out of time
8 to give a presentation
9 action points

40.5
1 To sum up, sales of our older products have fallen this year.
2 Stefan is on vacation and will be absent from this meeting.
3 I'll talk through the report and then I'll take questions.
4 Our poor sales figures will be on the agenda today.
5 Let's wrap up this meeting. It's almost one o'clock.

41

41.3
1 This is a difficult job. Make sure you **do everything by the book**.
2 Great! We're all **on the same page** about this marketing campaign.
3 This client will never be satisfied because he keeps **moving the goalposts**.
4 Health and safety in the warehouse involves a lot of **red tape**.

41.4
1 Could I touch base with you for a quick update on this project?
2 Rohit clinched the deal after offering the clients a discount.
3 We're losing money, so we need a game plan for increasing sales.

4 We don't know the exact costs, but here's a ballpark figure.

41.5

1 We expected a change of pace **after we received several large orders**.
2 This product will never sell. We're **throwing money down the drain**.
3 This client will never be satisfied because **he keeps moving the goalposts**.
4 They've cornered the **market with their new range of shoes**.
5 This is a difficult job. Make **sure you do everything by the book**.

41.6

A 2 B 6
C 1 D 7
E 4 F 5
G 3 H 8

42

42.4

1 Professional achievements
2 Career summary
3 Education
4 Key skills
5 Interests
6 References

42.5

1 recruitment agency
2 job ad (US) / advert (UK)
3 cover letter (US) / covering letter (UK)
4 portfolio

42.6

1 to manage
2 to have an interview
3 to negotiate
4 to organize
5 to supervise
6 to apply for a job
7 to collaborate
8 to fill out a form
9 to coordinate

42.7

1 I am **responsible for** six other staff members.
2 I have an **in-depth knowledge** of hair-coloring techniques.
3 I have a **proven track record** in the catering industry.
4 As an ex-car salesman, I have a **service-oriented** background.
5 I am **proficient in** all major types of accounting software.

43

43.3

1 determined
2 organization
3 public speaking
4 numeracy
5 flexible
6 competitive
7 practical
8 responsible
9 teamwork
10 research
11 punctual
12 initiative
13 fast learner
14 negotiating

43.4

professional, reliable, hardworking, responsible, administration, motivated, research, organized, calm

43.5

1 fluent in languages
2 attention to detail
3 time management
4 customer-focused
5 problem-solving

43.6

1 confident
2 patient
3 honest
4 research
5 innovative
6 ambitious
7 efficient
8 fast learner
9 organization
10 competitive
11 decision-making

43.7

1 ambitious 2 team player 3 energetic
4 interpersonal skills 5 efficient

44

44.4

1 B 2 C 3 D
4 A 5 F 6 H
7 E 8 I 9 G

44.5

1 passengers
2 platform
3 bicycle
4 pedestrian
5 commuters
6 coach
7 yacht
8 moped
9 van

44.6

1 train
2 helicopter
3 boat
4 ferry
5 camel
6 yacht
7 horse
8 taxi
9 van

44.7

A 4 B 10 C 1 D 11 E 6
F 9 G 3 H 15 I 2 J 14
K 8 L 13 M 5 N 12 O 7

45

45.3

1 seatbelt
2 car wash
3 fuel
4 to check the tires (US) / tyres (UK)
5 to brake
6 speed camera
7 wipers
8 to slow down
9 pedestrian crossing
10 steering wheel
11 to check the oil
12 traffic jam
13 parking ticket
14 to signal (US) / to indicate (UK)

45.4

1 trunk
2 diesel
3 mechanic
4 gasoline
5 traffic jam
6 headlight
7 steering wheel
8 parking attendant

45.5

1 hood (US) / bonnet (UK)
2 trunk (US) / boot (UK)
3 tire (US) / tyre (UK)
4 wheel

45.6
1. parking lot
2. flat tire
3. car wash
4. wipers
5. to slow down
6. insurance
7. speed limit
8. oil

45.7
1. traffic lights
2. parking lot
3. to pass
4. wheel clamp
5. road sign
6. to set off
7. speed limit

46

46.4
1. north
2. northeast
3. east
4. southeast
5. south
6. southwest
7. west

46.5
1. turn
2. block
3. mile
4. distance
5. footpath

46.6
1. street
2. roadmap (US) / streetmap (UK)
3. key
4. shoulder (US) / hard shoulder (UK)
5. yard
6. intersection (US) / crossroads (UK)
7. sidewalk (US) / pavement (UK)
8. one-way street
9. avenue

46.7
1. to go / turn left
2. to go / turn right
3. to take the second right
4. to take the first left
5. to stop at (the hotel)
6. to go straight ahead (US) / on (UK)
7. to ask directions

46.8
1 A 2 B 3 A 4 C 5 B

47

47.5
1. to make a reservation
2. to check in
3. to check out
4. to stay in a hotel

47.6
1. room service
2. passport
3. apartment
4. luggage
5. boarding pass
6. laundry service
7. passport control
8. en-suite bathroom (UK)
9. cabin
10. window seat
11. to go abroad
12. all-inclusive
13. double room
14. hostel

47.7
A 4 B 1 C 5 D 2 E 9 F 3
G 6 H 8 I 7 J 11 K 10 L 12

47.8
1. direct flight
2. to book a vacation
3. dorm
4. walking vacation
5. safe
6. one-way ticket
7. single room

48

48.2
1. We like to stay in places that are off **the beaten path**.
2. Zoe is really looking forward **to visiting the pyramids**.
3. We got hopelessly **lost when we tried to drive into Tokyo**.
4. The palace is such a tourist **trap in the summer**.
5. We're checking out **the zoo that you recommended**.
6. I love to get away **from it all when I'm on vacation**.
7. I'm taking Clara to look **around the park today**.
8. I save lots of money on train tickets **by booking in advance**.

48.3
1. I don't like going abroad because I **feel homesick**.
2. I save lots of money on train tickets by **booking in advance**.
3. We got **hopelessly lost** when we tried to drive into Tokyo.
4. We like to stay in places that are **off the beaten path**.

48.4
1. Brendan loves sports and has a real thirst for adventure.
2. I like to travel out of season, when it's nice and quiet.
3. This place is so different from home. It's such a culture shock.
4. Let's stop off at the gallery before we check into our hotel.
5. Dan's parents came to the airport to see him off.

48.5
1. This hotel looks very **run-down**. Let's stay somewhere else.
2. I don't like going abroad because I feel **homesick**.
3. I save lots of money on train tickets by **booking in advance**.
4. I love to **get away** from it all when I'm on vacation.
5. We don't need another suitcase. It's just a weekend **getaway**.

49

49.3
1. saddle
2. handlebar
3. pedal
4. frame

49.4
1. cycle pump
2. reflector
3. basket
4. bicycle lane

49.5
1. gear
2. hot drink container (US) / flask (UK)
3. campsite
4. tent
5. walking boots
6. pothole
7. camping stove
8. backpack / rucksack (UK)
9. lock

49.6
1 shower block
2 racing bike
3 unicycle
4 waterproofs
5 bike rack
6 tandem
7 campfire
8 caravan
9 tent
10 bicycle lane
11 barbecue
12 brakes

49.7
A 3 B 6 C 1 D 18 E 2
F 10 G 7 H 4 I 5 J 11
K 16 L 8 M 13 N 9 O 17
P 12 Q 15 R 14

50

50.2
1 surfing
2 picnic basket
3 beach ball
4 wet suit
5 wave
6 sunscreen (US) / sun cream (UK)
7 snorkel and mask
8 life preserver (US) / life ring (UK)
9 kite
10 towel
11 flip-flops
12 jet ski
13 shell
14 sunbathing

50.3
1 wet suit
2 swimsuit
3 swimming trunks
4 sandcastle
5 kite
6 bodyboarding
7 life preserver
8 jet ski

50.4
1 bodyboarding 2 windbreak
3 windsurfing 4 sea 5 crab
6 deck chair 7 flippers
8 picnic blanket 9 sandcastle

50.5
1 B 2 A
3 C 4 A
5 B 6 A

51

51.4
1 cool
2 stifling
3 freezing
4 downpour
5 Fahrenheit
6 overcast
7 chilly
8 thunder
9 raindrop
10 humidity
11 flood

51.5
1 thundery 2 rainy
3 cloudy 4 icy
5 windy

51.6
1 drought
2 blizzard
3 lightning
4 snowflake
5 snowstorm
6 heatwave
7 puddle
8 gale

51.7
A 7 B 1 C 3 D 8
E 6 F 2 G 5 H 10
I 4 J 9 K 12 L 11

52

52.2
1 wood
2 canyon
3 ocean
4 high tide
5 sand dune
6 grassland
7 wave
8 low tide
9 glacier
10 rocks
11 cave
12 mountain range
13 swamp
14 farmland

52.3
1 countryside
2 canyon
3 plateau
4 volcano
5 meadow
6 rain forest (US) / rainforest (UK)
7 mountain range
8 polar region

52.4
1 hill
2 forest
3 peak
4 stream
5 river

52.5
1 C 2 B 3 A 4 C
5 A 6 B 7 A

53

53.2
1 Fossil fuels such as coal and oil produce carbon dioxide.
2 Carbon dioxide is one of the best-known greenhouse gases.
3 Solar panels on your house can help you save electricity.
4 Factory emissions are a cause of global warming.
5 It can be much cheaper to use renewable energy.

53.3
1 endangered
2 global warming
3 wind power
4 solar power
5 alternative energy

53.4
1 We need to **tackle pollution** in our rivers.
2 Dinosaurs became **extinct** millions of years ago.
3 The traffic in our cities is **harmful to the environment**.
4 We can reduce pollution by using more types of **alternative energy**.
5 **Climate change** is a huge threat to many animals.

53.5
1 This **wind farm** has been running for several years.
2 We must work together to stop the **destruction** of our forests.
3 **Climate change** is a huge threat to many animals.
4 If we don't reduce pollution, Earth will undergo **irreversible change**.

54

54.4
1. hamster
2. to quack
3. doghouse (US) / kennel (UK)
4. fish
5. to squeak
6. rabbit hutch
7. parrot
8. basket

54.5
1. horse
2. turkey
3. sheep
4. to purr
5. to meow
6. mouse
7. to croak
8. donkey
9. collar

54.6
1. whiskers
2. tail
3. paws
4. claws

54.7
1. to scratch
2. goose
3. tortoise
4. aquarium
5. bird seed

54.8
A 10 B 6 C 3 D 1 E 2
F 5 G 7 H 4 I 9 J 8

55

55.3
1. B
2. A
3. B
4. C
5. C

55.4
1. koala
2. frog
3. giraffe
4. chipmunk
5. snake
6. bison
7. polar bear

55.5
1. bat
2. buffalo
3. hippopotamus
4. tiger
5. wolf
6. elephant
7. mongoose
8. jaguar

55.6
1. gazelle
2. lion
3. moose
4. zebra
5. to roar
6. panda
7. to burrow
8. yak
9. tapir
10. to swing
11. tiger
12. raccoon
13. to hunt
14. meerkat

56

56.4
BUGS:
moth, **spider**, **wasp**, **caterpillar**, **ant**, **snail**
BIRDS:
hawk, **vulture**, **penguin**, **duck**, **swan**, **dove**

56.5
1. to hatch
2. to hoot
3. to sing
4. to peck
5. to swoop

56.6
1. beak
2. wing
3. claw

56.7
1. claw
2. to flap
3. toucan
4. dove
5. pelican
6. seagull
7. beak
8. caterpillar

56.8
1. woodpecker
2. worm
3. eagle
4. butterfly
5. beetle
6. chicken
7. parrot
8. cockroach
9. pelican

57

57.3
1 B 2 D 3 A 4 E 5 C

57.4
1. jellyfish
2. turtle
3. squid
4. lobster
5. eel
6. shark

57.5
seahorse, dolphin, otter, mussel, lobster, ray, walrus, clam, swordfish, oyster, jellyfish, octopus, crab, seal

57.6
1 A 2 C 3 B 4 A 5 C 6 B

57.7
1. oyster
2. porpoise
3. killer whale
4. sea lion
5. a school of fish
6. lobster
7. squid
8. blue whale
9. eel

58

58.2
1. to make models
2. to do karaoke
3. to collect stamps
4. to take photos
5. to go camping
6. to fly a kite
7. to see a play
8. to have a picnic
9. to paint
10. to knit
11. to do puzzles

58.3
1 C 2 B 3 D 4 A

58.4
1 to collect stamps
2 to draw
3 to sew
4 to visit a museum
5 to stay home
6 to ride a horse
7 to bake
8 to do yoga
9 to go to a book club

58.5
1 to go jogging
2 to write
3 to go to a party
4 to do the gardening
5 to play video games
6 to play board games
7 to play a musical instrument
8 to go foraging
9 to go to the gym
10 to walk / to hike
11 to watch television
12 to listen to music
13 to do exercise
14 to arrange flowers

59

59.2
1 to run
2 to spell
3 to carry
4 to pull
5 to point
6 to taste
7 to sing
8 to think
9 to repair
10 to whisper
11 to work
12 to smell
13 to blow
14 to decide

59.3
A 2 B 3 C 1 D 6 E 4
F 5 G 7 H 10 I 8 J 14
K 13 L 9 M 12 N 11

59.4
1 B 2 A 3 D 4 E 5 C

59.5
1 C 2 A 3 A
4 B 5 C

60

60.3
1 skating
2 fishing
3 basketball
4 cricket
5 hockey
6 rugby
7 tennis
8 golf
9 archery

60.4
1 rock climbing
2 surfing
3 judo
4 motor racing
5 volleyball
6 paragliding
7 skydiving
8 skateboarding

60.5
1 B 2 C 3 B 4 A 5 B 6 C

60.6
1 badminton
2 baseball
3 gymnastics
4 cycling
5 squash
6 skateboarding
7 scuba diving
8 table tennis
9 skydiving
10 volleyball
11 abseiling
12 swimming

61

61.4
1 penalty
2 to be booked
3 half time
4 flag
5 red card
6 goalkeeper
7 corner kick
8 stoppage time (US) / injury time (UK)
9 field (US) / pitch (UK)
10 manager
11 substitutes
12 to be sent off
13 final whistle
14 linesman

61.5
1 to score a goal
2 to kick
3 to lose
4 final whistle
5 fans
6 mascot
7 to tackle
8 full time
9 to tie

61.6
A 4 B 1 C 5 D 2 E 3
F 7 G 6 H 9 I 8 J 10
K 12 L 11

61.7
1 to be booked
2 penalty spot
3 to kick
4 mascot
5 to tie
6 throw-in
7 forward
8 red card
9 linesman
10 bar
11 fans
12 midfielder

61.8
1 D 2 A 3 C
4 E 5 B

62

62.3
1 C 2 A 3 B
4 E 5 D

62.4
1 swimming cap
2 swimsuit
3 armband
4 float
5 swimming trunks
6 flipper

62.5
1 boxing ring
2 arrow
3 flipper
4 stopwatch
5 hurdles
6 bow
7 gym
8 skis
9 lifejacket
10 pool cue

62.6
EQUIPMENT:
skis, **pool cue**, **fishing rod**, **helmet**, **roller skates**, **baseball bat**
VENUES:
tennis court, **ice rink**, **stadium**, **ski slope**, **golf course**, **running track**

62.7
1 paddle
2 arrow
3 shuttlecock
4 snowboard
5 helmet
6 bowling pins
7 harness

63

63.4
1 science-fiction
2 autobiography
3 travel writing
4 crime fiction
5 e-reader
6 nature writing
7 biography
8 cookbook
9 novel
10 dictionary
11 textbook / course book
12 encyclopedia
13 gossip magazine
14 horoscope

63.5
1 author
2 novel
3 guidebook
4 romance
5 puzzles
6 hardback

63.6
1 I flipped through the guidebook **and decided to buy it**.
2 His new novel has received **glowing reviews from all the critics**.
3 I'm reading a crime novel. **It's a real page-turner**.
4 I find the plot difficult to **understand in most fantasy novels**.
5 Her latest novel is a **bestseller around the world**.

63.7
A 4 B 2 C 6 D 1 E 3
F 5 G 10 H 9 I 7 J 8

64

64.5
1 saxophone
2 flute
3 clarinet
4 trombone
5 guitar
6 violin
7 cello
8 electric guitar
9 keyboard

64.6
1 to perform
2 opera
3 to play the trumpet
4 rock
5 to conduct
6 to compose
7 classical
8 to listen
9 country

64.7
1 solo
2 lyrics
3 choir
4 guitar player
5 microphone
6 group
7 conductor
8 festival

64.8
1 C 2 C 3 A
4 B 5 B 6 A

65

65.3
1 opera
2 romantic comedy
3 thriller
4 horror
5 ballet

65.4
1 costumes
2 multiplex
3 script
4 popcorn
5 villain
6 usher
7 cartoon
8 stunt
9 director

65.5
1 script
2 hero
3 movie
4 dialog
5 encore
6 audience
7 box office
8 crime drama
9 props
10 villain

65.6
1 orchestra seating (US) / stalls (UK)
2 orchestra pit
3 stage
4 balcony
5 circle

65.7
1 screen
2 costumes
3 action movie
4 movie star
5 audience
6 cartoon
7 encore

66

66.4
1 children's show (US) / children's TV (UK)
2 comedy
3 news
4 cooking show
5 talk show (US) / chat show (UK)
6 period / costume drama

66.5
A 5 B 7
C 2 D 4
E 1 F 3
G 6 H 9
I 11 J 8
K 12 L 10

66.6
episode
documentary
channel
remote
satire
reporter
weather
drama
screen
preview
sitcom

66.7
1. to change channel
2. thriller
3. to record
4. season (US) / series (UK)
5. weather
6. to turn down the volume
7. talk show (US) / chat show (UK)
8. video on demand
9. shopping channel
10. couch potato
11. to turn off

66.8
1 weather 2 show
3 reporter 4 drama
5 interview 6 channel
7 crime 8 cartoon

67

67.2
1 Lee's **claim to fame** was that he could eat five burgers in five minutes.
2 **The opening night** of the show was a great success.
3 Lucinda is used to being **in the public eye**.
4 The success of her latest movie has **gone to her head**.

67.3
1 My favorite actors were on the red carpet this evening.
2 Social media has supported the rise of celebrity culture.
3 This singer's wedding was headline news last week.
4 Everyone was talking about her attention-grabbing dress.

67.4
1 John would really love to have **his name in lights**.
2 This morning's newspaper **headline is shocking**!
3 Kelly has had a truly meteoric **rise in the music industry**.
4 Some people go on talent **shows to become famous**.
5 Politicians can easily **be exploited by the media**.
6 The politician's lies were **exposed in the interview**.

67.5
A 6 B 1
C 4 D 3
E 2 F 5

68

68.6
1 C 2 B 3 A 4 B 5 C

68.7
1. sore
2. pain
3. bite
4. sprain
5. flu
6. high blood pressure
7. swollen

68.8
SICKNESS:
food poisoning, **diabetes**, **appendicitis**, **chickenpox**, **mumps**, **cold**
INJURIES:
broken bone, **wound**, **bruise**, **burn**, **sting**, **cut**

68.9
1. mumps
2. cut
3. asthma
4. stress
5. virus
6. migraine
7. symptoms
8. eczema

69

69.4
1 B 2 A 3 D 4 E 5 C
6 H 7 I 8 G 9 F

69.5
1. prescription
2. ambulance
3. appointment
4. syringe
5. to heal
6. to exercise
7. injection
8. treatment
9. to resuscitate

69.6
1. antiseptic wipes
2. adhesive bandage (US) / plaster (UK)
3. bandage
4. cotton pads (US) / cotton wool (UK)
5. adhesive tape
6. safety pin
7. ointment
8. scissors
9. painkillers
10. tweezers

69.7
stethoscope, physical therapy, operation, patient, blood test, inhaler, paramedic, bandage, ointment

69.8
A 13 B 4 C 14 D 1 E 15
F 5 G 2 H 6 I 8 J 3
K 7 L 9 M 11 N 16 O 10 P 12

70

70.3
1 A 2 E 3 B 4 F 5 C
6 G 7 D 8 I 9 H

70.4
1 B 2 B 3 A 4 A 5 A 6 C 7 A

70.5
1 Pedro has given up chocolate this month.
2 I'm trying to eat more vegetables because they're low in fat.
3 Brown bread is a good source of fiber.
4 You should eat smaller portions if you want to lose weight.
5 Convenience food saves people time, but isn't always good for them.

70.6
1 I'm trying to **cut down on** sugary drinks because I know they're bad for me.
2 Mia must not eat nuts because she's **allergic to** them.
3 I'm trying to eat more vegetables because they're **low in** fat.
4 It's okay to **eat** treats like cake **in moderation**.

71

71.5
1. circuit training
2. to skip
3. to cool down
4. locker room
5. spa
6. to meditate
7. to squat
8. aromatherapy
9. yoga

71.6
1 elliptical (US) / cross-trainer (UK)
2 weights
3 exercise mat
4 personal trainer
5 treadmill
6 exercise bike

71.7
1 to work out (US) / to keep fit (UK)
2 to sleep well
3 to stretch
4 to relax / to chill out
5 lockers
6 acupuncture
7 heart rate
8 push-up (US) / press-up (UK)
9 counseling (US) / counselling (UK)
10 massage
11 sit-up
12 jump rope (US) / skipping rope (UK)
13 boot camp

71.8
1 personal trainer
2 treadmill
3 to chill out
4 boot camp
5 spa
6 lockers
7 steam room

71.9
1 reflexology
2 exercise class
3 sauna
4 steam room
5 to sleep well
6 to warm up

72

72.2
1 town square
2 fountain
3 castle
4 store (US) / shop (UK)
5 town hall
6 restaurant
7 library

72.3
1 hospital 2 pharmacy
3 temple 4 factory
5 nightclub

72.4
1 B
2 A
3 C
4 A
5 C

72.5
1 post office
2 mosque
3 shopping mall
4 theater (US) / theatre (UK)
5 fire station
6 office building
7 village
8 cemetery
9 church
10 gas station (US) / petrol station (UK)
11 park
12 commercial district
13 law court
14 city

73

73.4
1 greengrocer
2 baker
3 fish dealer (US) / fishmonger (UK)
4 bookstore (US) / bookshop (UK)
5 boutique
6 toy store (US) / toy shop (UK)
7 butcher
8 street market
9 florist

73.5
1 to try on
2 bank
3 to sell
4 jewelers
5 to exchange
6 hardware store
7 to fit
8 to choose
9 delicatessen

73.6
1 You can buy almost anything you want at the **flea market** in town.
2 It's always worth **shopping around** when buying a new car.
3 I love going **bargain-hunting** at my local market.
4 I thought the restaurant was **overpriced**. The food was very disappointing.
5 The local hardware store has **slashed its prices**. You can find some real bargains.

73.7
1 a good deal
2 to slash prices
3 on a tight budget
4 a flea market
5 to shop around
6 a rip-off
7 bargain-hunting

74

74.4
1 exit
2 cashier
3 cash register (US) / till (UK)
4 shopping bag / carrier bag (UK)
5 checkout
6 shopping cart (US) / trolley (UK)
7 basket

74.5
1 convenient
2 receipt
3 special offer
4 basement
5 customer
6 guarantee
7 escalator

74.6
1 C 2 D
3 A 4 B

74.7
1 food court
2 upmarket
3 closed
4 price tag

74.8
A 3 B 1 C 6
D 2 E 4 F 9
G 12 H 5 I 7
J 10 K 8 L 11

75

75.2
1 There are lots of green **spaces** in the city for people to relax in the summer.
2 There's a greater **choice** of cafés and restaurants in large cities.
3 Moscow has a **lively** nightlife, with bars and nightclubs that stay open until dawn.
4 The **road** work meant that it took me two hours to arrive at the office today.
5 It's sometimes impossible to get on the bus during **rush** hour.
6 The **pollution** in my city can be terrible in the summer months.

75.3
1 Overcrowding on London's trains means it's often hard to find a seat.
2 I offer guided tours of the city's historic buildings.
3 Good infrastructure, such as roads and telecommunications, is essential for a modern city.

75.4
A 5
B 3
C 2
D 4
E 1

75.5
1 The **pace of life is much faster in the city** than in the countryside.
2 The **vandalism in my area makes** the buildings look very ugly.
3 A good **way to avoid traffic jams is to** travel by train.
4 The **road work meant that it took me** two hours to arrive at the office today.

76

76.3
1 password
2 artificial intelligence
3 e-reader
4 smartwatch
5 USB drive
6 camera
7 plug
8 wireless
9 MP3 player
10 smartphone
11 remote control
12 memory card
13 flashlight (US) / torch (UK)
14 hands-free headset

76.4
1 C
2 E
3 D
4 A
5 B

76.5
1 GPS
2 voice recorder
3 Wi-Fi
4 circuit
5 bulb
6 laptop
7 webcam
8 speakers
9 battery
10 router
11 remote control
12 power cord
13 tablet

76.6
1 computer desk
2 keyboard
3 mouse pad (US) / mat (UK)
4 mouse
5 wire

76.7
1 bulb
2 plug
3 tablet
4 camera
5 laptop
6 circuit

77

77.2
1 The car was expensive, but it will save us money in the long **run**.
2 Higher prices could be the **shape** of things to come.
3 It's only a matter of **time** before we sell one of these paintings.
4 Laila is **making** predictions about what will happen in the new year.

77.3
1 I really want to buy the latest model of their smartphone.
2 My uncle's a technophobe. He still uses a typewriter.
3 The internet has caused a revolution in the way we learn.
4 Seb's such a technophile. He has to have the latest phone.

77.4
1 You need **to be computer literate to** find a good job these days.
2 My new smartphone **is light-years ahead of** my old one.
3 CDs and cassettes have **become obsolete because of** online streaming.
4 In **this digital age, many** people have a laptop and smartphone.
5 The research scientists **made an amazing breakthrough**.

77.5
A 5
B 2
C 4
D 3
E 1

78

78.3
1 steam
2 to record
3 to observe
4 crystals
5 cloning
6 battery
7 hypothesis

78.4
1 safety goggles
2 microscope
3 Bunsen burner

78.5
1 crystals
2 pestle
3 to pour
4 cells
5 physics
6 to freeze
7 molecules

78.6
1 to boil
2 beaker
3 gas
4 to record
5 results
6 to burn
7 steam
8 reaction
9 static electricity

78.7
1 A
2 A
3 B
4 A
5 C

Word list

Numbers refer to the unit number. Words separated by a forward slash usually indicate the differences between US and UK spelling.

A

abilities 59
able to drive 43
abseiling 60
absent 40
accent 25
accessories 16
accident 68
accommodation 13, 47
Accounts (department) 36
accurate 43
ache 68
across from 46
act 59
action movie 65
action points 40
actions 59
actor 34
acupuncture 71
adaptable 43
add 33, 59
adhesive bandage 69
adhesive tape 37, 69
administration 43
Administration (department) 36
adults 20
advertising industry 36
adverts 66
aerobics 71
aeroplane 44
aerospace industry 36
afternoon 3
aftershave 16
against the clock 8
agriculture 36
ahead 46
ahead of the game 41
air bed 49
air mattress 49
airplane 44
airport 44, 72
alarm goes off 4
album 64
Alice band 16
Allen keys 12
allergic to something 70
allergies 68, 70
all-inclusive 47
alternative energy 53
always 3
amazed 19
amazing 6
ambitious 43
ambulance 69
American 1
American football 60
amused 19
anemone 57
angry 19
ankle 14
annoyed 19
annoying 6
annual leave 35
annual vacation 35
ant 56
antelope 55
antiseptic 69
antiseptic wipes 69
anxious 19
any other business 40
AOB 40
apartment block 9
apartments 13, 47
appearance 17
appendicitis 68
appetizer 33
applause 65
apple 29
application form 42
apply for a job 42
appointment 69
apprentice 35
approachable 18
apricot 29
April 3
aquarium 54
archery 60
architect 34
architecture 23
Argentina 1
Argentinian 1
arm 14
armadillo 55
armband 62
armchair 9
aromatherapy 71
arrange flowers 58
arrest somebody 27
arrive late 4
arrogant 18
arrow 62
art 23
artichokes 30
article 63
artist 34
ask directions 46
asparagus 30
assertive 18
assistant 35
asthma 68
ATM 38
attachment 7
attend a meeting 40
attend classes 24
attention to detail 43
attention-grabbing 67
attic 9
attract 78
aubergines 30
audience 65
August 3
aunt 20
Australia 1
Austria 1
Austrian 1
author 63
auto repair shop 45
autobiography 63
autumn 3
avenue 46
avocados 30
awful 6
ax / axe 12

B

baby 20
baby carriage 22
baby changing facilities 74
baby equipment 22
baby monitor 22
babygro 22
back up 76
backache 68
backpack 16, 49
bacon 28
bad 6
bad omen 26
badge 16
badminton 60
bag 32
bagel 31
bait 62
bake 33, 58
baker 73
balanced diet 70
balcony (building) 9
balcony (theater / theatre) 65
bald 17
ball 22, 61, 62
ball is in your court 41

ballet 65
balloon 22
ballpark figure 41
banana 29
band 64
bandage 69
bank 38, 73
bank loan 38
bank statement 38
bar (goalpost) 61
bar (pub) 33, 72
barbeque 49
bargain 74
bargain-hunting 73
bark 54
baseball 60
baseball bat 62
basement 9, 74
basil 31
basket 49, 54, 74
basketball 60
bat 55
bath 4, 9
bathrobe 15
bathroom 9
bathroom equipment 10
bathtub 9
battery 76, 78
be booked 61
be delayed 47
be laid off 35
be on the fence 8
be sent off 61
beach 50, 52, 58
beach ball 50
beak 56
beaker 78
beans 30
bear 55
beard 17
beautiful 6, 17
beauty 16, 74
beaver 55
become a celebrity 67
bed 4, 9
bed and breakfast 47
bedroom 9
bedside table 9
bee 56
beef 28
beer 32
beetle 56
beginner's luck 26
behind 46
beliefs 26
believe in something 26
belt 16
bend in the road 46
benefits 35
bestseller 63
between 46
bib 22
bicycle 44, 49
bicycle lane 49
big 5
bike 44, 49
bike rack 49
bilingual 25
bill 33
bills 13, 38
bin 9, 37
bin liner 11
binder clip 37
biography 63
biologist 78
biology 23, 78
bird seed 54
birds 56
birdwatching 58
biscuit 31
bison 55
bite 32, 68
bitter 32
black 5
black hair 17
blackberries 29
blackcurrants 29
bleach 11
bleat 54
bleed 68
blender 10
blink 14
blizzard 51
block 46
block of flats 9
blond hair 17
blood test 69
blouse 15
blow 59
blue 5
blue eyes 17
blue whale 57
blueberries 29
blush (action) 14
blush / blusher (make-up) 16
boar 55
board a plane 47
board games 22, 58
board of directors 40
boarding pass 47
boat 44
bodyboarding 50
body, parts of 14
bodysuit 22
boil 33, 78
boiled egg 28
boiling 51
boiling point 51
bolt 12
bonnet (car) 45
bonus 35
book 63
book a holiday 47
book a vacation 47
book club 58
book in advance 48
bookcase 9
booked 61
bookshop 73
bookstore 73
boot (car) 45
boot camp 71
booties 22
boots 16
bored 19
boring 6
bottle 22, 32
bottle opener 10
bottom of the career ladder 39
boutique 73
bow (archery) 62
bow (gesture) 14
bow tie 16
bowl (container) 10, 32
bowling 60
bowling pins 62
box 32
box office 65
boxer shorts 15
boxes 13
boxing 60
boxing gloves 62
boxing ring 62
boy 20
boyfriend 20
bra 15
bracelet 16
brakes 45, 49
brave 18
Brazil 1
Brazilian 1
bread 31
break down 45
break even 38
break up with someone 21
breakfast 4, 33
breakfast TV 66
breakthrough 77

breast 28
breathe 14
breathtaking 6
bribery 27
bridge 72
briefcase 16
brilliant 6
bring someone up 21
bring up someone 21
British 1
broccoli 30
broil 33
broken bone 68
brooch 16
broom 11
brother 20
brother-in-law 20
brown 5
brown eyes 17
brown hair 17
browse the internet 58
bruise 68
brunch 33
brush 11
brush your hair 4
brush your teeth 4
bucket 11
bucket and spade 50
buckle 16
budget 38
buffalo 55
buffet 33
buggy 22
bugs 56
build a fire 49
building blocks 22
building bricks 22
bulb 76
bull 54
bulletin board 37
bump into someone 21
bungalow 13
bungee jumping 60
Bunsen burner 78
burger 28
burglary 27
burn 68, 78
burrow 55
bus 44
bus station 72
bus stop 44
business 41
business as usual 41
business card 7
business studies 23
businesslike attitude 43
businessman 34
businesswoman 34
busk 64
butcher 34, 73
butter 28
butterfly 56
butternut squash 30
button 15
buy 73
buy groceries 4
buzz 56

C

cabbage 30
cabin 47
cabinet 9
cable TV 66
café 4, 33, 72
cage 54
cake 31
calcium 70
calendar 3, 37
call a friend 4
call friends 58
call in sick 35
call your family 4
calm 18, 19, 43
calorie-controlled diet 70
calories 70
camel 44, 55
camera 76
camper van 49
campfire 49
camping 49, 58
camping stove 49
campsite 49
can 32
can opener 10
Canada 1
Canadian 1
candy 31
canoeing 60
canyon 52
cap 16
car 45
car accident 45
car park 45
car theft 27
car wash 45
caravan 49
carbohydrates 70
carbonated 32
cards 58
career path 39
career summary 42
caring 18
carnival 75
carrier bag 74
carrots 30
carry 59
carton 32
cartoon 65, 66
cash machine 38
cash register 38, 74
cashew nut 29
cashier 74
cast 65
castle 72
casual 17
cat 54
catch 59
catch a train 44
catch the bus 4
catch the train 4
catch-up TV 66
catering industry 36
caterpillar 56
cauliflower 30
cautious 18
cave 52
celebrity 67
celebrity culture 67
cell phone 37
cell phone number 7
cello 64
cells 78
Celsius 51
cemetery 72
century 3
cereal 31
chain 49
chair 9, 37
chalet 47
change (clothes) 15
change a lightbulb 12
change channel 66
change money 38
change of pace 41
change the sheets 11
changing mat 22
changing room 71, 74
changing table 22
channel 66
chapter 63
chat show 66
check (payment) 38
check (restaurant) 33
check in 47
check out 47
check out something 48
check something out 48
check the oil 45
check the tires / tyres 45
check your emails 4

checked / checkered 15
checkout 74
cheek 14
cheerful 19
cheese 28
cheesecake 31
cheetah 55
chef 33, 34
chemical industry 36
chemicals 78
chemist 78
chemistry 23, 78
cheque 38
cherries 29
chess 58
chest 14
chest of drawers 9
chew 32
chicken 28, 54, 56
chickenpox 68
child-care provider 34
children 20
children's department 74
children's show 66
children's TV 66
chili / chilli flakes 31
chill out 71
chilled 32
chilly 51
chin 14
China 1
Chinese 1
chipmunk 55
chips 28
chives 31
chocolate 31
choir 64
cholesterol 70
choose 73
chop 33
chopping board 10
chopsticks 10
chores 11
church 72
chutney 31
cilantro 31
cinema 65, 72
circle 65
circuit training 71
city 7, 72
city centre 72
claim to fame 67
clam 57
clap 14
clarinet 64
class 23
classical 64
classroom 23
claw(s) 54, 56, 57
clean 5
clean the bathroom 11
clean the windows 11
clean up 11
cleaner 34
cleaning 11
cleaning fluid 11
clear distinction 24
clear the table 4, 11
click 76
click with someone 21
client 35
cliff 52
climate 51
climate change 53
climb 59
climbing frame 22
clinch the deal 41
clinic 69
clipboard 37
cloning 78
close friend 21
closed 74
cloth 11
clothes 15
clothes line 11
cloud 51
cloudy 51
coach 44
coat 15
cockpit 44
cockroach 56
coconut 29
cod 28
coffee 4, 32
coins 38
cola 32
colander 10
cold (sickness) 68
cold (temperature) 5, 51
cold feet 8
collaborate 42
collar (pet) 54
collar (shirt) 15
colleague 35
collect stamps 58
college 23
coloring / colouring book 63
colors / colours 5
comb 16
comedy 65, 66
comic 63
commercial break 66
commercial district 72
commit a crime 27
commuters 44
company 35
company name 7
compare and contrast 24
compass 46
competitive 43
compose 64
composer 64
computer 37
computer desk 76
computer literate 77
computing 43
concert 58, 64
concert hall 72
condiments 31
conditioner 10
conduct 64
conductor 64
conference call 40
confident 18, 19, 43
confused 19
confusing 6
considerate 18
construction industry 36
construction worker 34
consume 53
contact 7
containers 32
continuous assessment 24
convenience food 70
convenient 74
conversational 25
cook 58
cook dinner 4
cookbook 63
cooker 9
cookie 31
cooking show 66
cool 51, 78
cool down 71
coordinate 42
copy 59
coriander 31
corkscrew 10
corn 30
corner 46, 61
corner kick 61
corner the market 41
correction fluid 37
cosmetics 74
cosmopolitan 75
costume drama 66
costumes 65
cot 22
cottage 13
cottage cheese 28
cotton 15

cotton pads 69
cotton wool 69
couch 9
couch potato 66
cough 14, 68
counseling / counselling 71
count 59
countries 1
country 64
countryside 52
courgettes 30
course book 63
cousin 20
cover 63
cover / covering letter 42
cow 54
co-worker 35
crab 28, 50, 57
cranberries 29
crawl 59
cream (colour) 5
cream (dairy) 28
creative 43
credit card 38
crib 22
cricket 60
crime 27, 66
crime drama 65
crime fiction 63
crime rate 75
crime wave 27
criminal record 27
crisps 28
critical 18
croak 54
crockery 10
crocodile 55
croissant 31
crossroads 46
cross-trainer 71
crow (bird) 56
crow (cockerel) 54
cruise 47
cry 14
crystals 78
cucumbers 30
cuff 15
cufflinks 16
culture shock 48
cup 10
cupboard 9
cupcake 31
curious 19
curly hair 17
currant 29
currency 38
current affairs 66
curtain 65
cushion 9
customer 74
customer service 43, 74
customer-focused 43
cut (food preparation) 33
cut (wound) 68
cut corners 8
cut down on something 70
cutlery 10
cutting board 10
cutting-edge 77
cycle pump 49
cycling 49, 60
cycling helmet 49
cycling trails 49
Czech Republic 1

D

dad 20
daily 3
dairy 28, 70
dairy-free 70
dance 59, 64
dark green 5
dark skin 17
data analysis 43
date 29
daughter 20
day 3
day off 35
dead-end job 39
debit card 38
debt 38
decade 3
December 3
decide 59
decimals 2
decision-making 43
deck chair 50
deep 5
deep breathing 71
deer 55
defender 61
degree (qualification) 23, 24
degrees (temperature) 51
delayed 47
delete 7, 76
delicatessen 73
delicious 6, 32
delighted 19
denim 5, 15
dental floss 10
dentist 34
deodorant 10
department store 74
departments (workplace) 36
departure gate 47
deposit 13
depressed 19
derelict buildings 75
desert 52
design and technology 23
designer 34
designer labels 74
desk 9, 37
desktop computer 76
desserts 31, 33
destruction 53
detached houses 13
determined 43
detox 70
diabetes 68
dialog / dialogue 65
diaper 22
diarrhea / diarrhoea 68
diary 37
dictionary 63
diesel 45
dig 59
digital age 77
dine 32
dining room 9
dinner 4, 33
dinnerware 10
diploma 23
dire consequences 53
direct flight 47
direction 46
director 65
dirty 5
disappointed 19
disappointing 6
disastrous 6
discus 60
disgusted 19
disgusting 6, 32
dishes 4, 11
dishonest 18
dishwasher 9
dishwashing liquid 11
dissolve 78
distance 46
distracted 19
diving 60
diving board 62
DNA 78
do 59
do exercise 58
do homework 4
do karaoke 58
do pottery 58
do puzzles 58

do something by the book 41
do the dishes 4, 11
do the gardening 58
do the housework 4
do the ironing 11
do the laundry 11
do the weeding 12
do up 15
do yoga 58
doctor 34, 69
doctor's surgery 69
documentary 66
dog 54
doghouse 54
doll 22
dollhouse / doll's house 22
dolphin 57
donkey 54
door 9
dorm 47
double room 47
dove 56
download 76
downpour 51
downstairs 9
downtown 72
draft 7
drama 23, 65, 66
draw (art) 58
draw (sports result) 61
drawer 37
drawing pin 37
dress 15
dresser 9
dressing gown 15
drift apart 21
drill 12
drink 32
drink tea or coffee 4
drink water 69
drive 4
drive a car 44
driver 34
driver's licence / license 45
driving 45
drop a hint 26
drop someone off 45
drought 51
drug dealing 27
drum 64
dry 51
dry cleaners 73
dry the dishes 11
dry your hair 4
drying clip 11
duck 54, 56
dummy 22
dumplings 31
duplex 13
dust 11
duster 11
dustpan 11

E

eagle 56
ear 14
earn 35
earphones 76
earrings 16
ears 54
east 46
eat 32
eat breakfast 4
eat dinner 4
eat lunch 4
eat something in moderation 70
eccentric 18
economic downturn 38
economics 23
ecstatic 19
eczema 68
education 23, 36, 42
eel 57
efficient 43
egg 28
egg white 28
eggplants 30
Egypt 1
Egyptian 1
eight 2
eighteen 2
eighth 2
eighty 2
elbow 14
electric guitar 64
electric shock 78
electrical appliances 74
electrician 34
electronics industry 36
elegant 17
elephant 55
elevator 74
eleven 2
eleventh 2
elliptical 71
email 7
email address 7
embarrassed 19
employee 35
employer 35
employment 35
encore 65
encyclopedia 63
endangered 53
energetic 43
energy 70
energy drink 32
energy industry 36
enforce the law 27
engine 44, 45
engineer 34
engineering 23
English 23
enrol on 24
enroll in 24
en-suite bathroom 47
entertainment industry 36
enthusiastic 18
entrée 33
envelope 37
environment 53
episode 66
eraser 37
e-reader 63, 76
escalator 74
essay 23
estate agent 13
evaporate 78
evening 3
evening class 58
every day 3
every other day 3
exam 23
exchange 73
exchange business cards 7
exchange rate 38
excited 19
exciting 6
exclusive interview 67
excursion 47
exercise 58, 69, 71
exercise bike 71
exercise book 23
exercise class 71
exercise mat 71
exhausted 19
exit 74
expenditure 38
experiment 78
exploit 67
expose 67
extinct 53
extraordinary 6
eyebrow 14
eyelashes 14
eyeliner 16
eyes 14, 17
eyeshadow 16

F

fabric 5
face 14
face the music 8
face wash 10
facial hair 17
Facilities (department) 36
factory 72
Fahrenheit 51
fail 23
fair skin 17
fairy tale 26
fall (action) 59
fall (season) 3
fall in love with someone 21
fall out with someone 21
families 20, 21
fans 61
fantastic 6
fantasy 63
far 5
farm animals 54
farmer 34
farming 36
farmland 52
fashion designer 34
fashion industry 36
fast food 28, 33
fast learner 43
fasten 15
fast-paced 75
father 20
feather 56
February 3
feed the cat 4
feed the dog 4
feed the pets 11
feedback 24
feel better 69
feel homesick 48
feel under the weather 8
feelings 19
female 20
ferret 54
ferry 44
festival 64
fever 68
fiber / fibre 70
fiction 63
field (land) 52
field (sports) 61, 62
fifteen 2
fifth 2
fifty 2
fifty percent off 73
fig 29
file 12
files 37
filing cabinet 37
fill out a form 42
fill up 45
film 65
film star 65
fin 57
final whistle 61
finance 38
Finance (department) 36
finance industry 36
find somebody guilty 27
find somebody not guilty 27
fine 27
finger 14
finish work 4
fire station 72
fired 39
firefighter 34
first 2
first aid kit 69
first draft 24
first floor 74
first name 7
fish 28, 54, 57
fish dealer 73
fish slice 10
fish tank 54
fishing 60
fishing industry 36
fishing rod 62
fishmonger 73
fit 15, 73
fit a carpet 12
fitness 71
five 2
fix a puncture 49
fixed menu 33
flag 61
flamingo 56
flap 56
flashlight 49
flask 32, 49
flat tire / tyre 45
flats 13
flavorings 31
flea market 73
flexible 43
flick through 63
flight attendant 34
flip through 63
flip-flops 16, 50
flippers 50, 62
float 62, 78
flood 51
florist 73
flour 31
flu 68
fluent in (languages) 25, 43
flute 64
fly 56, 59
fly a kite 58
fog 51
foggy 51
fold clothes 11
folders 37
folding chair 49
folding table 49
folklore 26
food court 74
food industry 36
food poisoning 68
food stall 33
foot 14
football 60
football boots 62
footpath 46
foraging 58
forehead 14
forest 52
fork (cutlery) 10
fork (gardening) 12
formal 17
fortnight 3
forty 2
forward (email action) 7
forward (soccer player) 61
fossil fuels 53
foundation 16
fountain 72
four 2
fourteen 2
fourth 2
fox 55
fractions 2
frame 49
France 1
fraud 27
freckles 17
free time activities 58
freeway 46
freeze 78
freezer 9
freezing 51
freezing point 51
French 1
fresh 32
fresher 24
freshman 24
Friday 3
fridge 9
fried egg 28
friendly 18

friends 4
fries 28
frightened 19
frightening 6
frizzy hair 17
frog 55
front desk 47
frost 51
frosty 51
frown 14
fruit 29
fruit salad 31
frustrated 19
fry 33
frying pan 10
fuel 45
full time 61
fun 6
funny 18
fur 54
furious 19
furnished 13
furniture 9
future-proof 77

G

gadgets 76
gain weight 69
gale 51
gallop 54
game plan 41
game show 66
games 22
garage 45
garbage bag 11
garden 9
gardener 34
gardening 12, 58
garlic 30
gas station 45, 72, 78
gasoline 45
gazelle 55
gear 49
gecko 54
generous 18
genetic engineering 78
geographical features 52
geography 23
geology 23
gerbil 54
German 1
Germany 1
get a degree 24
get ahead 39
get along with someone 21
get away from it all 48
get changed 15
get cold feet 8
get down to business 41
get dressed 4
get fired 35
get in a taxi 44
get into debt 38
get off a bike 49
get off a bus 44
get on a bike 49
get on a bus 44
get on with someone 21
get out of a taxi 44
get the ball rolling 41
get up 4
get your hair cut 17
getaway 48
geyser 52
gill 57
ginger 31
giraffe 55
girl 20
girlfriend 20
give a presentation 40
give and take 39
give birth 21
give notice 13
give someone a lift 44
give someone a ride 44
give someone feedback on something 24
give something up 70
give up something 70
glacier 52
glamorous 17
glass 5, 32
glasses 16
glide 56
global warming 53
gloves 16
glowing reviews 63
gluten-free 70
go abroad 47
go ahead 46
go birdwatching 58
go camping 58
go foraging 58
go home 4
go jogging 58
go left 46
go on a cruise 47
go on a holiday 47
go on a vacation 47
go on an excursion 47
go on holiday 58
go on maternity leave 35
go on vacation 58
go out 4, 38, 58
go past 46
go right 46
go shopping 58
go sightseeing 47
go straight on 46
go the extra mile 39
go to a book club 58
go to a café 4
go to a concert 58
go to a party 58
go to an evening class 58
go to bed 4
go to school 4
go to somebody's head 67
go to the beach 58
go to the gym 58
go to the shops 11
go to the store 11
go to work 4
goalkeeper 61
goalpost 61
goat 54
goatee 17
goggles 62
golden raisin 29
golf 60
golf club 62
golf course 62
gone off 32
good 6
good deal 73
good ear for languages 25
good omen 26
good source of something 70
goose 54, 56
gooseberries 29
gorilla 55
gossip 26
gossip magazine 63
government building 72
GPS 76
graduate 23, 24
graffiti 27
grammar 25
grandchildren 20
granddaughter 20
grandson 20
grapefruit 29
grapes 29
grassland 52
grate 33
grateful 6, 19
grater 10
gray / grey 5
gray / grey eyes 17
gray / grey hair 17
great 6

greater choice 75
Greece 1
Greek 1
green 5
green energy sources 53
green eyes 17
green spaces 75
greengrocer 73
greenhouse gases 53
grill 33
grin 14
ground floor 74
groundsheet 49
group 64
grow up 21
grow your hair 17
guarantee 74
guava 29
guesthouse 47
guidebook 47, 63
guided tour 47
guilty 27
guinea pig 54
guitar 64
guitar player 64
gulp 32
guy rope 49
guyline 49
gym 58, 71
gymnastics 60, 62

H

hacking 27
hacksaw 12
haggle 73
hailstone 51
hair 17
hair band 16
hair cut 17
hair dye 16
hair gel 16
hair spray 16
hairbrush 16
hairdresser 34
half 2
half time 61
ham 28
hammer 12
hamster 54
hand 14
handbag 16
handkerchief 16
handlebar 49
handsome 17
hands-on experience 39
hang clothes 11
hang gliding 60
happy 19
hard drive 76
hard shoulder 46
hardback 63
hardware store 73
hardworking 43
harmful to the environment 53
harmless 6
harmonica 64
harness 62
hat 16
hatch 56
have a bath 4
have a break 4
have a car accident 45
have a day off 35
have a good ear for languages 25
have a heart of gold 8
have a picnic 58
have a shower 4
have a sneaking suspicion 26
have an impact on something 77
have an interview 42
have breakfast 4
have dinner 4
have lunch 4
have serious doubts 26
have serious misgivings 26
have something in common 21
have tea or coffee 4
have your hair cut 17
have your hands full 39
have your name in lights 67
hawk 56
hay fever 68
hazel eyes 17
hazelnut 29
head 14
head over heels 8
headache 68
headlight 45
headline 63
headline news 67
headquarters 35
headset 37
heal 69
healthcare 36
healthy eating 70
hear something on the grapevine 8
heart of gold 8
heart rate 71
heat 78
heatwave 51
heavy 5
hedge 52
helicopter 44
helmet 62
herbal tea 32
herbs 31
here 46
hero 65
hex keys 12
high 5
high blood pressure 68
high chair 22
high heels 16
high in something 70
high jump 60
high tide 52
highbrow 63
highlighter 37
hike 58
hill 52
hip 14
hip-hop 64
hippopotamus 55
hiss 54
historic buildings 75
historic quarter 72
history 23
hit 59
hit the nail on the head 8
hitchhike 44
hockey 60
hockey stick 62
hoe 12
hold 59
hold a position 39
hold your breath 14
hole punch 37
holiday 47, 58
home furnishings 74
home improvements 12
homework 4, 23
honest 18, 43
honey 31
hood (car) 45
hood (clothing) 15
hook 62
hooliganism 27
hoot 56
hop 54
hopelessly lost 48
horoscope 63
horrible 6
horror 65
horse 44, 54
horse riding 60
hose 12
hospital 69, 72
hospitality 36
host 66
hostel 47

hot 5, 32
hot air balloon 44, 51
hot chocolate 32
hot dog 28
hot drink container 32, 49
hot tub 71
hotel 47, 72
hour 3
hourly 3
hourly rate 35
house 9
house number 7
household chores 11
household name 67
housemate 13
house-warming party 13
housework 4
Human Resources / HR (department) 36
humidity 51
hummingbird 56
humor / humour 63
humpback whale 57
hundred 2
hunt 55
hurdles 62
hurricane 51
hurt 68
husband 20
hypothesis 78

I

ice 51
ice cream 31
ice hockey 60
ice rink 62
ice skates 62
ice tea 32
iceberg 52
iced 32
icy 51
iguana 54
ill 31, 68
illustration 63
immature 18
impact 77
impatient 18
important 6
impulsive 18
in a nutshell 41
in front of 46
in the long run 77
in the public eye 67
in the red 41
inbox 7
including utilities 13
income 38
incredible 6
independent 43
in-depth knowledge 42
India 1
Indian 1
indicate 45
indicator 45
indigestion 68
Indonesia 1
industries 36
infection 68
information technology 23
Information Technology (department) 36
infrastructure 75
inhaler 69
initiative 43
injection 69
injury time 61
innovation 77
innovative 43
insect repellent 49
insects 56
insensitive 18
insomnia 68
insurance 45
intelligent 18
interest rate 38
interested 19
interesting 6
interests 42
intern 35
interpersonal skills 43
interrupt 40
intersection 46
interview 42, 66
intrigued 19
introduce yourself 7
invoice 38
iron 70
iron a shirt 4, 11
ironing 11
ironing board 11
irreversible change 53
irritated 19
irritating 6
island 52
IT 43
IT (department) 36
itchy 68
itchy feet 48

J

jacket 15
jaguar 55
jam 31
janitor 34
January 3
Japan 1
Japanese 1
jar 32
javelin 60
jazz 64
jealous 19
jeans 15
jellyfish 57
jet ski 50
jewelers / jewellers 73
jewelry / jewellery 16
jigsaw (tool) 12
jigsaw puzzle 22
job ad / advert 42
job title 7
jobs 34, 42
jockey shorts 15
jog 71
jogging 58
journalism 36
journalist 34
judge 27, 34
judo 60
juice 32
July 3
jump 59
jump rope 22, 71
jumper 15
junction 46
June 3
junk mail 7
jury 27

K

kangaroo 55
karaoke 58
kayaking 60
kebab 28
keep an eye on 8
keep fit 71
kennel 54
ketchup 31
kettle 10
key 46
key skills 42
keyboard 64, 76
keys 13
kick 59, 61
kickoff 61
killer whale 57
kilometer / kilometre 46
kind 18
kitchen 9
kitchen implements 10
kitchen knife 10

kitchenware 74
kite 22, 50
kiwi (bird) 56
kiwi fruit 29
knee 14
knickers 15
knife 10
knit 58
knock on wood 26
koala 55

L

laboratory 23, 78
laces 16
ladder 12
ladle 10
ladybird 56
ladybug 56
laid-back 18
laid off 35, 39
lake 52
lamb 28
lamp 9, 37
land at the airport 47
landlord 13
language barrier 25
languages 23, 25
laptop 37, 76
last name 7
latest model 77
latin 64
laugh 14
laundry 11
laundry basket 11
laundry detergent 11
laundry service 47
law 23, 27
law court 27, 72
lawn 9
lawn mower 12
lawyer 27, 34
lazy 18
lead (electrical) 76
lead (for a pet) 54
leadership 43
lease 13
leash 54
leather 5, 15
leave the house 4
leave work 4
lecture 23
lecturer 23
leeks 30
left 46
leg 14, 28
leg of a journey 48
leg of a trip 48
Legal (department) 36
leggings 15
legs 54
legumes 70
leisure center / centre 72
lemon 29
lemonade 32
lemongrass 31
lend a hand 8
leopard 55
let the cat out of the bag 8
let your hair down 8
letter 7, 37
lettuce 30
level 12
librarian 34
library 23, 72
lick 14, 59
lie down 69
life preserver 50
life ring 50
lifeguard 50
lifejacket 62
lift 44, 59, 74
light 5, 9
light shower 51
lighting 51, 74
light-years ahead 77
lime 29
line 74
linesman 61
lingerie 74
lingua franca 25
lion 55
lips 14
lipstick 16
liquid 78
listen 59, 64
listen to music 58
listen to the radio 4
listening 25
litter box 54
litter tray 54
little 5
lively nightlife 75
living room 9
lizard 55
llama 54
load the dishwasher 11
lobster 28, 57
local 13
lock 49
locker room 71
lockers 71
locust 56
lodger 13
log in 76
log out 76
lonely 19
long 5
long hair 17
long jump 60
look around 48
look forward to something 48
look up to someone 21
loose 5
lorry 44
lose 61
lose weight 69
loud 5
lovely 6
low 5
low in something 70
low tide 52
loyalty card 74
lucky 19
luggage 47
lunch 4, 33
lychees 29
lyrics 64

M

mackerel 28
mad 19
made redundant 35, 39
magnet 78
magnificent 6
mail 7
main character 65
main course 33
main objective 40
main road 46
make 59
make a loss 38
make a reservation 33, 47
make a wish 26
make curtains 12
make friends with someone 21
make models 58
make predictions 77
make the bed 4, 11
make yourself understood 25
male 20
manager 35, 42, 61
mandarin 29
mango 29
manufacturing industry 36
maps 46
marbles 22
March 3
margarine 28
Marketing (department) 36

marmalade 31
mascara 16
mascot 61
mash 33
massage 71
materials 5
maternity leave 35
math / maths 23
mature 18
May 3
mayonnaise 31
meadow 52
meals 33, 58
mean 18
measles 68
meat 28
mechanic 34, 45
media 67
medical treatment 69
medication / medicine (healthcare) 69
medicine (subject) 23
mediocre 6
meditate 71
medium height 17
meerkat 55
meet a deadline 24
meet friends 58
meetings 40
melon 29
melt 78
memo 7
memory card 76
men's wear 74
menu 33
meow 54
meringue 31
metal 5
meteoric rise 67
meter / metre 46
Mexican 1
Mexico 1
microphone 64
microscope 78
microwave 10
middle name 7
middle-aged 17
midfielder 61
migraine 68
mild 51
mile 46
milk 28
milkshake 32
millennium 3
million 2
mince 33
minerals 70
mining industry 36
mint 31
minus 51
minute 3
miserable 19
miss a deadline 24
miss a train 44
mix 33
mobile 22
mobile banking 38
mobile number 7
mobile phone 37
moisturizer 10, 16
mole (animal) 55
mole (skin) 17
molecules 78
molt / moult 54
mom 20
Monday 3
money 38
Mongolia 1
Mongolian 1
mongoose 55
monkey 55
monkey wrench 12
month 3
monthly 3
moods 19
moose 55
mop the floor 11
moped 44
morning 3
mortar 10, 78
mortgage 38
Moses basket 22
mosque 72
mosquito 56
moth 56
mother 20
motivated 43
motor home 49
motor racing 60
motorbike / motorcycle 44
motorway 46
mountain 52
mountain bike 49
mountain range 52
mouse (animal) 54
mouse (computer) 76
mouse mat 76
mouse pad 76
mousse 31
moustache 17
mouth 14
mouthwash 10
move 59
move in 13
move out 13
move the goalposts 41
movie 65
movie star 65
movie theater 65, 72
moving 13
moving truck 13
mow the lawn 12
mug 10
mugging 27
multiplex 65
mum 20
mumps 68
museum 72
mushrooms 30
music 23, 64
music channel 66
music store 64
musical 65
musical instrument 58
musician 34
mussel 28, 57
mustache 17
mustard 31

N

nail 12
nail polish 16
name 7
napkin 33
nappy 22
narrow 5
nasty 6
nationalities 1
native speaker 25
nature documentary 66
nature writing 63
navy blue 5
near 5
neck 14
necklace 16
nectarine 29
negotiate 42
negotiating 43
nephew 20
nervous 18, 19
net 61, 62
Netherlands 1
never 3
New Zealand 1
news 66
news anchor 66
newspaper 63
newspaper headline 67
newsreader 66
next to 46
nibble 32

nice 6
niece 20
night 3
nightclub 72
nine 2
nineteen 2
nine-to-five 39
nine-to-five job 35
ninety 2
ninety-nine percent 2
ninth 2
no vacancies 47
nod 14
non-carbonated 32
non-fiction 63
noodles 31
north 46
northeast 46
northwest 46
nose 14
nosebleed 68
nostrils 14
not guilty 27
note 7
notepad 37
notes 38
notice board 37
nought point five 2
novel 63
November 3
numbers 2
numeracy 43
nurse 34, 69
nursery 22
nuts 12, 29

O

oars 62
oasis 52
observe 78
obsolete 77
ocean 52
October 3
octopus 28, 57
odd 6
off (food) 32
off the beaten path 48
off the beaten track 48
off, percent 73
office building 72
office equipment 37
Office Services (department) 36
often 3
oil (car) 45
oil (cooking) 31
ointment 69
old 17
old-fashioned 6
olive skin 17
omelet / omelette 28
on a tight budget 73
on the agenda 40
on the ball 8
on the corner 46
on the fence 8
on the left 46
on the right 46
on the same page 41
once a week 3
once-in-a-lifetime 48
one 2
one hundred 2
one million 2
one percent 2
one point seven 2
one thousand 2
one-way street 46
one-way ticket 47
onions 30
online banking 38
online chat 7
online shopping 74
only a matter of time 77
only child 20
only time will tell 77
open 74
opening night 67
open-plan 13
opera 64, 65
opera house 65
operation 69
opinions 6
opposite 46
optimistic 18
orange (colour) 5
orange (fruit) 29
orangeade 32
orchestra 64
orchestra pit 65
orchestra seating 65
order 33
organization 43
organize 42
organized 43
ostrich 56
otter 57
out of date 77
out of season 48
outbox 7
outgoing 18
outlay 38
outstanding 6
over the top 8
overcast 51
overcrowding 75
overdraft 38
overpriced 73
overtake 45
overtime 4, 35
owl 56
oyster 28, 57

P

PA 34
pace of life 75
pacifier 22
pack 13, 59
pack your bags 47
packet 32
paddle 62
page 63
page-turner 63
pail and shovel 50
pain 68
pain in the neck 8
painful 68
painkillers 69
paint 12, 58
paint a room 12
paint the house 12
paintbrush 12
pajamas 15
Pakistan 1
Pakistani 1
pale green 5
pale skin 17
pancakes 31
panda 55
panties 15
pants 15
pantyhose 15
paparazzi 67
papaya 29
paper 5
paper clips 37
paperback 63
paragliding 60
paramedic 34, 69
park (recreation area) 72
park (vehicle) 45
parking attendant 45
parking lot 45
parking meter 45
parking space 13
parking ticket 45
parrot 54, 56
parsley 31
partner 20
part-time 35

party 58
pass (overtake) 45
pass (succeed) 23
pass with flying colors / colours 24
passengers 44
passion fruit 29
passionate 18
passport 47
passport control 47
past 46
pasta 31
patient (hospital) 69
patient (personality trait) 18, 43
pavement 46
paws 54
pay 35, 73
pay cut 35
pay rise 35
pay separately 33
peach 29
peak 52
peanut 29
peanut butter 31
pear 29
peas 30
peck 56
pedal 49
pedestrian crossing 45
pedestrianized street 46
pedestrians 44
peel 33
peeler 10
peg 11
pelican 56
pen 37
penalty 61
penalty spot 61
pencil 37
pencil sharpener 37
penguin 56
pepper 31
peppers 30
percentages 2, 73
perform 64
performance 65
perfume 16
perfumery 74
period drama 66
permanent 35
personal assistant 34
personal statement 42
personal trainer 71
personality traits 18
perspire 14
pescatarian 70
pestle 10, 78
pestle and mortar 10
petrol 45
petrol station 45, 72
petroleum engineering 36
pets 54
pharmaceutical industry 36
pharmacy 72
Philippines 1
philosophy 23
phone 37
phone call 7
photocopier 37
photographer 34
phrasebook 47
physical education 23
physical therapy 69
physicist 78
physics 23, 78
physiotherapy 69
pick someone up 45
pick something up quickly 25
pickpocketing 27
picnic 58
picnic basket 50
picnic blanket 50
pig 54
pigeon 56
Pilates 71
pills 69
pilot 34
pin 16
PIN 38
pineapple 29
pink 5
pistachio 29
pitch (sports) 61, 62
pitch a tent 49
pizza 28
plain (adjective) 15
plain (landscape) 52
plan your route 46
plane 12
planner 37
plant bulbs 12
plaster 69
plaster the walls 12
plastic 5
plate 10
plateau 52
platform 44
play (action) 59
play a musical instrument 58
play board games 58
play cards 58
play chess 58
play the trumpet 64
play video games 58
playground 22
playing cards 22
playpen 22
plays (performance) 65
pleasant 6
pleased 19
pliers 12
plot 63
plug in 76
plum 29
plumber 34
poach 33
poached egg 28
pocket 15
point 59
Poland 1
polar bear 55
polar opposites 24
polar region 52
police 27
police officer 34
police station 72
Polish 1
polish 11
polite 18
polka dot 15
pollution 75
pomegranate 29
pond 52
ponytail 17
pool 60
pool cue 62
pop 64
popcorn 65
pork 28
porpoise 57
port 44
portfolio 42
portion 70
Portugal 1
Portuguese 1
post 7
post office 72
postcode 7
postgraduate 24
potatoes 30
pothole 49
pottery 58
potty 22
pour 33, 78
power cord 76
PR 36
practical 43
practice / practise 64
pram 22
prawn 28
prescription 69
presentation 40

presenter 66
press-up 71
pretty 6
preview 66
price tag 74
print 7
printer 37
prison 27
problem-solving 43
processed food 70
Production (department) 36
professional 43
professional achievements 42
professional attributes 43
professor 23
proficient in 42
program / programme 65
programme (TV) 66
project management 43
projector 37
promotion 35
pronunciation 25
property 13, 36
props 65
protein 70
proud 19
proven track record 42
prowl 55
prune trees 12
psychologist 34
psychology 23
Public Relations 36
public speaking 43
pudding 33
puddle 51
pull 59
pulling your leg 8
pulses 70
punctual 43
puppet 22
Purchasing (department) 36
pure luck 26
purple 5
purr 54
purse 16, 38
push 59
push-up 71
put on (clothes) 15
put on make-up 4
put the children to bed 4
put up shelves 12
put your foot down 21
puzzles 58, 63
pyjamas 15

Q

quack 54
qualification 23
quarter 2
queue 74
quiet 5
quince 29
quiz show 66

R

rabbit 54
rabbit hutch 54
raccoon 55
racing bike 49
rain 51
rain forest / rainforest 52
rainbow 51
raincoat 15
raindrop 51
rainy 51
raise 35
raisin 29
rake 12
ranch house 13
rap 64
rapids 52
raspberries 29
rattle 22
ray 57
razor 10
reach a consensus 40
reach a verdict 27
reaction 78
read 58
read a map 46
read a newspaper 4
reading 25, 63
real estate 13, 36
reality show 67
reality TV 66
realtor 13
reasonable 18
receipt 38, 74
reception 47
receptionist 34
record 64, 66, 78
recover 69
recruitment agency 42
recycling bin 11
recycling industry 36
red 5
red card 61
red carpet 67
red hair 17
red tape 41
redcurrants 29
reduce your carbon footprint 53
reference (landlord) 13
references (employer) 42
reflector 49
reflexology 71
refrigerator 9
refund 73
rehearse 64
relationships 21
relax 71
relaxed 19
relaxing 6
reliable 18, 43
remarkable 6
remember 59
remote 66
removal van 13
renewable energy 53
rent 13
rent a cottage 47
renting 13
repair 59
repel 78
reply 7
reply all 7
reporter 66
Republic of Ireland 1
research 43
Research and Development / R & D 36
residential area 13
resit 23
respectable 6
responsible 43
responsible for 42
rest 69
restaurant 33, 72
results 78
resuscitate 69
retire 35
return ticket 47
review 23
review the minutes 40
revise 23
revolution 77
rhinoceros 55
rice 31
ride 44, 59
ride a bike 44
ride a horse 44, 58
right 46
ring 16
rip-off 73
river 52
road sign 45
road work / roadworks 75
roadmap 46

roar 55
roast 33
robbery 27
rock (music) 64
rock climbing 60
rocks 52
ROI 1
roll (action) 33
roll (bread) 31
roller (paint) 12
roller skates 62
roller-skating 60
rolling pin 10
romance 63
romantic comedy 65
romper suit 22
roof 9
room service 47
room with a view 47
roomer 13
roommate 13
rooms 9
round-trip ticket 47
router 76
row houses 13
rowing 60
rowing machine 71
rubber 37
rubber band 37
rubber gloves 11
rucksack 16, 49
rude 18
rug 9
rugby 60
ruler 37
run 59, 71
run in the family 21
run out of time 40
run-down 48
running 60
running a marathon 60
running track 62
runny nose 68
rush hour 75
Russia 1
Russian 1
rusty 25

S

sad 19
saddle 49
safe 47
safety goggles 78
safety pin 69
sailing 60
salad 28
salary 35
sale 74
Sales (department) 36
sales assistant 34
salmon 28, 57
salt 31, 70
salty 32
sand 50
sand dune 52
sandals 16
sandbox 22
sandcastle 50
sandpit 22
sandstorm 51
sandwich 28
sardines 28
satellite TV 66
satire 66
satnav 76
saturated fat 70
Saturday 3
saucepan 10
sauna 71
sausages 28
save 38
savory / savoury 32
saw 12
saxophone 64
scale (fish) 57
scales (measure) 46, 69
scallops 28
scanner 37
scared 19
scarf 16
school 4, 23
school of fish 57
science 23, 78
science fiction 63, 65
scientist 34, 78
scissors 10, 37, 69
score a goal 61
scouring pad 11
scrambled eggs 28
scratch 54
screen 65, 66, 76
screw 12
screwdriver 12
script 65
scrub the floor 11
scuba diving 60
sea 50, 52
sea creatures 57
sea lion 57
sea urchin 57
seafood platter 28
seagull 56
seahorse 57
seal 57
seasons 3, 66
seatbelt 45
second 2
second floor 74
secretive 18
security 61
security guard 34
see 59
see a play 58
see eye to eye with someone 21
see off somebody 48
see somebody off 48
seesaw 22
self-help 63
selfish 18
sell 73
semester 24
semi-detached houses 13
send 7
sensationalize 67
sensitive 18
sent off 61
sentence somebody to something 27
September 3
series 66
serious 18, 19
serious doubts 26
serious misgivings 26
serve a sentence 27
service charge 33
service the car 45
service-oriented 42
set menu 33
set of beliefs 26
set off 45
set the table 11
set your sights on something 39
sets 65
seven 2
seventeen 2
seventh 2
seventy 2
sew 58
shake 59
shake your head 14
shallow 5
shampoo 10
shape 12
shape of things to come 77
shark 57
sharp 5
shave 4, 17
shaving foam 10
shears 12
sheep 54
shell 28, 50, 57

shelves 74
shin 14
ship 44
shipping industry 36
shirt 15
shiver 14
shocked 19
shocking 6
shoe shop 73
shoe store 73
shoes 16
shop 11, 72
shop around 73
shoplifting 27
shopping 58, 73
shopping bag 74
shopping cart 74
shopping channel 66
shopping mall 72
shopping trolley 74
short 5, 17
short hair 17
shorts 15
shoulder (body) 14
shoulder (road) 46
shoulder-length hair 17
shout 59
show of hands 40
shower 4, 9
shower block 49
shower gel 10
shows 65, 66
shredder 37
shrimp 28, 57
shrug 14
shuttlecock 62
shy 18
sick 68
side 33
side order 33
sideburns 17
sidewalk 46
sieve 10
sigh 14
sightseeing 47
signal 45
signature 7
signpost 46
silk 5, 15
silly 18
silverware 10
simmer 33
sing 56, 59, 64
sing in a choir 58
Singapore 1
singer 64
single room 47
sink (action) 78
sink (household fixture) 9
sip 32
sister 20
sister-in-law 20
sit an exam 23
sit down 59
sit on the fence 8
sitcom 66
sit-up 71
six 2
sixteen 2
sixth 2
sixty 2
skateboard 62
skateboarding 60
skating 60
ski slope 62
skiing 60
skip 71
skipping rope 22, 71
skirt 15
skis 62
skydiving 60
skyscraper 72
slash prices 73
sleep well 71
sleeping bag 49
sleeve 15
slice 33
slide 22
slippers 16
sloth 55
Slovakia 1
slow down 45
small 5
smart 17
smartwatch 76
smell 59
smile 14
smog 51
smoothie 32
smuggling 27
snack 28, 33
snail 56
snake 55
sneakers 16
sneaking suspicion 26
sneeze 14, 68
sniff 54
snore 14
snorkel and mask 50
snorkeling / snorkelling 60
snort 54
snow 51
snowboard 62
snowboarding 60
snowdrift 51
snowed under 39
snowflake 51
snowstorm 51
snowsuit 22
snowy 51
soap 10
soap opera 66
soccer 60, 61
soccer cleats 62
social networking 7
socks 15
sofa 9
soft toy 22
solar panel 53
solar power 53
solid 78
solo 64
sometimes 3
son 20
sorbet 31
sore 68
sore throat 68
soul 64
soup 28
sour 32
south 46
South Africa 1
South Korea 1
southeast 46
southwest 46
soy sauce 31
spa 71
spaghetti 31
Spain 1
spam 7
Spanish 1
spanner 12
sparkling 32
spatula 10
speak 59
speak accurately 25
speaking 25
special 6
special effects 65
special offer 74
specials (menu) 33
speed camera 45
speed limit 45
speed up 45
speeding 27
spell 59
sperm whale 57
spices 31
spicy 32
spider 56
spinach 30

spine 63
spinning top 22
spirit level 12
splinter 68
split the bill 33
split the check 33
sponge 10, 11
spoon 10
sports 60, 62
sports center / centre 72
sports drink 32
sports programme 66
sports show 66
spotted 15
sprain 68
spread a rumor / rumour 26
spring 3
sprinkler 12
squash 60
squat 71
squeak 54
squid 28, 57
stadium 62
staff 35
stage 65
stair gate 22
stairs 9
stalls 65
stand up 59
standing ovation 65
stapler 37
staples 37
starfish 57
starfruit 29
start a rumor / rumour 26
start work 4
starter 33
state 7
state-of-the-art 77
static electricity 78
stationery 37
stay (at) home 58
stay in a hotel 47
steam 78
steam room 71
steering wheel 45
step down 39
stepbrother 20
stepmom 20
stepmother 20
stepmum 20
stepsister 20
stethoscope 69
steward 61
stick up for someone 21
sticky notes 37
stifling 51
still (drink) 32
sting 56, 68
stir 33
stitches 69
stock exchange 38
stomach 14
stomachache / stomach ache 68
stop at 46
stop off 48
stoppage time 61
stopwatch 62
storage 13
store 11, 72
stork 56
storm 51
stormy 51
stove 9
straight hair 17
straight on 46
strange 6
strategy 40
strawberries 29
stream 52
street address 7
street crime 27
street map 46, 72
street market 73
stress 68
stressed 19
stretch 71
striker 61
strikingly different 24
striped 15
stroke of luck 26
stroller 22
strong 32
stubble 17
student 23
study 9
study a subject 23
studying 23, 24
stuffed animal 22
stunning 6
stunt 65
style your hair 17
styles 15, 17
stylist 34
subject 7
substitutes 61
subtitles 66
subtract 59
suburb 75
suck 14
sugar 31, 70
suit (clothing) 15
suit (someone) 15
suitcase 47
sultana 29
sum up 40
summer 3
sun 51
sunbathing 50
sun cream 50
Sunday 3
sunglasses 16
sunny 51
sunscreen 50
superb 6
superfoods 70
supermarket 74
supervise 42
supportive 18
surf the internet 58
surfboard 62
surfing 50, 60
surgeon 34
surprised 19
sushi 28
swallow 32
swamp 52
swan 56
sweat 14
sweater 15
sweep the floor 11
sweet 32
sweet potatoes 30
sweetcorn 30
sweets 31
swimming 60
swimming cap 62
swimming gear 62
swimming pool 62, 72
swimming trunks 50, 62
swimsuit 50, 62
swing 55
swings 22
Swiss 1
Switzerland 1
swollen 68
swoop 56
swordfish 57
symptoms 68
synagogue 72
syringe 69

T

table 9
table tennis 60
tablet (gadget) 76
tablets (medicine) 69
tackle 61
tackle pollution 53
tackle something head-on 39

tail (airplane / aeroplane) 44
tail (animal) 54, 55
take a bath 4
take a flight 44
take a shower 4
take a test 24
take a year off 24
take a year out 24
take after someone 21
take an exam 24
take away 33
take minutes 40
take off 15, 39
take on someone 39
take out 33
take out the rubbish 4, 11
take out the trash 4, 11
take photos 58
take questions 40
take someone on 39
take something with a pinch of salt 8
take the bus 44
take the first left 46
take the second right 46
take the train 44
talent show 67
talented 18
talk 59
talk show 66
talkative 18
tall 17
tambourine 64
tan / tanned skin 17
tandem 49
tape measure 12
tapir 55
taste 32, 59
tasty 32
tattletale 26
taxi 44
taxi driver 34
taxi rank 44
taxi stand 44
tea 4, 32
teacher 23, 34
teacher's pet 8
team player 43
teamwork 43
technology 23, 76, 77
technophile 77
technophobe 77
teddy bear 22
teenagers 20
teeth 14
telephone 37
telephone manner 43
television 9, 66 *see also* TV
tell a white lie 26
telltale 26
temperature 51, 68
temple 72
temporary 35
ten 2
tenancy agreement 13
tenant 13
tennis 60
tennis court 62
tennis racket 62
tent 49
tent peg 49
tent pole 49
tenth 2
term 24
terraced houses 13
terrarium 54
terrible 6
terrified 19
test 23
test results 69
test tubes 78
text message 7
textbook 23, 63
Thailand 1
theater / theatre 65, 72
there 46
thermometer 69
thesis 23
thick 5
thigh 14
thin 5
think 59
think outside the box 41
think the world of someone 21
third 2
thirst for adventure 48
thirteen 2
thirty 2
thousand 2
three 2
three times a week 3
thrilled 19
thriller 65, 66
thrilling 6
throw 59
throw money down the drain 41
throw-in 61
thumb 14
thumbtack 37
thunder 51
thundery 51
Thursday 3
ticket 44
tidy 11
tie (clothing) 15
tie (sports result) 61
tie your hair back 17
tiger 55
tight 5
tights 15
tile the bathroom 12
till 38, 74
time 3
time management 43
tin 32
tin opener 10
tip 33
tire 45, 49
tired 19
tiring 6
title 7
toast 31
toaster 10
toddler 20
toe 14
toilet 9
toilet block 49
toilet paper 10
toiletries 10
tomatoes 30
tonsillitis 68
tool box 12
tools 12
tooth 14
toothbrush 10
torch 49
tornado 51
tortoise 54
toucan 56
touch base 41
touch wood 26
tour guide 34
tourism 48
tourism industry 36
tourist attraction 75
tourist information 72
tourist office 72
tourist trap 48
towel 9, 50
town 72
town hall 72
town square 72
toy shop 73
toy store 73
toys 22
traffic jam 45, 75
traffic lights 45
tragedy 65
train 44, 71
train driver 34
train set 22
train station 44, 72

trained in 42
trainers 16
tram 44
transfer money 38
translation 25
transportation 44
transportation industry 36
trash 7
trash can 9, 37
travel 44, 47, 48
travel agent 34
travel writing 63
trays 37
treadmill 71
treatment 69
trial 27
trim a hedge 12
triplets 20
trombone 64
trousers 15
trout 57
trowel 12
truck 44
trumpet 64
trunk 45, 55
try on 73
t-shirt 15
Tuesday 3
tumble dryer 11
tuna 57
turkey 54
Turkey 1
Turkish 1
turn / turning 46
turn left 46
turn off 66, 76
turn on 66, 76
turn right 46
turn signal 45
turn up the volume 66
turtle 57
tusk 55
TV 9, 66
TV guide 63, 66
TV schedule 66
TV set 66
tweezers 69
twelfth 2
twelve 2
twentieth 2
twenty 2
twenty-first 2
twenty-one 2
twenty-two 2
twice a week 3
twin beds 47
twins 20
two 2
two hundred 2
two weeks 3
tyre 45, 49

U

UAE 1
ugly 6
UK 1
umbrella 16
unanimous agreement 40
unapproachable 18
unblock the sink 12
uncle 20
unclog the sink 12
undergraduate 24
understand 59
undo 15
unenthusiastic 19
unfasten 15
unfriendly 18
unfurnished 13
unhappy 19
unicycle 49
uniform 15
unimpressed 19
United Arab Emirates 1
United Kingdom 1
United States of America 1
university 23
unkind 18
unload the dishwasher 11
unpack 13
unpleasant 6
unreasonable 18
unreliable 18
unsaturated fat 70
unshakable belief 26
unspoiled 48
up 15
up to your ears 39
up to your eyeballs 39
upload 76
upmarket 74
upset 19
upstairs 9
urban life 75
urban myth 26
US 1
USB drive 76
useful 6
useless 6
usher 65
usually 3

V

vacancies 47
vacation 47, 58
vacuum cleaner 11
vacuum the carpet 11
valley 52
van 44
vandalism 27, 75
vegan 70
vegetables 30
vegetarian 70
vet 34
veterinary medicine 23
vice / vise 12
video games 58
video on demand 66
view a house 13
villa 47
village 72
villain 65
vinegar 31
violin 64
virus 68
visit a gallery 58
visit a museum 58
vitamins 70
vocabulary 25
voicemail 7
volcano 52
volleyball 60
volunteer 42
vomit 68
vulture 56

W

wages 35
waist 14
waiter 33, 34
waiting room 69
waitress 33, 34
wake up 4
walk 44, 58
walk the dog 4
walking boots 49
walking holiday 47
walking vacation 47
wallet 16, 38
walnut 29
walrus 57
want 73
wardrobe 9
warm 51
warm up 71
wash the car 11
wash the dishes 4

wash your face 4
wash your hair 4
washing line 11
washing machine 11
washing up liquid 11
wasp 56
watch 16
watch a movie 58
watch television / TV 4, 58
watch your weight 70
water 32
water cooler 37
water the flowers 12
water the plants 11
waterfall 52
watermelon 29
waterproofs 49
wave (gesture) 14
wave (water) 50, 52
wavy hair 17
wear 15
weather 51, 66
weather forecast 66
website 7
Wednesday 3
weeding 12
week 3
weekend 3
weekly 3
weights 71
well-being 71
west 46
western 65
wet 51
wet suit 50
wet wipe 22
whales 57
what the future holds 77
wheel 45
wheel clamp 45
wheelbarrow 12
whisk (action) 33
whisk (equipment) 10
whiskers 54
whisper 59
white 5
white-collar crime 27
wide 5
wide range 74
widow 20
widower 20
wife 20
Wi-Fi 76
wild animals 55
wind 51
wind farm 53
wind power 53
windbreak 50
window 9
window seat 47
window shopping 73
windsurfing 50, 60
windy 51
wine 32
wing (airplane / aeroplane) 44
wing (bird) 28, 56
wink 14
winter 3
win-win situation 41
wipers 45
wire 76
wireless 76
withdraw money 38
witness 27
wok 10
wolf 55
women's wear 74
wonderful 6
wood (landscape) 52
wood (material) 5
wooden spoon 10
woodpecker 56
wool 5
woolen / woollen 15
word of mouth 26
work 4, 59
work from home 35
work full-time 35
work opportunities 75
work out 71
work overtime 4
work part-time 35
work shifts 35
work well under pressure 43
working 39, 41
working environment 39
workplace 43
world of difference 24
worm 56
worried 19
wound 68
wrap (sandwich) 28
wrap up 40
wrench 12
wrinkles 17
write 58
writer 34
writing 25
written communication 43

X

X-ray 69

Y

yacht 44
yak 55
yard (garden) 9
yard (measurement) 46
yawn 14
year 3
yellow 5
yellow card 61
yoga 58, 71
yogurt 28
yolk 28
young 17
yo-yo 22

Z

zebra 55
zip / zipper 15, 16
zip code 7
zucchini 30

Acknowledgments

The publisher would like to thank:
Sarah Edwards, Carrie Lewis, Daniel Mills, Aisvarya Misra, and Christine Stroyan for editorial assistance; Rabia Ahmad, Debjyoti Mukherjee, and Sonakshi Singh for design assistance; Simon Mumford for national flags; Viola Wang for additional illustration; Steph Lewis for proofreading; Elizabeth Wise for indexing; Christine Stroyan for audio recording management; and ID Audio for audio recording and production.